BOB SLOSSER
WITH CYNTHIA ELLENWOOD

CHANGING THE WAY AMERICA THINKS

WORD PUBLISHING
Dallas · London · Sydney · Singapore

Changing the Way America Thinks

Library of Congress Cataloging in Publication Data

Slosser, Bob.
Changing the way America thinks / Bob Slosser with Cynthia Ellenwood.
p. cm.
Bibliography: p.
1. Christianity and culture. 2. United States—Moral conditions. 3. Evangelicalism—United States. 4. Fundamentalism. I. Ellenwood, Cynthia, 1944- . II. Title.
BR115.C8S57 1989 89-32541
277.3'0828—dc20 CIP

ISBN 0-8499-0657-1

9 8 0 1 2 3 9 AGF 9 8 7 6 5 4 3 2 1

Printed in the United States of America

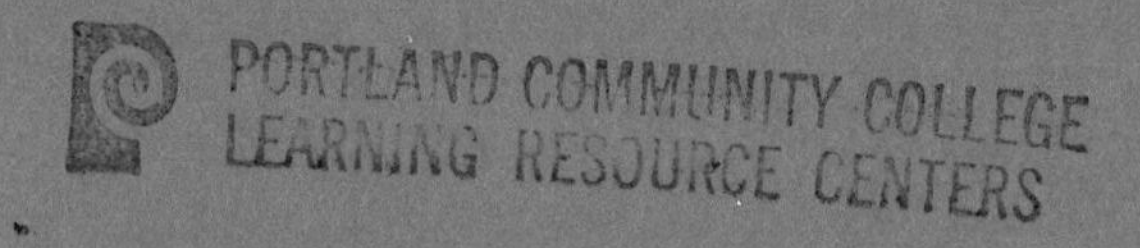

CHANGING THE WAY AMERICA THINKS

To our good friends
at CBN University

Don't let the world around you
squeeze you into its own mold, but
let God re-make you so that
your whole attitude of mind is
changed. Thus you will prove in
practice that the will of God's
good, acceptable to him and perfect.

(Rom. 12:2, PHILLIPS)

Contents

Preface

By one way of counting, this book began to develop in 1985, shortly after the author was elected by the Board of Regents to be the president of CBN University. The totality of the Gospel of Jesus Christ was sending wave after wave of awe upon me as I was thrust into the midst of a collection of men and women struggling to understand and articulate the full implications of that gospel upon their intellectual and professional disciplines.

It sounds a bit trite to say I was at last recognizing that this was a "thinking" matter; I had theretofore been jousting with symptoms as I watched the corruption and deterioration of many parts of American life. My predecessor at the university, Richard Gottier, had perceived and taught the reality of "the renewed mind" as laid out in Holy Scripture, and that perception was key. The minds given by Almighty God are wonderful, and to reach fulfillment they must be presented to Him as a living sacrifice. They must be offered so that the comforting, helping, teaching Holy Spirit and Holy Bible can enable us to walk—to think, to live—in the will of God.

The powerful faculty, administrative staff, and student body were already moving, some faster than others, toward meaningful service to these diverse United States of America, which had been launched as one nation under God. In the intervening time, all of us have grown more certain that America can be restored to that godly heritage, that together with the larger body of Christ we can, in reality, change the way America thinks.

The author and coauthor are indebted to literally hundreds of people who played a role in the development and writing of this book, and it would take many pages to name them. Thus we must be selective.

Ruth Ann Arnold of Fort Worth, Texas, wife of George Arnold, the former director of academic services at CBNU, was very important to the early development of the book; she encouraged, exhorted, and spent hours putting ideas on paper. Rick Quintana, former television producer at CBN, was also instrumental. Then there were Herbert W. Titus, provost and dean of the CBNU College of Law and Government and rediscoverer of the biblical principles in which our nation's law and government are immersed; CBNU professors Clifford W. Kelly, who uncovered the biblical roots of American journalism, and Robert J. Schihl, who communicated the Roman Catholic heritage in the Christian church; CBNU professors Gary T. Amos, Walter W. Davis, Joseph N. Kickasola, Terrence R. Lindvall, John C. Munday, Jr., and Wellington Boone, president of New Generation Campus Ministries, who helped revise early manuscript drafts; Melanie Kaharl Ciccarello and Curt McCutchan, whose prayer and research assistance were invaluable; and my secretary, Janice Bullard.

The author is also indebted to the following: Homer J. Allen, Robert J. Barth, Devi Anne Moore Chancey, Lesley Wilson Claster, Gerald L. Cooper, William F. Cox, Jr., Scott Dixon, Garland R. Hunt, Jerry W. Horner, George L. Jefferson, Jr., Eva L. Kiewitt, Duane A. Larson, Linda Lutz, Kerry L. Morgan, David Outten, Jack L. Ralston, W. George Selig, Gerald R. Thompson, Gailon M. Totheroh, Clifford L. Whitehouse, and the invaluable counsel of Jim Nelson Black.

In his book, *The Recovering of the Christian Mind,* Harry Blamires wrote, "When we ponder into whose hands we have increasingly placed the keeping of our cultural inheritance and the responsibility of transmitting it to generations, can we feel other than worried?"

In this book, we join hands with our British brother in his concern that those who control the transmission of our cultural heritage are increasingly hostile toward God and His Word. We pledge to do what we can to change the thinking of our people, through Jesus Christ our Lord.

Prologue

Herb Titus strode angrily toward the steps of his roughed-out cedar house, his mind boiling with the injustices of American society. High on a hill, nestled among Pacific Northwest trees, the house and family should have been a welcome respite from the struggles of the thirty-seven-year-old lawyer. His wife and four children, however, were continually shut out of the driving liberal activism that ruled his life.

As a volunteer legal counsel for the Oregon Civil Liberties Union, Titus was involved in the prison reform movement and had just represented before a parole board a man convicted of sodomizing a teenager. As a homosexual rights advocate, Titus felt he had clearly presented his case. "This man is not violent," he had told the board, gesturing passionately with the strength of his convictions. "It is his constitutional right to practice as he pleases."

The prisoner, articulate and popular with his cellmates, had stood up to the board. Titus had admired his boldness and conviction. "No, I will not assure you that I will never have sex with a teenager if you release me," the man had said.

The request was denied. Titus was convinced the man had been deprived of his religious liberty. Everything he stood for in 1974 demanded parole for the confessed pedophile. As a law professor at the University of Oregon, well known for the liberal convictions of its faculty, he helped unify various elements in the people's drive for power against unjust government regulations and incompetency.

From the time he arrived at the assortment of brick, stucco, and concrete buildings that made up the Oregon campus, Titus had been a leader.

Teamed with local lawyers and other sympathizers, he helped to organize an antiwar group that eventually strangled draft boards coast to coast. He was involved in successful drives to decriminalize marijuana in Oregon. With two others, he helped lead the Upper Willamette Valley Anti-Pollution League to confront pollution by the giant Weyerhauser Corporation.

"I thought the world was bad," Titus said later. "I thought there was something terribly wrong with America. I decided that everything had to be changed."

In his law classes he urged students into political activism, drilling them on legal manipulations to accomplish their goals through the court system. "The legislative process won't bring social change," he told them. "It's too slow, too inaccessible. You need to litigate! Not everybody can get into the legislative halls. Not everybody can get into the governor's office. If you persist and persist and persist in the courts, pretty soon you'll get victory. They'll want to get you off their backs."

His students, roused to anger over the Vietnam War, began to plot illegal protest activities. Many of their attempts were unsuccessful. He risked being arrested for aiding and abetting, but he never turned them in.

He hated to fail. This incident with the parole board kept replaying in his mind, until a jarring thought suddenly invaded his consciousness: "What if one of your sons became a homosexual?" He had three sons, ages eight, six, and five. With a strange chill, he thought, "I wouldn't like that." He dismissed the unwelcome thought. That was just one of the contradictions with which he had learned to live.

Life is full of contradictions, he decided. That's just the way life is. There's no way I'll ever be reconciled within myself. I still have to follow what I believe, even if everything inside me says it's wrong.

Often he blamed his parents and teachers for his double-mindedness. After all, it took time to undo all the damage caused by their generation's insistence that people adhere to certain absolute standards of right and wrong. That was one reason American society had to be dismantled. It was trying to force people to live by an outdated morality.

The next generation will be different, he comforted himself. My children won't have the same problems because they'll be raised correctly. I'm just carrying over my generational prejudice because that's what was planted in me. There's nothing I can do about it. I'm helplessly schizophrenic.

Meanwhile, his family suffered. Titus and some of his fellow activists treated their women as quasi servants. The men were the heroes, the draft resisters, the risk takers. The women were supposed to keep the home warm and the children obedient and offer up sexual favors when the conquering heroes returned. Some refused to marry their women so they didn't have to take on that responsibility. Many women decided that if that was what men were like, they would have no part of it. They became feminists and lesbians.

One women's right the men supported was the right to an abortion. Even before the 1973 *Roe v. Wade* decision, they said, "It's her body, isn't it?"

Titus's wife, Marilyn, had a brief but frightening experience with a hydatidiform mole, a bizarre pseudopregnancy characterized by an uncontrolled growth. When Marilyn became pregnant again she told him, "Honey, I'm scared about this pregnancy. Do you think we should consider an abortion?" "No!" he said instantly. Contradictions. They plagued his life.

"We talked about love in this movement," Titus said, "but I didn't see any. People wanted to get what they could from me, to get my services for free, to put my house up for their bail, to take all my assets into a commune.

"But I was as selfish as they were. The lack of love I saw in others I saw in myself. I knew that for a long time. I didn't love anybody. I didn't love my wife. I didn't even love myself."

Finally, he decided there was one contradiction he could escape from—his family. "I didn't feel like a husband and father," he said. "I didn't act like a husband and father. The solution was to cease to be one."

Within a year of the parole board episode with the pedophile, a year of continuing agony over who he was and what he believed, he made a decision to get out of the marriage. Marilyn hadn't yet told him, but she was ready to let him go.

As the last weekend of July 1975 approached, he was again startled by his own thoughts. This time it seemed like an urgent command: "Start a new life with your wife."

He couldn't shake it, couldn't rationalize it away. His options were running out. That Friday night, for the first time in their thirteen years of married life, he began to tell his wife about the painful struggles warring inside him.

They talked most of the night. "I confessed my failures as a father," Herb recalled, "and as a husband. All I could think of was 'Please forgive me. Please understand me.'" Marilyn forgave him, but she couldn't understand him.

"When my wife said, 'I forgive you,'" Herb said, "I knew I was forgiven. Then we tried to figure out how we had made such a mess of our lives. We had everything that Americans are supposed to have and we were miserable."

Finally, in the early hours of the morning, his wife asked, "Will you buy me a new car?" "I didn't want to buy her a new car," he admitted, "even though I knew she needed one. But I said yes. This was the first act of love that I ever made toward my wife. I had never done anything for her according to her need unless I had a need that was commensurate or identical to it."

Marilyn had another request. Although she was not a deeply religious person, she believed in God and thought families should go to church.

Herb was an atheist. Along with the ACLU he had fought to remove a cross from a hill in Eugene. He was anti-business, anti-government, and anti-Christian. "I never went around like Madalyn Murray O'Hair, but I certainly agreed with her," he said. "I thought Christianity was stupid."

That weekend, he agreed to go to church, "not because I wanted to go, not because the answers were there, but because I would do it for her. It wasn't entirely altruistic, though. I wanted a new life."

Saturday morning, after two or three hours sleep, they went out and bought a new car. Back at home, they stretched out on a large pillow on the floor.

Herb couldn't believe his eyes. Unfolding on the woodbeamed ceiling above him was a color painting full of human figures. He began to describe it to Marilyn, who was looking out the window at the trees. "There's a large crowd of people," he said, "and at the center of the crowd there's a woman." A strange, creamy quality was creeping into his voice. "They're all dressed in robes, and across the woman there's a figure superimposed, something she's holding."

Marilyn wondered what in the world was going on. Here they were at the greatest crisis of their lives, and he was describing a painting that didn't exist. Yet because he used such careful detail, she began to ponder what it meant.

As she turned to look, he said, "You won't see it," not knowing why he said it, and she didn't. Neither of them could explain the phenomenon, and neither believed in miracles.

That afternoon they chose a church, the Oak Hill Orthodox Presbyterian Church, from a newspaper ad. Then they spent another night talking hour after hour, sharing the brokenness of their lives.

On Sunday morning, they drove up to a modest, fairly new church of contemporary design. While Marilyn was settling their sons into their Sunday school classes, Titus went to the kitchen. Over coffee and tea a church member tried to strike up a conversation with him.

"Are you new to Eugene?" he asked.

"No," Titus responded.

"Are you traveling through?"

"No."

"Are you Orthodox Presbyterian?"

"No."

After that he had no more questions, so Titus asked, "What's Orthodox Presbyterian?"

"We teach the Bible and nothing but the Bible," he answered.

Titus said nothing, but inwardly cringed. "Oh, yuk. Wrong church."

"Neither of us went in expecting anything," he said later. "We were looking for a new circle of friends. We needed to get out of the university lifestyle that seemed to be killing us."

The Sunday school teacher, who was also the pastor, opened the class by describing two difficult teaching experiences from a Christian youth camp. Titus was struck by the examples. They were almost identical to difficulties he was having teaching in law school. He had just told Marilyn about them that weekend.

"From then on," Titus recalled, "he began to take exact words, exact phrases from those all-night conversations. We'd had lots of questions because we couldn't figure out what went wrong. The only difference was, he started giving us answers out of the Bible.

"I remember the first Scripture that touched my heart was Rom. 2:14–15, where it says man without the Bible is a law unto himself, accusing or excusing. That was my life. I accused others who did things I didn't do and excused myself and others for things that I did wrong and they did wrong."

Herb and Marilyn had difficulty maintaining their composure. "I knew if I looked at Marilyn she would start crying," Herb said, "so we just sat there."

After the class, no one tried to find out what was happening to their visitors, unaccustomed to seeing anyone so deeply moved. When they were alone, Titus asked his wife with amazement, "How did he know?"

"God the Father told him," Marilyn answered simply. It was a revelation to her.

"Why?"

"Because He loves us. Now I know why God became a man, so that He could reach out to us without scaring us. Now I know that Jesus is who He says He is."

As soon as she spoke, Herb knew it was the infant Jesus he had seen in the painting. At the same moment, he recalled, "All the guilt, all the shame, all the burden of sin was gone. I was born again, but I didn't know it because there was nothing in the Sunday school lesson about being born again."

They were out in the parking lot, laughing, crying, and hugging each other before they realized that their sons were still in the church. With a feeling of incredible lightness, Titus told the pastor that they would like to stay but, "We have an awful lot of things to talk about."

Within twenty-four hours they had a new marriage. In another twenty-four hours the whole family was off on a camping vacation in eastern Oregon. As they drove through the night, Titus had an incredible urge to read the Bible. Neither of them had one along. Herb didn't even own one. So they settled on a plan. There was a public library in the town about nine miles from the campground. They could go into town, read the Bible every morning, return to camp and swim in the afternoon, then walk and talk in the evening.

At the end of the week, Marilyn said, "God has done so much for us. Are we supposed to continue to ask Him questions?" Her husband didn't know. On Saturday of their camping vacation, they looked in the newspaper for a church they could attend the next day. It was easy. A sermon title they found said "Becoming a New Christian, Part 2."

Sunday morning, at the beginning of the service, the pastor called the children up for a special message. Marilyn had an unexplainable urge to go with them. Holding up the hook from the top of a metal coat hanger, he asked, "Who can tell me what this is?"

The inevitable response was "A broken coat hanger." Another tried: "It looks like a fishhook." "Look again," said the pastor. "It's a question mark," someone said. "That's right," he encouraged them. "Does God want us to ask questions? Yes, He does, because that's how we learn about Him."

That remarkable answer to Herb and Marilyn's question was followed by a sermon that once more echoed words and phrases from their recent conversations. They had no more doubts. This God was alive.

GOD IN AMERICAN HISTORY

Herb Titus began to investigate the God who had loved him enough to grant him a new life. With a scholar's intensity he began to study the Bible and look at history for evidence of God at work. He was stunned. Wherever he looked, God was there. Biblical principles were intertwined in American law and government. They formed the foundation of science. They explained why immorality caused such problems for society. He discovered that the Bible held the keys to America's successes and the reasons for its failures.

God began to take the zeal that had driven Titus to change America by litigation and make it conform to His will. He hammered and shaped that zeal until Titus wanted nothing else more than God's plan for America.

The only reason America has survived is because God-fearing men wrote into our country's founding documents the plain truth about God. The Declaration of Independence calls Him the source of rights, the Creator, the Supreme Judge of the world. The Constitution was signed "in the year of our Lord."

God has always had a place in America. The trouble is, Americans love to sing "God Bless America," but they don't want God to tell them how to think. The platform of "God and country" is erected for special occasions and then dismantled when the moment passes. It takes more than a few thrilling moments of patriotism to bring God's blessing on the land.

Most Americans don't know how to think biblically any more. Public schools forbid it, churches ignore it, and families are too busy to make it stick. That's why I wrote this book, to explain what it means and why it is so necessary that we learn how to think and weigh our decisions biblically.

Herb Titus was an atheist, a liberal, and a member of the American Civil Liberties Union. Some people believe that thinking biblically means you blame all of America's problems on people like that. The truth, however, is that every one of us is to blame. None of us has given God full access to our minds.

The Mind of Christ

When I worked as an editor for the *New York Times,* I struggled with some of the same questions that plagued Titus. As an arrogant journalist I acted as though I sat on the perfect perch to judge America. At night, however, I used to pace the floor after my wife and children were in bed. I remember crying out, "What is life all about?" As an atheist and an existentialist I had no answers, no hope that anyone was listening. Life was absurd. I was only speaking to the darkness.

Then, through the efforts of John McCandlish Phillips, a fellow *Times* newsman, I met a pastor in Westchester County who began to give me answers. One day this pastor, Harald Bredesen, prayed with my wife, Gloria, and me to acknowledge and accept Jesus Christ as our Savior.

That episode was a remarkable turning point in our lives. It gave me strength and hope for the future. It helped me escape the garbage polluting my life. Unfortunately, however, it had little impact on my thinking about the world.

My language was cleaned up and many of my bad habits were changed, but I didn't understand that although salvation is a *personal* experience it is not a *private* one. God is to be Lord of *all* of our lives, including our thought lives and work lives. If not, He is in reality the Lord of nothing.

I became a much more decent and likable person, but my mind had not been renewed (Rom. 12:2). I never considered that the Bible might apply to the news stories I worked on every day—crises in government, crime, civil rights, the family.

I suspect that many Christians are just like I was. After all, for more than a century the church has been in retreat from public life, leaving the running of the country to others who claimed they were better qualified.

Solomon wrote, "He that troubleth his own house shall inherit the wind" (Prov. 11:29, KJV). For the last sixty-five years, Christians have thought that statement applied to them. If they spoke out on the issues in biblical terms they would surely trouble the house and divide the nation. Religion and politics don't mix.

There is a new move afoot to reject that kind of thinking. There is a new militancy thrusting itself onto the American scene. God's people are coming alive again. Although they have scant experience and are making some mistakes, they are also having some successes. They are calling it a lie that committed Catholics and evangelicals are a danger to America. Instead, they believe that God's people are the country's only hope.

Those who have been accustomed to ruling the house unhindered don't like this unnerving bunch of newcomers. Just when they thought they had succeeded in discrediting those annoying "religious" people they find them swarming everywhere.

These zealous Christians can survive for a short time on prayer and sheer nerve, but if they are to make a lasting impact on the nation they must know the Word. Like America's Founders, they must have a firm grasp on specific biblical principles to inform their zeal.

As you read this book, you will encounter these principles in a variety of forms. Some of the things you read may shock you. Some will seem impossible. As you read, I want to ask you to do three things.

1. *Ask God to show you the truth and to cleanse your thinking of all the confusion of the past.* Submit your mind totally to

Him. Tell Him you are willing to give up everything that does not conform to His Word. As the Apostle Paul wrote: "We demolish arguments and every pretension that sets itself up against the knowledge of God, and we take captive every thought to make it obedient to Christ" (2 Cor. 10:5).

2. *Listen for God's voice as you read.* Allow the Holy Spirit to "guide you into all truth" (John 16:13, KJV). Discard everything that I or anyone else says that does not agree with His Word. Fill your mind with a new way of thinking until you have the "mind of Christ" (1 Cor. 2:16, KJV).
3. *Do whatever He tells you to do.*

The first place I want to take you on this journey is a country courthouse in Dayton, Tennessee. The year is 1925. A death grapple occurred in that building which changed the course of American history. Our history was not altered because of what happened there but because false reports emanating from that courthouse have become a part of American culture. Those lies have been a cancer eating away at our relationship with God. Let me show you what I mean.

Part 1

Education

The Religion then of every man
must be left to the conviction and
conscience of every man; and it is
the right of every man to exercise it
as these may dictate. This right is
in its nature an unalienable right.

James Madison

1

Death Grapple in the Light

In 1925, Dayton, Tennessee, was a friendly town of pleasant lawns, paved roads, and well-stocked stores. Many of its citizens were college graduates and regular church goers who had a strong sense of community. No one could have suspected it would soon be described by the nation's newspapers as the "forlorn backwaters of the land," filled with "thousands of unregulated or ill-balanced minds." Nor did anyone realize it would set the stage for the most effective campaign ever launched to change the way America thinks about God. Chances are you've probably swallowed some of the lies yourself. Let me tell you how it all got started.

Dayton's high school football team was coached by a popular twenty-four-year-old science teacher named John Thomas Scopes. With his tall, slim frame, freckled face, and wavy blond hair, Scopes could have been mistaken for one of his students.

An obliging young man, he accepted an invitation to a friendly discussion in a local drugstore. Three of the town's citizens were discussing a new law forbidding the teaching of evolution in the public schools.

The regulation forbade teachers employed by the Tennessee public schools "to teach any theory that denies the story of the Divine Creation of man as taught in the Bible, and to teach instead that man has descended from a lower order of animals." The fine to be levied for each misdemeanor ranged from $100 to $500.

George Rappleyea, a coal-mining engineer originally from New York, had read a news story given to the Tennessee papers by the American Civil Liberties Union. The group sought someone willing to go to trial in a test case over the new law. Rappleyea was convinced that Dayton should take the challenge in order to get free publicity and provide a public forum for a creation/evolution debate.

To Rappleyea, the Bible was simply an attempt at history, but most of the Dayton people believed it all. They thought a literal interpretation of the Bible excluded any type of evolution or, like Scopes, assumed creation could be reconciled with it. Almost everyone agreed that God had created man in a special creative act—one separate from the animals—as someone to love Him and be loved in return. They considered the theory of man's descent from apes, without God, as a heresy that would deceive their children and lead them away from God.

Although Scopes was reluctant to have an arrest on his record, he agreed to let Rappleyea swear out a warrant for his arrest for teaching evolution. He wasn't the only one in Tennessee ignoring the law, Scopes reasoned, and he couldn't see any way to teach biology without including evolution. His state-endorsed textbook mentioned Darwin approvingly, although it stated that none of the animals was considered an ancestor of man. To Scopes, a test case seemed like a simple method to resolve a local curriculum issue.

As soon as Rappleyea notified the ACLU, it wired back a promise of financial support, publicity, and lawyers, whom it pledged would take the case all the way to the Supreme Court, if necessary. Scopes later described the chain of events as a drugstore discussion that got out of hand.

SCOPES IS ARRESTED

On 7 May 1925, Scopes was arrested and charged with teaching evolution on April 24. In the first of many falsehoods to be disseminated from Dayton, Scopes later admitted he had skipped the evolution lesson that day. The students didn't remember one way or another, so the youthful "witnesses" were helpfully coached before the trial by Scopes's lawyer. (Contrary to the 1955 play *Inherit the Wind,* by Jerome Lawrence and Robert E. Lee, Scopes never spent a moment in jail.)

Meanwhile, the ACLU vigorously promoted a nationwide drive for support of Scopes's case. The Tennessee law, it said, struck a blow at scientific teaching and must be reversed. The ACLU was supported by the editors of most general circulation newspapers across the country.

Although the first 150 years of American journalism had been dominated by Bible-believing crusaders, that had all changed by the twentieth century. Instead of seeking to glorify God, the country's newspapers had begun to rule Him out of the equation entirely with so-called objective reporting. Thus, members of the press were eager and willing to use their power to bring down whatever vestiges of God remained in education.

They saw to it that not only editorials but also a flood of news stories from Dayton attacked Tennessee's "quarantine against learning."

In Europe, the reaction to the Scopes trial was no less intense. George Bernard Shaw, quoted in the *New York Times,* warned: "The world without the concept of evolution would be a world wherein men of strong mind could only despair."

The *Times* endorsed evolution in nearly religious terms in a 26 July 1925 editorial: "If man has evolved, it is inconceivable that the process should stop and leave him in his present imperfect state. Specific creation has no such promise for man. . . . No Legislature should (nor can) rob the people of their hope."

In a way, it was a plea for the union of evolutionism and the state. Americans had in the past assumed that they had a Creator who was the source of their rights to life, liberty, pursuit of happiness, and child rearing. Those rising to power in the press, education, and law, however, thought it was high time for man's thinking to evolve beyond such antiquated concepts. The civil government, not parents, should decide what was best for the children's education. The state should refuse any religion-tainted guidance from families or the church.

Those were the beliefs of the self-proclaimed agenda setters, but they were not the general beliefs of the people of Tennessee. Unlike their "enlightened" fellow citizens, they had not rejected the Creator and the Bible, and they wanted both to stay in their children's curriculum.

John Washington Butler, the Tennessee state legislator who had sponsored the anti-evolution bill, believed that man was created by God and had fallen into sin. Belief in evolution wasn't his source of hope because he knew evolution would never change anybody's heart. Man's true hope was a relationship with God through His Son, Jesus Christ. Only Christ could make someone a "new creation" (2 Cor. 5:17).

As a parent, Butler believed that books on evolution could be read in the home but should be banned from the tax-supported public schools. As a citizen, he believed the Creator should retain the place He had always held in American public life. He wrote: "In the first place, the Bible is the foundation upon which our American Government is built. . . . The evolutionist who denies the Biblical story of creation, as well as other Biblical accounts, cannot be a Christian. . . . It goes hand in hand with Modernism, makes Jesus Christ a fakir, robs the Christian of his hope and undermines the foundation of our Government."

When Butler said "the evolutionist who denies the biblical account of creation," he pointed out something that almost all the international hoopla missed. Evolution as one of many scientific theories was one thing.

Evolution as a substitute for the Creator was out of the question. Although the prosecution would bring in witnesses who said their Christian faith was compatible with creation, the agenda of Scopes's out-of-town lawyers was to replace outmoded notions of creation with twentieth-century, atheistic evolution. Roger Baldwin, founder of the ACLU, called it a case of "the Good Book against Darwin, bigotry against science, or, as popularly put, God against the monkeys."

The ACLU hired Clarence Darrow, one of the nation's most prominent trial lawyers, to defend Scopes and the theory of evolution. The rumpled appearance of the sallow-skinned, cynical lawyer masked a brilliant legal mind. At sixty-eight, Darrow had successfully defended a great number of famous—and infamous—clients. When it suited him, he could plead his case with quiet gentleness or biting scorn. An agnostic, he was perfectly cast in his role as the avenger of evolution against the "bigoted" believers of Tennessee.

Darrow's warm welcome by the townspeople, most of whom opposed the teaching of evolution, was typical of the lack of animosity between the creationists and evolutionists in Dayton. Scopes, for example, was often invited to dinner by the creationist families and carried suitcases for both sides as they arrived in town.

BRYAN HEADS PROSECUTION

The prosecution team had the services of a famous orator and statesman, William Jennings Bryan, a rather mediocre lawyer who hadn't been active in law for many years. He was primarily known for his three campaigns for the presidency on the Democratic ticket and for his ability to rally a crowd behind his Christian beliefs. With ringing oratory and comfortable humor, the man was irresistible.

When the sixty-five-year-old Bryan spoke, one had the illusion that a hidden megaphone magnified his clear baritone. In 1925 he was still recognized as one of the great American orators of all times, although the same aging process that expanded the waistline of his athletic frame and grayed his dark curly hair had diminished his volume and added a lisp.

Bryan's performance in Dayton was no exception. The night he arrived, the townspeople assembled for a dinner in his honor. After watching the diabetic Bryan gorge himself on forbidden foods, including part of Scopes's dinner, they listened to his dramatic summation of the events to come. He said: "The contest between evolution and Christianity is a duel to the death. It has been in the past a death struggle in the darkness. From this time on it will be a death grapple in the light. If evolution wins in Dayton, Christianity goes—not suddenly, of course, but gradually—for the two cannot stand together. They are as antagonistic as light and darkness, as good and evil."

Bryan called it "a death grapple in the light." Dramatic words, perhaps, but in the years to come they were to prove prophetic because the forces ostensibly arrayed to rescue Scopes from bigotry had a bigger agenda. They knew they couldn't win in Dayton, but they intended to use the publicity and subsequent appeals, not to supplement creation according to standards of academic inquiry, but to supplant it. They knew that the Genesis account of creation was the archenemy of their godless version of evolution. They had no intention of simply wounding the adversary. Their plan was "shoot to kill."

By the time the proceedings began, 120 to 150 reporters had descended on Dayton. The coverage was enormous. The *New York Times* alone printed an average of 10,000 words—some ten or eleven columns—every day.

Even in 1925, journalists were developing a marked similarity of opinion on the issues, and one that increasingly diverged from the mainstream of American thought. At the turn of the century, the first dean of the University of Missouri's journalism school, Walter Williams, wrote a "Journalist's Creed." In it he said, "I believe that the journalism which succeeds best—and best deserves success—fears God and honors man." When the reporters came to Dayton, however, most of them had long since decided that the fear of God was definitely out of place. They associated such thinking with reactionary minds and acrimonious debate.

As a result, they were surprised to find such pleasant people there. H. L. Mencken, for example, who covered the trial for the *Baltimore Sun,* said that he saw no "evidence of that poisonous spirit which usually shows itself when Christian men gather to defend the great doctrine of their faith."

With little dissension to write about, some journalists, bored with the proceedings, took time out to go swimming. Their friends, and even Scopes himself, wrote stories under their bylines. When events dragged, a few reporters created their own stories. Other reporters badgered Scopes mercilessly, trying to find some new angle.

The now famous clash of beliefs occurred in a building that strained and groaned under the weight of the multitude. Dayton's red brick courthouse stood in a two-acre park near the center of town. Surrounded by stately oaks and graying maples, the two-story building boasted arches and a tall clock tower.

On the second floor of the creaky wooden courtroom, the judge, jury, accused, and lawyers sat on a low, railed platform beneath the windows. Although the courtroom was designed to accommodate 250 spectators, during the trial it held upwards of 1,000. Until the trial's seventh day, when Judge John T. Raulston moved the trial outdoors to preserve the courthouse, the assembled multitude sat and stood in every conceivable corner, day after sultry day.

When Raulston sat in his new judge's chair, purchased by the town in honor of Dayton's shining hour, he nearly always smiled. His round, red face and nose added a geniality to his austere position. Caught up in the journalistic spirit, he allowed long photo-taking sessions in the courtroom.

An almost carnival atmosphere existed outside the courtroom, including banners, refreshment stands, sideshows, and musicians. Added to the local population were sidewalk crusaders and evangelists, legitimate and lunatic alike.

Those evangelists who had a legitimate call to Dayton saw the trial as Bryan did: a death grapple between the forces of God and the forces of Satan. Although the course of events has been distorted beyond recognition in the intervening years, in 1925 there were sincere, intelligent Christians who knew there was something seriously wrong with a massive national campaign to dispense with the Bible. This was no dispute over whether creation took six days or six eons. It was an outright rejection of God's role in creation and, ultimately, of His very existence. It was a denial of the nature of man as made in God's image, subject to His Law, saved by His grace, and destined for heaven. The negation of biblical inerrancy may have been started by unbelievers, but many of those who today call themselves Christians have since joined their side. The late Francis Schaeffer called this defection "the great evangelical disaster."

OPENS WITH PRAYER

On the trial's opening day, Judge Raulston invited the Reverend L. M. Cartwright to pray. As the people quieted, reverently bowing their heads, Darrow and his associates, Dudley Field Malone and Arthur G. Hays, gazed stonily out the window. Cartwright prayed: "Oh God, our divine Father, we recognize Thee as the Supreme Ruler of the universe, in whose hands are the lives and destinies of all men. . . . We pray that the power and the presence of the Holy Spirit may be with the jury and with the accused and with all the attorneys interested in this case."

After the third day of opening prayers, Darrow complained, "I do not object to the jury or anyone else praying in secret or private, but I do object to the turning of this courtroom into a meeting house in the trial of this case. You have no right to do it."

In reality, the court's acknowledgment of God's presence was entirely appropriate. Before the famous statue of Lady Justice had been satirically blindfolded centuries earlier, she had always been seen open-eyed with a sword pointing at an open Bible. At the U.S. Supreme Court, litigants can see a depiction of Moses the Lawgiver. The Declaration of Independence appealed to the Supreme Judge of the World.

Darrow, however, had no use for such reminders of God. The mention of His name was a reproach to Darrow's campaign to gain favorable treatment for his special witnesses, brought in to critique divine creation and ridicule biblical inerrancy. Judge Raulston allowed Darrow and his defense team to call these expert witnesses, but he excluded the jury each time, ruling that the issue raised by the ACLU—creation vs. evolution—was irrelevant to the charge of "whether or not a school-teacher has taught a doctrine prohibited by statute." As a result, by the end of the trial, the jury Rev. Cartwright prayed for had spent little time in the courtroom.

In the eyes of journalists sympathetic to Darrow's cause, the trial was a vindication of the intelligent people who promoted evolution and a disgrace for Bryan and the simple-minded folk who believed in creation. They falsely reported that Darrow coolly and skillfully exposed Bryan as a pathetic old man whose outmoded doctrines were gradually stripped away. This misconception has persisted to the present day, greatly enhanced by the popular but highly inaccurate play and movie *Inherit the Wind.*

According to the official court record, Darrow was the one who lost his temper while Bryan maintained a stable, consistent oratory. Darrow's acrimony reached a peak on Friday, July 17, when he harshly contradicted the judge. Raulston had ruled that Bryan had a right to cross-examine all of Darrow's witnesses, including the experts brought solely to discredit creation and exalt evolution. Darrow disagreed, demanding the special privilege of parading his experts unchallenged through the witness stand just so he could enter them into the record. Darrow wanted the testimony recorded intact so that he could use it in future appeals. Any challenges to the information's accuracy would have been counterproductive. His goal was to attack the Butler Act as bad law and get it repealed, not obtain an acquittal of Scopes. He fumed at the judge: "They have no more right to cross-examine than to bring in the jury to hear this issue. We want to submit what we want to prove. That is all we want to do. . . . Counsel well knows what the judgment and verdict in this case will be. We have a right to present our case to another court and that is all we are after."

Throughout the day Darrow continued to harass and interrupt the judge. On Monday morning, he was slapped with a fine of $5,000 for contempt of court.

Over the weekend, Darrow had cooled off. When the judge informed him of the fine, Darrow humbly apologized, saying he realized after reading the court record that he was at fault.

Judge Raulston responded grandly:

> My friends, and Colonel Darrow, the Man that I believe came into the world to save man from sin, the Man that died on the cross that man might be redeemed, taught that it was godly to forgive, and were it not for the forgiving nature of Himself I would fear for man. . . . I am sure that if he had had time to have thought and deliberated he would not have spoken those words. . . . I feel that I am justified in speaking for the people of the great state that I represent when I speak as I do to say to him that we forgive him and we forget it and we commend him to go back home and learn in his heart the words of the Man who said: "If you thirst come unto Me and I will give thee life."

There was wild applause, and the judge adjourned the proceedings to the courthouse lawn. One can only imagine Darrow's reaction when told he was rescued by Christ's forgiveness.

SCIENTIST STATES CASE

Some of Darrow's experts told the court that teaching children that they were descended from lower forms would have no harmful effect on religion. Kirtley F. Mather, chairman of the department of geology at Harvard University, said that, in fact, evolution had made him a better Christian. We shall see later what his definition of "Christian" entailed.

As a scientist, Mather said he left the mystery of the soul to the theologian. He warned theologians to leave the evolution of life to the scientists. If the church continued to attack evolution, he said, it would destroy America: "Withdraw this theory, and every department of physical research would fall back into heaps of hopelessly dislocated facts, with no more order or reason or philosophical coherence than exists in a basket of marbles. . . . We should go back into chaos if we took out . . . this great doctrine of evolution. Chaos would inevitably destroy the whole moral fabric of society." Mather had neatly dissected theology from science, a practice increasingly prominent after the popularization of Darwin's theories.

In earlier centuries, leading scientists based their research on a stable system where belief in the Creator avoided chaos, not caused it. According to Darwin's model, however, everything was left to chance, which was hardly a remedy for chaos. In random evolution, man, instead of living in a universe given moral and physical order by the loving

Creator, became one of many cosmic accidents. His only hope was that there would be enough accidents to make mankind better. That may be sufficient hope for those who can wait for eons, but individuals with problems *right now* find it extremely depressing. No wonder suicide is on the rise.

Final Assault on the Bible

When Darrow's experts had finished their testimony, he made a final, dramatic move, not to prove his client's innocence, as most trial lawyers would do, but to attack the religious beliefs of those who supported the law. He called Bryan to the stand in order to contrast the cool-headed scientists he had just paraded through the witness stand with someone who had the audacity to believe in miracles. He spoke to the scientists with respect but to Bryan with dripping sarcasm.

Darrow proceeded to interrogate Bryan on a list of biblical teachings he found ludicrous and that he contended would be rejected by all thinking men. For ninety minutes he mercilessly grilled Bryan about Jonah's fish, the sun standing still, dates for Creation and the Flood, the source of Cain's wife, and whether the serpent once walked on its tail.

Bryan was ill-equipped for such ruthless probing and told Darrow he was not prepared to explain scientifically all the implications of his beliefs, such as the cataclysmic effects of the earth's stopping its revolution.

What Bryan didn't know was that Darrow and his experts operated according to the faulty assumption that the only route to truth is the modern version of the scientific method, which begins from a position of doubt and attempts to accumulate proof. Scientists of the past had not reasoned that way. They had accepted the Bible as a given, an absolute. They believed Jesus when He said, "If you abide in My word, then you are truly disciples of Mine; and you shall know the truth, and the truth shall make you free" (John 8:31–32, NASB). The scientists' results were reliable when they conformed to the unchanging system of physical laws put in place by God Himself. They proceeded deductively from fact to application. If the universe were solely a product of chance, nothing could be accurately analyzed or predicted.

Bryan fell right into Darrow's trap, trying to use faulty methods of reasoning to prove that there is a God. He tried desperately to explain the unexplainable to those with hardened hearts and no ears to hear.

Bryan's inability to satisfy the cynical lawyer with specific rebuttals delighted many reporters and temporarily lost him the support of the crowd. The court record, however, bears no resemblance to the account in Lawrence and Lee's play where a humiliated Bryan (under the name of

Matthew Brady) begins babbling the names of the books of the Bible and then collapses into his wife's arms crying, "Mother. They're laughing at me, Mother!"

According to the court record, Bryan never ceased to react with a fervent counterpoint to Darrow's innuendoes. Here is one such heated exchange:

> Gen. A. T. Stewart [chief of the prosecution]: What is the purpose of this examination?
>
> Bryan: The purpose is to cast ridicule on everybody who believes in the Bible, and I am perfectly willing that the world shall know that these gentlemen have no other purpose than ridiculing every Christian who believes in the Bible.
>
> Darrow: We have the purpose of preventing bigots and ignoramuses from controlling the education of the United States.

These exchanges continued until Bryan said to the judge:

> Bryan: Your honor, I think I can shorten this testimony. The only purpose Mr. Darrow has is to slur at the Bible, but I will answer his question. I will answer it all at once, and I have no objection in the world. I want the world to know that this man, who does not believe in a God, is trying to use a court in Tennessee . . .
>
> Darrow: I object to that.
>
> Bryan: (continuing) to slur at it, and while it will require time, I am willing to take it.
>
> Darrow: I object to your statement. I am [examining] you on your fool ideas that no intelligent Christian on earth believes . . . [Outcries from the crowd. Bedlam.]
>
> Judge Raulston: Court is adjourned until 9 o'clock tomorrow morning.

The following day, Judge Raulston announced that since Bryan's testimony could not benefit the higher court it would be stricken from the record.

A GUILTY VERDICT

Inevitably, according to prearranged plan, Darrow asked for a guilty verdict for his client to speed Scopes on his way to a higher court. He said: "We have no witnesses to offer, no proof to offer on the issues that the court has laid down here, that Mr. Scopes did teach what the children said he taught, that man descended from a lower order of animals—we do not mean to contradict that, and I think to save time we will ask the court to bring in the jury and instruct the jury to find the defendant guilty."

The jury took nine minutes to convict Scopes, but the remaining steps in the ACLU scenario never took place. The plan to send Scopes's case to the U.S. Supreme Court was stopped at the state level when the conviction was overturned by the Tennessee Supreme Court on a technicality. Judge Raulston had imposed on Scopes a $100 fine with inferred but not specific instructions from the jury. A retrial could have been ordered, but since Scopes was no longer in the service of the state, the court essentially closed the book for the sake of the "peace and dignity of the State."

Hays, the codefense attorney for Scopes, finally realized that the ACLU's Roger Baldwin had been premature in predicting victory over what the press had labeled "Fundamentalism." Hays commented wryly, "We are dealing with astute church people in that case, and I guess we did not credit them with the astuteness that they really possessed."

After the "Monkey Trial" ended, however, gleeful reports went out that Bryan was a broken man. In *Inherit the Wind,* he collapsed while still in the courtroom and died.

In reality, Bryan showed few immediate ill effects, continuing his crusade with releases such as this one: "For the first time in history, so far as I have been able to learn, a militant minority, made up of atheists, agnostics and other dissenters from orthodox Christianity, is seeking to use the courts to compel the majority to pay teachers to undermine the religious faith of their children."

Bryan had hit on a key point of controversy, something those who would later capitulate were unable to see. Lawmaking was supposed to be the work of elected officials who represented their constituency and, originally, conformed to God's law.

Instead, a group of out-of-town crusaders had tried to force the courts to challenge the sovereignty of local government and impose their own standards of truth. It was the same strategy Herbert Titus taught his Oregon law students before his conversion to Christ and one that continues to be a force for social change. It is extremely dangerous because it accepts no absolute standards nor local control.

Instead of allowing tax-paying parents to determine the content of curriculum used for their children, crusading lawyers, scientists, and journalists made it their business to invade a peaceful town and tell the people what should be taught. The parents' beliefs differed from their superior, "objective" position, so the parents must be defeated.

This usurpation of the parents' rights was contrary to the First Amendment right to free exercise of religion. It recalled the days when Virginia's established church told people what to think and what to believe, all at the taxpayers' expense. Thomas Jefferson, author of the Virginia Act for Religious Freedom that still stands today, said that it was "sinful and tyrannical" to "compel a man to furnish contributions of money for the propagation of opinions which he disbelieves and abhors." Thus, since 1786 the established church has been ruled unconstitutional, but in Virginia, as in Tennessee and the rest of the country, the established school has taken its place.

As taxpayers and parents, the people of Tennessee considered it their right to control what their children learned. They did not consider mention of the Creator to be a religious belief but a universal truth. Because most of Tennessee's teachers, lawmakers, and judges also understood this truth, creation prevailed in 1925. Before long, as we shall see, even those authorities would join the chorus of voices calling for an end to biblical influence.

Creation could never have been expurgated from the public school curriculum if Christians had stood unashamedly for the truth of Scripture and taken positions of prominence in journalism, law, and education. Instead, they retreated before the crafty Clarence Darrows of the world and listened to preachers who told them to stay out of politics, the media, and the public schools. Now they must share the blame for the staggering blows continually being struck against American life and liberty.

Without hope and without God, America's deranged citizens have shot schoolchildren at random, killed their neighbors in the nation's urban ghettoes, succumbed to drugs, and stolen the pittances of the helpless elders of the country. Where will it end? It will end only when thinking in America begins to conform to the biblical model, when love of God and love of neighbor bring hope and healing to those in despair.

DEATH FEEDS THE FIRE

Five days after the Scopes trial, following a heavy round of speeches, Bryan died suddenly in his sleep. Death was attributed to extreme heat, exhaustion, and uncontrolled diabetes.

For a time, Bryan's death seemed to fuel the fires of the creationists, giving them a martyr and enhancing their efforts for years to come. The prohibition against teaching evolution remained on the law books of Tennessee for the next forty-two years.

After the trial, Darrow received supportive letters from admirers, and this commendation from Kirtley Mather: "Clarence, you say you're not a Christian; but from those letters, you're a much better Christian than most of those who call themselves Christians." Darrow snorted, "Oh, I just did what I had to do because I'm made that way, I guess."

The man who had fought so long for the doctrine that man is a product of chance spoke of himself as "made" and did not argue with Mather's assumption that a "Christian" could be someone who doubted the existence of the Creator God. The number of churchgoers who today hold a similar position is a sad commentary on the success of the antibiblical propaganda and the elimination by the church of unalterable creeds.

For centuries, creeds had informed and united the church with words about the Creator like these from the Nicene Creed: "I believe in one God the Father Almighty, Maker of heaven and earth . . . and in one Lord Jesus Christ, the only-begotten Son of God . . . By whom all things were made." Without them, it became easy to dismiss Christ's embarrassing role in Creation and begin Christianity at the cross.

Mather complimented Darrow's Christianity, but others around the country were not so kind. Even liberal Christians, not known for their sympathy to biblical inerrancy, sent a flood of letters to the ACLU, protesting Darrow's mistreatment of Bryan. As a result, the ACLU, responding to public opinion and complaints from within its own leadership, tried to disengage itself from Darrow before he could take the case to the U.S. Supreme Court. Some feared he would insult those justices as he had Raulston. However, the outcome at the state supreme court level rendered Darrow's dismissal irrelevant.

Before he died, Bryan released a speech he had planned to give in the courtroom. In it he refuted the outrageous assertion that Christianity and education were enemies. He contended: "Religion is not hostile to learning. Christianity has been the greatest patron learning has ever had. But Christians know that 'the fear of the Lord is the beginning of wisdom,' now just as it has been in the past, and they therefore oppose the teaching of guesses that encourage godlessness among the students."

He quoted from a book by eminent biologist George John Romanes who spoke wistfully of the time before his faith in evolution replaced his faith in the Creator: "I am not ashamed to confess that with this virtual negation of God the universe to me has lost its soul of loveliness. . . . I think, as think at times I must, of the appalling contrast between the hallowed glory of that creed which once was mine, and the lonely mystery of existence as now I find it."

If such despair results from the teaching of evolution, Bryan cried, "can the fathers and mothers of Tennessee be blamed for trying to protect their children from such a tragedy?"

After the trial, John Butler wrote of the anti-evolution statute he introduced to Tennessee: "I am not afraid of investigation. . . . Truth is mighty and will prevail. . . . The Dayton trial is the beginning of a great battle between infidelity and Christianity. . . . This is the controversy of the age."

Butler was fearless, as was Bryan, and they won the day in Dayton. In the intervening years, however, the historical truth of their accomplishment has been totally rewritten. Most Christians have not investigated why they think the way they do about Scopes, creation, and evolution.

Henry Morris, whose 1961 book *The Genesis Flood* is credited with a resurgence of interest in creation, said that Christians in general went into retreat. He said that in the years after the Scopes trial, Christians apparently decided, "We'll emphasize evangelism and the spiritual life, just get people saved and ready for heaven and don't get involved in controversial issues like science, history, and politics."

As a result, when a balanced treatment of evolution became law in Arkansas and Louisiana in 1981, few believers held the influential positions needed to give the law a fair hearing. Popular opinion was heavily on the side of the teaching of creation alongside of evolution, but the common people had lost the ability to exert their will. The ACLU and other anticreation forces, however, had not stood idly by during the fifty-six years following the *Scopes* decision. With their expertise and the growing hostility by the agenda setters to anything promoted by religious groups, the deck was stacked against the people. By that time, even the courts had taken sides against God. While at the Scopes trial the ACLU complained that excluding evolution was nonscholarly, this time they no longer made even a pretense of promoting academic freedom. As Norman Geisler observed wryly, they said that "it would be religious bigotry to allow two models of origins to be taught."

The people of Arkansas wanted their children to hear at least something about the Creation story that has filled art and story telling since the beginning of history. When Judge William R. Overton ruled against the people's desire, he cited the unconstitutional establishment of religion. Herbert Titus observed that in order to do this, Overton had to stray outside the realm of case law into the heady atmosphere of defining "What is truth?" and "What is science?" In the process he usurped the role of parents, teachers, and school boards, not to mention the sovereign state legislature, to determine what was best for their children.

The Medieval church's role in condemning the theories of Copernicus and Galileo is ridiculed today, but no one seems to notice that America's courts are acting the same way. The courts, relying on the ACLU, have no more ability to judge the virtues of scientific theories than the medieval clergy did by relying on Greek mythology.

Anticreation propaganda has flourished in this century. *Scopes* and the aftermath are one reason, but the most enduring cause is the country's massive public school system. It teaches Americans how to think and most of the time it teaches them not to think about God. In the twentieth century, that philosophy can be traced to John Dewey, the father of twentieth-century progressive education, and humanistic facets of teacher education. His opposition to the Creator and his dislike for orthodox Christianity is obvious from his writings and from his signature on the Humanist Manifesto of 1933:

- "The universe [is] self-existing and not created."
- "The time has passed for theism. . . . Religion consists of those actions, purposes, and experiences which are humanly significant."

In 1973, humanists reaffirmed these beliefs and added that belief in God was still wrong and belief in salvation, they said, was "harmful, diverting people with false hopes of heaven hereafter. Reasonable minds look to other means for survival."

The psalmist wrote, "The fool says in his heart, 'There is no God'" (Ps. 14:1). How foolish the Humanist Manifesto sounds to those who know better. Belief in God is as natural as breathing. Children are born with it. It is belief in evolution that requires a leap of faith. Evolution is the religion that has no answers. Bernard Ramm, of the American Baptist Seminary of the West, said that evolutionists have been unable to explain:

- The sudden appearance of new forms throughout the history of the universe.
- A First Cause. Nature can't create itself.
- Evolution's contradiction of the Second Law of Thermodynamics. The universe is degenerating, not improving.
- The impossibility that chance could account for intricate sense organs, sense of beauty, capability for rational thought, and, indeed, man's universal yearning after God.

God's people need to start asking those hard questions of themselves and others. They need to recommit themselves to the Creator and then start a crash program to educate children in the truth—at home, in church, in after-school Bible clubs. They must refuse to allow public funds to be used to suppress the truth. God is waiting for His people to rise up on His behalf. If we love Him, we have no other choice.

For Further Reading

L. Sprague de Camp. *The Great Monkey Trial.* Garden City, N.Y.: Doubleday & Co., 1968.

Ray Ginger. *Six Days or Forever?* London: Oxford University Press, 1958.

Peggy Lamson. *Roger Baldwin: Founder of the American Civil Liberties Union.* Boston: Houghton Mifflin Co., 1976.

Jerome Lawrence and Robert E. Lee. *Inherit the Wind.* 1955; New York: Bantam Books, 1979.

Henry M. Morris. *The Biblical Basis of Modern Science.* Grand Rapids, Mich.: Baker Book House, 1984.

Bernard Ramm. *The Christian View of Science and Scripture.* Grand Rapids, Mich.: William B. Eerdmans, 1954.

The World's Most Famous Court Trial: State of Tennessee v. John Thomas Scopes—Complete Stenographic Report. New York: Da Capo Press, 1971.

2

A Call to Arms

As evening fell on the small frame houses and rutted roads of the city, Paul Revere left his silversmith's shop, turned left, and strolled across a drawbridge into Boston. Behind the Old State House, near the darkened Fanueil Hall, he furtively entered an alley leading to the Edes and Gill printing office, home of the *Boston Gazette.* He wasn't there for purely newspaper business.

By light of day, Revere was a respected artisan. By night, he was a revolutionary. All their lives, Revere and his compatriots had been taught that God ruled in the affairs of men. They were convinced God was displeased as much as they were with the oppression they suffered from the British. They were counting on Him to deliver them, but first they were building a base of support by training the people in the biblical principles of freedom.

In secret councils, newspapers, and messages sent by horseback courier over hundreds of miles, they discussed the long train of abuses they would later list in the Declaration of Independence. These included:

- Establishing tyranny.
- Preventing citizens from exercising their right to representation.
- Suspending assemblies.
- Usurping power.
- Destroying the lives of the people.
- Inciting domestic insurrections.

The people of the colonies were still marrying, buying homes, carrying on businesses, and raising families. Nevertheless, because the civil government controlled by England refused to recognize their God-given rights, they were willing to go to war.

For all the talk about "rights" today, most Americans are ignorant of the unalienable rights for which the Founders fought. After generations of public education they don't think biblically about freedom. That is why these seeds are sprouting again:

Establishing tyranny:

- Government policy that schools must deny God's existence.
- State control of children's thinking through twelve years of public school.

Preventing equal representation:

- Harassment of Christian teachers in public schools.
- Court hostility to religious exercise.

Suspending assemblies:

- Closing down Christian schools.
- Forbidding school Bible studies.

Usurping power:

- Regulating every school—public, private, or home.
- Dictating what school a child must attend and which teacher he must have.

Destroying the lives of the people:

- Allowing illiteracy to flourish.
- Forcing taxpayers to pay for their grandchildren's murders (through abortions for their daughters).

Inciting domestic insurrections:

- Forcing parents with high moral values to pay for teaching their children promiscuity.

- Taxing parents for advisers who counsel their children in secrecy.

It is time for a new revolution. Like the Founders, we must launch it by changing the way we think.

Preparing for Revolution

Revere and his coconspirators who met secretly at Edes and Gill were all literate men. Although no names were recorded for reasons of security, it is known that the "Long Room Club" included men like Samuel Adams, John Hancock, James Otis, and Joseph Warren. At least eleven Harvard graduates were among the sixteen regulars. Even artisans like Revere attended strict schools until the age of thirteen when they began their apprenticeships. His training was so sound that he was able to read complicated chemistry texts related to his gold- and silversmith work with no further education.

To the Puritan, an upbringing lacking in intellectual depth was a sign of moral debasement and religious error. "Hence," wrote historian N. Porter, "whenever he builds a church, he erects a school-house." At the time of the Scopes trial, Christians were portrayed as the enemies of education because they objected to man's evolution from the apes. The ignorant people who made that charge had no knowledge that education has held an honored place in both branches of the church since the time of the Reformation. Christians knew that citizens informed by the Bible, the classics, and the great literature of the ages possessed mighty weapons against state tyranny.

In colonial Boston, parents knew that God required them to educate their children. Therefore, they taught them at home or joined with other townspeople to pay a teacher. Because of their forebears' experiences with religious persecution, no one considered relinquishing the tender minds of their children to British brainwashing. Nor would they have allowed out-of-town strangers to dictate what their children learned. The right education was a powerful weapon. The wrong education was a sinister evil.

The schoolchildren, who were mostly boys, had no vacations, summer or winter, only a few days off for Thanksgiving, fasting and prayer days, elections, funerals, or one of the frequent fire emergencies in the city. Local ministers kept tabs on the schools to make sure they were maintaining their standards.

The adults who educated their fellow citizens in the principles of liberty likewise kept themselves independent of outside authorities. The success of the revolution, which they hoped and prayed would never come to armed warfare, was dependent on literate communicators who could understand the rock-bottom principles of freedom and explain them to others through meetings and newspapers.

Since the freedoms of religion, speech, press, and assembly were all intertwined in the success of the colonists' crusade, they later perpetuated these freedoms in the First Amendment.

A PRINCIPLED REVOLUTION

After a night of planning, reasoning, and debating, the men of the Long Room Club would convert their ideals to print and commit their crafted paragraphs to the Edes and Gill hand press.

One of their greatest communicators in print, Sam Adams, was also one of the greatest teachers. No citizen was too lowly to be taught the biblical principles of freedom. At sites like the North End's Salutation tavern, Sam Adams patiently schooled the working men of the city in the knowledge of their rights. Socratic in style, he never dominated their thinking but posed challenging questions that demanded an answer.

In his day, Adams was the acknowledged father of the American Revolution. With incredible patience, he worked for years instilling in the men of Boston a love for liberty and a knowledge that freedom was their right as Englishmen and an unalienable right from God. Through his writings, his Committees of Correspondence, and his backroom teaching, Adams helped lay the foundation for a remarkable nation.

Adams was also the driving force behind the Sons of Liberty, the more visible, activist arm of the protest movement. Their disciplined excursions, however, stand in stark contrast to today's revolts of ungodly, sanctioned terrorism. Historian Esther Forbes wrote of these American patriots:

> It was they who established a mob rule in Boston which was stronger than any law courts. . . . [But] it was, as a puzzled observer wrote back to England, "a trained mob." . . . To their unending honor—they did not take one life in Boston nor inflict serious or permanent physical injury. . . . No European country, torn by its variously colored shirts, has been more bitterly divided than Boston was before the Revolution broke into warfare. To a modern newspaper reader the mildness and order of the Sons of Liberty is hard to understand.

The difference between those Boston revolutionaries and other oppressed people was their belief in God. The French were fomenting revolution in the same era as the Americans, but their philosophy was guided by the Enlightenment. Their source of rights and truth came from the mind of man, not the Spirit of God. They were primarily deists who thought of God as a distant watchmaker, someone who had set the universe in motion and then departed.

The Americans believed in a personal God who judged men and nations. Sam Adams and others gathered their families twice daily for prayers. They knew that they were answerable to the Supreme Judge of the world. Because they recognized the absolute sinfulness of fallen man, the Americans made sure their constitution had checks and balances against dictatorship.

Enlightenment thinkers were opposed to the Bible and anything supernatural because they believed man's reason was all-sufficient. Without biblical absolutes and an allegiance to King Jesus, they committed terrible atrocities in the name of liberty, equality, and fraternity and gave birth to new generations of instability and oppression.

Religious Freedom in America

Since Enlightenment thinking had not yet penetrated the American continent when Paul Revere was still a pupil, his schoolwork was filled with biblical allusions and examples. On Sundays, like many Boston families, the Reveres attended a Congregational church. The Puritans considered the Anglican church an agent of the British government, preferring the freedom to rule themselves and not answer to a bishop appointed by the king.

Colonial preachers spoke boldly about the application of the Bible to all areas of life. They did not play parlor games with religion, endlessly discussing how they could get the most for themselves from God. They believed that the health and safety of the nation depended on the survival of biblical principles. Pastors exercised their liberty in three-hour sermons by teaching the people how the Bible applied to politics, law, corruption, local scandals, and current events. No subject was off-limits because they knew their rights. The people were electrified by the implications of their faith. It gave them the zeal they would later need to fight a mighty empire.

As in every age, rivalries developed and accusations of heresy flew back and forth between the churches. In the early days of the Massachusetts Bay Colony, Puritans distrusted unbelievers and monopolized the local government. They gradually yielded to the demands of others to be involved in self-government.

In Virginia, the established church that took citizens' money and required their attendance eventually yielded to demands for religious freedom. Thomas Jefferson wrote in Virginia's Act for Religious Freedom: "Almighty God has created the mind free. . . . All men shall be free to profess, and by argument to maintain, their opinions in matters of religion, and that the same shall in no wise diminish, enlarge or affect their civil capacities."

It is the premise of this book that, until Christ returns, it is never appropriate for one sect to impose its beliefs on the nation by law. God created the mind free.

The Calvinists explained that in public life a distinction was made between the roles of God as Creator and as Redeemer. The evidence of His creative role was everywhere and required no "preacher" to proclaim it. Every child was born with a sense of God's presence, and anyone who looked at nature could see His mighty works. Thus it is entirely appropriate for America to have as its motto, "In God We Trust."

The Redeemer is not so obvious. Humanity knows that it is sinful and, like Adam and Eve, is ashamed of its sin, but not everyone knows that God sent His Son as an atonement for sin. The communication of that truth is the urgent commission of the Christian, but it is not an appropriate role of the civil government. As the Founders said in the First Amendment to the Constitution, Congress cannot establish an official religion.

Moreover, the Founders also decreed that Congress may not prohibit the free exercise of religion. During the period leading up to the Revolution, the rival sects learned a lot from each other, modifying certain practices to form the union. George Washington, an Anglican and a devout believer, was the unanimous choice as Commander-in-Chief.

If today's government still enforced both the establishment and the free exercise clauses of the First Amendment, Christianity would have just as much access to the minds of the American people—children and adults—as does secularism, humanism, atheism, or any other religion in today's so-called pluralistic society. Instead, the establishment clause was enlarged and the free exercise clause was diminished, until Christianity began to be treated as a threat to the nation.

As a result, not only public schools, but also private churches and schools are increasingly monitored by the state lest they communicate the full message of the Gospel—the Lordship of Christ over *all* of life.

The Revere family attended the "Cockerel" Church—so named because of a young member who crowed derisively from the weather vane at a rival church. Paul's father allowed him to take a job ringing the bells of the disfavored Christ's Episcopal Church, but without permission Paul also slipped off to the West Street Church to hear the fiery young Jonathan

Mayhew, a man who in January 1750 preached what John Adams later called "the opening gun of the Revolution."

Mayhew's sermon—widely distributed as a pamphlet—said that Christians were only bound by God to obey "just" rulers. He labeled as blasphemy the demand "to call tyrants and oppressors God's ministers." There was no divine right of kings. Nations must be ruled by law, not the arbitrary whim of a ruler nor the bloodthirsty rule of a mob. As the Declaration of Independence would later say, governments are instituted among men to secure God-given rights, not to control them. Mayhew died before the "shot heard round the world," but his words started fifteen-year-old Paul and many others on the path to revolution.

After volunteering in the French and Indian Wars and listening for years to the messages of the patriots, Revere was willing to do whatever God and country required of him. On 18 April 1775, he received word that British troops were set to confiscate weapons and arrest the leaders of colonial dissent. A veteran of many long rides in the saddle as courier for the rebels, Revere knew that he was engaging in high treason by spreading the message that night, but for him the law of God took precedence over the law of man.

His first stop was at the familiar Christ's Episcopal where he sent Robert Newman up the stairs with two lanterns to warn the patriots in Charlestown: "Two if by sea."

Somehow he slipped through the troops milling near his house and was rowed across the water under a bright, cold moon. At John Larkin's house he was given his compatriot's best horse. They all knew how many lives depended on the success of his mission.

Revere rode past an iron cage containing the remains of a slave executed twenty years earlier for treason and left there in chains as a warning. He spotted two British officers before they spotted him and took off across the field on his light-footed steed. The officers mounted their horses and pursued him, but their heavy parade horses bogged down in the mud. Revere's horse ran free.

Everywhere he went, bedlam followed. "The regulars are out!" he shouted, and men leaped from their beds, grabbed their muskets and powder horns, and rode off to tell others. Bells rang. Drums beat. Women and children ran for the swamps.

When he reached Clark's Parsonage, he met Sam Adams and the nattily attired John Hancock, who could scarcely be restrained from joining the first battle. Inevitably, Revere was captured, but he knew the Minute Men had been aroused and the fight for freedom had begun.

A NEW TYRANNY

Henry Wadsworth Longfellow later wrote, "The fate of a nation was riding that night." Yet by the time he penned those words, a new force rode across the land. It promised greater freedom than Americans had ever known, but it was only a new tyranny in disguise.

The dark specter that began its ride in Longfellow's time was compulsory, secular education. No less a menace than the arbitrary rule of tyrants, it began in the villages and farms of Massachusetts but eventually captured the soul of the nation. It carried the imported Enlightenment message that America could be a heaven on earth if its citizens were given the best worldly wisdom. With insufficient biblical knowledge to refute it, Americans volunteered for the yoke.

Secular education, funded and enforced by the government, is no less dangerous than oppression by a tyrant or civil rule by the clergy because it allows the state to become the master of the mind. God gave freedom of heart and mind to humankind. The state did not give that right, and it cannot legally take it away, but it often tries.

Religious freedom was the first casualty when Horace Mann and the early advocates of compulsory education insisted on a program free from the tenets of sectarianism. In order to produce properly docile citizens for the state, the schools eliminated anything considered inflammatory, such as the fact that there is one God and one Lord Jesus Christ by whom all persons must be saved. Thus, from the beginning, state-funded, anti-Christian schools were in direct conflict with the First Amendment. They should never have been allowed.

Consider these recent developments:

- Christians who say that they believe that Jesus Christ is the Savior of the world willingly refrain from speaking His name in the public forum.
- Christian teachers in the public schools are harassed by their superiors.

Kenneth Roberts, a fifth-grade teacher in Adams County, Colorado, was forbidden to read his Bible to himself in his classroom during student reading times and forced to remove a Bible and Bible storybook from the classroom library. In an opinion on 5 January 1989, the federal district judge said, "The students are, in a real sense, a captive audience to even silent forms of religious indoctrination." (How true—all the more reason to have some Bibles around to counteract the anti-God religion schoolchildren pick up every day.)

- Publishers, in order to sell textbooks, remove all mention of religion from history, government, and contemporary life.

Paul Vitz wrote in *Censorship: Evidence of Bias in Our Children's Textbooks* that in his review of forty social studies texts commonly used for grades one through four, twenty-five did not have a single word or picture of a religious activity. Half of the books that did mention religion placed it in the past, usually in references to Puritans and Spanish missions. No modern story character went to a church or synagogue.

- Textbooks ignore the godly, patriotic men who built America.

After reviewing 670 reading stories for grades three and six, Vitz found only five stories that were remotely patriotic, and none of these had the slightest hint of the Founders' beliefs or sense of commitment. Paul Revere had been replaced by a girl named Sybil Ludington, who dressed like a man in order to warn the colonials of the British march on Concord and Lexington. Vitz wrote, "This story is in many respects a feminist piece, and it has little of a specifically patriotic character."

- Christian schools are unconstitutionally regulated and closed when they offer an alternative to secular education. Several lawsuits are currently pending.
- An elite minority of secularists is exerting its will over Christians trying to get an advanced education.

The Institute for Creation Research discovered through the news media in December 1988 that its pending accreditation had been denied by the state of California. School Superintendent Bill Honig told the press that the college could no longer grant a graduate degree in science because it emphasized creation. Although the program differed in no other way from secular science courses, Honig asserted, "The vast bulk of what they learn is not science." The ill-treated school is appealing.

- Religious freedom is redefined as the absence of religion.

State-financed schools endeavor to convince children that it is the task of all people to create an earthly utopia with no help from God. Horace Mann and John Dewey, Mann's twentieth-century successor, considered faith in God as an option, a frill. The real work in society was done by people who were not inherently sinful but inherently good and becoming better by evolving toward perfection.

Dewey promoted the idea of a common faith that all people would agree on, as long as nobody insisted on believing in God. The Founders knew that would never happen, and should never happen. That is why they wrote the First Amendment. No Christians worth their salt would agree to a religion that pretends it has no need for Christ, and no one who rejects Christ can be forced by the state to accept His atonement. Religion is an individual decision. The government that promotes one faith is tyrannical.

- Compulsory education has produced subdued masses of common people with little or no quality education, unable or unwilling to question the autocratic policies of the state.

The devastating condition in the public schools is described in the next chapter. Unlike the Founders, today's citizens are simply not being equipped with the information in the Bible, the classics, and history that could protect them from a tyranny of the strong.

- The communications media have been commandeered by public school graduates with no use for the Bible.

In 1985, press researchers Stanley Rothman and S. Robert Lichter found that half of the media elite had no religious affiliation.

- Outside influences dominate local education systems under the pretense of national harmony.

After the Civil War, Congress was temporarily dominated by Northerners. They took the opportunity to push through federally funded school programs to remedy the Southerners' "ignorance and illiteracy," which they contended had contributed to the war. They believed that only an expanded program of national education could preserve the union.

In 1867, a future president, James Garfield, in cooperation with increasingly powerful educators, pushed through Congress a National Bureau of Education. Representative Samuel Wheeler Moulton of Illinois used persuasive logic when he said, "We want all these school systems over all the land brought under one head so that they may be nationalized, vitalized and made uniform and harmonious as far as possible." This blurring of individuality among the states eventually brought on a national disaster: the authority over children's minds came to be concentrated in the hands of powerful education "experts" far removed from the local scene.

In 1931, there were 259,000 school districts. In 1980, these independent entities had been compressed into 16,000 megadistricts. As a result, schools came under the control of individuals who had no accountability to local patrons.

John Silber, president of Boston University, warned that Americans must insist on a "major devolution of authority from the states to the local schools. The ideal is surely to make public school patrons as powerful over their schools as private school patrons now are."

- The state began to define truth.

As a result of this uniformity movement, the state—via the schools and the courts—began to define not only what constituted a harmonious school system, but also what was true and what was not. The Bible fell in disfavor because it offered an alternative to the evolving kingdom of people. As Herbert Titus wrote, "The justices know that the Bible, as the foundation of all wisdom and knowledge, poses the greatest threat to the man-centered philosophy that dominates every subject in the state-operated schools today."

The nation's Founders believed that truth resided in the person of Jesus Christ. They taught in their schools that the fear of the Lord is the beginning of wisdom. Succeeding generations of secular educators, however, denounced these standards as a sectarian doctrine unfit for a "harmonious" educational system. As education analyst Samuel Blumenfeld said, "Public education, which had been instituted in the Puritan colony as a means of guaranteeing the survival of pure religion, would now be used to destroy it."

- Faith was labeled as the enemy of a stable society.

Secular educators portray religious faith as the activity of an uneducated, unreasoning minority. They consider it contrary to the sound education system that they have developed based on reason alone. However, said theology professor John Frame in his book, *Doctrine of the Knowledge of God:*

> When the unbeliever attacks Christianity for being based on "faith" as opposed to "reason" it is important to reverse the complaint. The unbeliever, too, has presuppositions that he does not question and that govern every aspect of his thought and life. Thus in a relevant sense, he too has "faith." He too argues in a circle. It is not as if the two are equal, however, for the non-Christian has no basis for trusting reason, except his blind faith. If this world is ultimately the product of chance plus matter, of space and time, why should we assume that events in our heads will tell us anything reliable about the real world?

CULTURAL ILLITERACY

In terms of their knowledge of American culture, our children are paying a heavy price for the hysteria over church-state issues. When religious references from the past must be hidden from children, their portion of history is meager indeed. The resulting cultural illiteracy has crippled education. Allan Bloom in his book, *The Closing of the American Mind,* lamented: "We are like ignorant shepherds living on a site where great civilizations once flourished. The shepherds play with the fragments that pop up to the surface, having no notion of the beautiful structures of which they were once a part."

Progressive education has inserted blanks into our intellectual ammunition. To restore the real thing, E. D. Hirsch, Jr., proposed a list of forty-five hundred words and phrases that all high school graduates should master. In his popular *Cultural Literacy: What Every American Needs to Know,* he urged a return to the national vocabulary people once shared, which, as several have noted, included a healthy dose of the Bible and the classics. Without these works, our thinking is shallow and uninformed. Our conversation resembles a mindless television commercial. We are vulnerable to tyranny because we have no lessons from the past to warn us otherwise.

John Dewey believed, like Darwin, that all life is in a constant state of flux and change. Nothing in the past has inherent value because everything is outdated. Bloom wrote that Dewey "saw the past as radically imperfect and regarded our history as irrelevant or as a hindrance to rational analysis of our present."

In *Experience and Education,* Dewey branded as "reactionary" the notion that education was the "transmission of the cultural heritage" and that certain subject matter was essential to education. Teachers trained over the years under Dewey's progressive education model often come to see themselves as superior to the religious and tradition-bound parents of their students.

Parents in Crisis

The majority of American public school teachers have little confidence in the parents of their students. They say that parents are not involved enough in helping their children and they can never get them to come to meetings.

There is no doubt about it. A great number of parents have relinquished control over their children's education to the public schools. This abdication is not without cause, however. From the time that the parents were pupils themselves, they have been trained to think that only a professional is qualified to teach children anything valuable. Parents can love and feed their children, but they don't have what it takes to train their minds.

It is time to put a stop to these lies. America needs a revolution in the home. Parents need to snap out of their hypnotic state and look at what the schools are doing to their children and their families by removing God from the classroom.

God told children to honor their parents, not despise their teaching ability. He told parents to teach their children. They may designate someone of their choosing to teach in their place, but a teacher only serves *in loco parentis*—in the temporary place of the parent. Parents must repent before God of so easily giving up their children to the state; teachers need to repent of placing themselves above the parents; and the state needs to resign from the mind-control business and let parents run their children's education.

Several models have been offered for resolving this problem:

- home schools
- private schools
- Christian schools
- parents' choice of a public school
- voucher system

When Larry and Mary Bevis lived in Bloomington, Minnesota, they had one conflict after another with the public schools. Mary said, "They challenged us on every level of our values, educational goals and parenting by ignoring our concerns no matter how involved we tried to be in the system *and* by actually instructing our kids to develop values and goals of their own, even if they conflicted with social norms or family principles."

The following year the Bevises took Bryna (eighth grade), Jocelyn (fourth grade), and Christopher (second grade) out of this impossible environment. They had a "delightful" time of home schooling, Mary said.

In 1988, they moved to nearby Burnsville, where they visited the public schools and found a pleasant surprise. As Mary wrote in a homemakers' magazine that she edited, "I'm sure there is no such thing as a perfect school, but I'm also certain we can successfully work with the Burnsville system. . . . We've always believed parents know what's best for their kids and this district seems willing to work with that."

The Bevises are unusual because they refused to accept the inferior status imposed on them by the arrogance of the Bloomington school authorities. They were fortunate that they lived in a state that recognized the parents' right to educate their children at home.

Ghetto families, however, may be just as upset with their children's education, the daily dangers they face, and the way parents are degraded. These families cannot afford home lessons or move to a new locale. One solution being offered to them is called "Choice."

A few localities allow parents to investigate several nearby schools until they find the one that best meets the academic and emotional needs of their children. When schools lose too many patrons, they face a mandate to improve their programs. Meanwhile, parents are given a more active role.

The voucher system is a more radical approach. Any parents with school-age children would receive a voucher from the state, good for whatever amount would be spent to educate the children in the local public school. The parents are free to cash in that voucher at any school of their choice: Christian, private, or public. Although it is doubtful that the agents of public funds will ever allow such freedom, allowing parents to choose their children's schooling is the proper thing to do.

The only solution that would meet both constitutional and biblical guidelines would be to close down the public schools altogether. Parents could use the savings in tax money to educate their children, with absolutely no involvement by the state. One cannot imagine a greater upheaval than that development would cause.

EDUCATIONAL REFORM

One crucial step to educational reform, said Lamar Alexander, former governor of Tennessee, is to challenge and defeat the power-hungry education elite. In his first term in the statehouse, he set out to improve the state's economy by attracting new industry. He discovered, however, that no one wanted to relocate in Tennessee. The state's public schools were not producing graduates whom businesses wanted to hire.

Tennessee was part of a national trend. Today's high school graduates are so inferior to their predecessors that one in three corporations has had to introduce basic skills training for its employees. In 1988, American businesses spent $200 million to compensate for the nation's faulty public schools. Costs in business for remedial education in the future could reach $25 billion annually.

Governor Alexander presented the Tennessee legislature with a sweeping educational reform package, including a proposal to recognize those who were outstanding master teachers and raise their salaries. To his surprise, he was immediately challenged by the Tennessee Education Association (TEA), an affiliate of the National Education Association (NEA). When the NEA came out swinging, the legislature refused to fight.

Alexander decided to get in the ring himself. "When the legislature passed an across-the-board teacher pay raise," he said, "I vetoed it. 'No reforms, no money,' I had vowed." In a statewide voters' poll, Tennesseans overwhelmingly endorsed his stand and rejected the TEA's position that teachers could not be evaluated fairly and that pay incentives would damage morale. The legislature listened to the people. A reform program was enacted and financed. Students and teachers would be tested. The master teachers could receive a bonus of up to $7,000. Tennessee's educational reforms succeeded.

The state also launched an attack on the education courses that discouraged so many potential students from entering the teaching profession. Dean Robert Saunders of Memphis State University's College of Education replaced the studies designed only to grant certification with requirements for postgraduate work in academic majors. The program included an opportunity to work alongside a master teacher as an apprentice during the day while taking required courses at night. With only fifty openings in the program, some three hundred applied. The plan was so successful that the Carnegie Foundation for the Advancement of Teaching has now recommended a similar program for all teacher certification programs.

Better Teachers Not the Whole Answer

Tennessee may be on its way to excellence in teaching methods, but a 1986 lawsuit by Vicki Frost and other parents contended that the state's textbooks promoted secular humanism, which they understood as an unconstitutional establishment of religion. The parents immediately became the laughingstock of the press. A member of the Hawkins County school board's legal team sniffed, "Lift the petticoat and look underneath, and it's just censorship."

"Censorship" is a common, faulty dodge guaranteed to win support against anyone who tries to change the content of curriculum. Don't accept it without a fight.

The term secular means simply "of, or pertaining to, the world." Christians have no problem with that. We all live in the world. "Secularism" or "secular humanism," however, is a *religion,* a belief system that insists that the only source for knowledge and morality is in human beings and in this present life. Belief in God or any consideration of a future life are excluded. Christians do have problems with that.

The secularist represents a view that defies Christianity head on. It is never, never, in any way a neutral system. You are either for God or against Him. Secularism is not simply non-Christian. It is counter-Christian, and it has been growing relentlessly in public education for a long, long time.

At first, there were subtle hints that God, although He exists, was not at the center of things; decisions did not have to be made with God as the starting point or with concern about His revealed Word. Education could set Him off to the side. Even people in the church began to tamper with the truth, vacillating and then denying the inerrancy of the Bible.

Generally speaking, Tennesseans are churchgoers, but, unlike the days of the Scopes Trial in 1925, only a few understood what was at stake in the quarrel over secular humanism. After an initial favorable ruling, Frost and the parents lost the suit. All was not lost, however. Tennessee is in the process of seeking equal treatment for creation and evolution.

THE LOVE OF GOD

Our ancestors realized that children studying the physical universe cannot help but see God at work, unless they are told otherwise. God is not *part* of nature, but, as Paul wrote to the Romans, His attributes are *revealed* by His creation. His beauty is seen in the autumn leaves of Vermont, His majesty in the rugged snowslopes of Mount Rainier, His power in the surf at Waikiki, His love in the tenderness of a child.

Paul wrote that we cannot see God with the naked eyes because He is Spirit, but "God's invisible qualities—his eternal power and divine nature—have been clearly seen, being understood from what has been made" (Rom. 1:20).

Without God, the universe is little more than particles and atoms and pieces lacking wholeness. It has no meaning, no hope, no love. The

American public school system, to the best of its ability, contributes to this devastation. Those who deny what is clearly seen, Paul said, are "without excuse," and their "godlessness and wickedness" incur God's wrath.

Watching the public school system falling apart at the seams, one cannot help but see the judgment of God. God loves the world. The world, the American nation, are far too important to be left to the control of secularists, yet that is exactly what has been done. Jesus said, "God loved the world so much that he gave his only Son, so that everyone who believes in him should not be lost, but should have eternal life. God has not sent his Son into the world to pass sentence upon it, but to save it—through him" (John 3:16–17, PHILLIPS). How can children be expected to make sense of anything—from science to social studies—if the puzzle always has the central piece missing?

Americans live in a nation where freedom of speech is a basic right, yet they have been led to believe that schoolteachers, unless they profess secularism, are forbidden to exercise this right. They live in a country that claims to be "One Nation Under God," yet they have allowed a small minority to convince them that it is somehow noble to pretend every school day that He does not exist.

Doesn't it give you pause to think what an impact that godlessness has had upon the minds of your children? Can you imagine how it grieves our Heavenly Father when we cooperate in suppressing the truth about Him? Like Peter, we have denied the Lord, and, like him, we should weep.

Without God, America's children—and the adults they become—have no hope and no reason to be good. Some may never learn until it is too late that God holds them accountable for their deeds. Meanwhile, children think there is no one to whom they answer, except teachers and parents, whom they can manage to outfox at least some of the time. Schools are a combat zone because no one dares mention absolute standards of right and wrong and the law of God. George Washington said it plainly in his Farewell Address: "Let us with caution indulge the supposition that morality can be maintained without religion. Whatever may be conceded to the influence of refined education on minds of peculiar structure, reason and experience both forbid us to expect that national morality can prevail in exclusion of religious principles."

America needs more than a few religious Band-aids to heal its bleeding public school system. The next few chapters describe what others are doing in the desperate attempt to help children attain a basic education once taken for granted—things like reading, math, science, and the truth that God exists. Much more is needed.

The need is just as great as that night when Paul Revere warned the people that the nation was in grave danger. Take this seriously. No volunteer is too insignificant for the cause.

Like the Founders, start your own training sessions in biblical principles of freedom. Covenant together to teach children the full truth. Encourage pastors to fire their guns at secularism from the pulpit and march into the local schools to find out what is going on there. Start newspapers and newsletters by the hundreds to sound the alarm across the land. Unite with groups like CBN, Focus on the Family, the American Family Association, and Concerned Women for America. Insist on the enforcement of the First Amendment in the public schools. Take a stand for freedom regardless of the cost. Remember the sacrifices of our forefathers.

"The weapons we fight with," said the Apostle Paul, "are not the weapons of the world. On the contrary, they have divine power to demolish strongholds" (2 Cor. 10:4). Take up those arms and go to war. Polish your knowledge of God's Word until it is truly a sword of the Spirit. Refuse to compromise on your rights or your ethics. Pray until you see those mountains move. Love your enemies until you win their minds. Forget those who despitefully use you. Let God deal with them.

In 1983, when a presidential commission published its scathing criticism of the public school system, *A Nation at Risk,* the members told parents that they did not have to accept the passive role imposed on them by the educational bureaucracy. They wrote, "You have the right to demand for your children the best our schools and colleges can provide. Your vigilance and your refusal to be satisfied with less than the best are the imperative first step."

For Further Reading

Samuel L. Blumenfeld. *Is Public Education Necessary?* Old Greenwich, Conn.: Devin-Adair Co., 1981.

John Dewey. *Experience and Education.* 1938; New York: Collier Books, Macmillan Publishing Co., 1963.

Esther Forbes. *Paul Revere and the World He Lived In.* New York: Literary Classics, 1942.

John M. Frame. *The Doctrine of the Knowledge of God.* Phillipsburg, N.J.: Presbyterian and Reformed Publishing Co., 1987.

Benjamin Hart. *Faith and Freedom.* The Christian Roots of American Liberty. Dallas: Lewis and Stanley, 1988.

Peter Marshall and David Manuel. *The Light and the Glory.* Old Tappan, N.J.: Fleming H. Revell, 1977.

Cotton Mather. *The Great Works of Christ In America: Magnalia Christi Americana.* 1702; Edinburgh: Banner of Truth Trust, 1979.

The National Commission on Excellence in Education. *A Nation at Risk: The Imperative for Educational Reform.* April 1983.

N. Porter. *The Educational Systems of the Puritans and the Jesuits Compared.* Library of American Civilization 40011. New York: M. W. Dodd, 1851.

Paul C. Vitz. *Censorship: Evidence of Bias in Our Children's Textbooks.* Ann Arbor, Mich.: Servant Books, 1986.

3

The Basics

When Jonathan Kozol began his career as a fourth-grade schoolteacher in Boston's Roxbury district, he found it "a world of suffering, of hopelessness and fear." The school's footworn floors and marred desks matched the rough, hardened prejudices of the teachers. Convinced the children had no intellectual capital from which to draw, the teachers collected salaries without improving minds. Kozol titled one of the books he wrote about it *Death at an Early Age.*

One of his principals had advised him to keep aloof from the parents. "Let the parents come to you," he urged. "Don't you go down to them." This arrogance is typical of, but not limited to, the schools in the ghetto. Parents have become for most educators in America an unwelcome intrusion on their day.

In spite of the warning, Kozol found himself drawn to the homes. With a coworker, he hesitantly made his way through the cluttered, noisy streets and began knocking on doors. At first the parents were frightened to see them, certain that their son or daughter must be in serious trouble. Eventually, they relaxed and talked, sharing their lives and expressing their hopes that their children would have a better life.

Often they invited the teachers to dinner. "I loved those dinners," wrote Kozol years later. "They saved me from my fear. They taught me of the generosity and kindness of some of the poorest and most poorly treated people in our nation."

Kozol has had a heart for the poor ever since and has become a vocal advocate for their needs. One of the problems he continues to fight is their desperate illiteracy. In some ways, this blight on America resembles the era before the Civil War when slaves were kept ignorant—under threat of dire punishment—to keep them under control. That age has passed, but the illiteracy rate is so high today that, intended or not, one group of people wields enormous power over another group because only the elite can read.

Illiteracy is so pervasive in American schools today that it is no longer limited to crumbling cities, nor even to rural shacks. Illiteracy has become an equal-opportunity disgrace. The city of Boston, once the literacy capital of America, was described recently by a disgusted businessman as "not only second rate, but a disaster, a waste basket."

Even with no other signs to indicate the failure of the public schools, it would be enough to exclaim that one-third of America's adult population is functionally illiterate. Parents can't help their children get an education and build a new life when they have never learned to read themselves. Kozol observed, "Twenty-five million American adults cannot read the poison warnings on a can of pesticide, a letter from their child's teacher, or the front page of a daily paper. An additional 35 million read only at a level which is less than equal to the full survival needs of our society."

The average illiterate American has spent eight years in school, yet he cannot read a phone book, fill out a job application, or follow instructions for public transportation. He can't vote or stop the school board from actions he abhors.

There is a solution to that problem. It works on the poor as well as the rich. It is so simple it is tragic. We already know how to teach almost every man, woman, and child in America to read, but our educational bureaucrats refuse to let us do it. In spite of the overwhelming evidence against their methods, the people who review school curricula continue to impose the same failed reading books on their students with their pretty pictures and empty promises.

The recalcitrance of reading educators has proved so devastating that the U.S. Department of Education reported in 1983, "The educational foundations of our society are presently being eroded by a rising tide of mediocrity that threatens our very future as a nation and a people." Test after test shows that even those American children who can read are ignorant of basic history, math, and science. They continually rate last when compared with other countries.

Literacy literally saved the American nation two hundred years ago because the Founders knew how to read the Bible and other great works that defined the principles of liberty. Will illiteracy defeat that same country? The threat is great. The answers are available. Something must be done about it now.

THE DISMAL RECORD

Americans were reading just fine until John Dewey began to promote the look-and-say method of reading as a part of his "progressive education" theory. Reading teachers nationwide had been using a reliable phonics method, teaching the sounds of the letters first, then applying them to the child's already extensive vocabulary. By contrast, the look-and-say method relied on memorization of whole words. Children could learn only a limited number of words each year, so during reading times they were encouraged to *guess* any words they didn't know.

The look-and-say method is hopelessly inept, and until Dewey's time was never seriously implemented. Such was Dewey's influence, however, along with that of the rapidly burgeoning educational powerhouse, that while families were busy trying to survive the Depression, educators slipped in a new reading curriculum in most of the country.

Rudolf Flesch described the dire consequences of these wholesale changes in his book, *Why Johnny Still Can't Read:* "That huge bonanza created problems. Look-and-say, after all, was still essentially a gimmick with no scientific foundations whatever. As it had for 150 years, it produced children who couldn't accurately read unfamiliar words. From the fourth grade up, textbooks in all subjects had to be 'dumbed down' to accommodate them. Grade promotions had to be based on age rather than on achievement. High school diplomas were given to functional illiterates. Colleges had to adjust to an influx of students who couldn't read. The national illiteracy rate climbed year after year after year."

It is only recently that Americans have been startled to hear about America's watered-down educational system, but, as the late Rudolf Flesch noted, the gruel had been simmering for years. Why has phonics been suppressed? Phonics doesn't fit the eclectic educational philosophy which assumes that no single reading system could possibly work for all children. It is academic relativism with a vengeance.

God created human minds consistent with one another in their ability to associate sight and sound. Reading is another of His miracles, but one to which He has given us many keys. If there was not such entrenched resistance to phonics, even Dewey's pragmatic test of experience would confirm that phonics works and look-and-say doesn't.

MAKING PHONICS FUN

Several years ago, Sue Dickson, a schoolteacher, left the Christian school where she had been teaching and took a public school job in New Jersey. She was shocked by what she found. "They couldn't read 'cat,'" she said in an interview. "I had been in a Christian school where they could read the King James Bible after second grade. I thought surely everybody's caught on to phonics by now."

The night before she got the job, she had been discouraged about the direction her life was taking. She "cried out to God," she said. "I told Him, 'I did what you told me to do. You show me what to do now.'" A short time later, she said, "a song popped into my mind" for teaching phonics.

She knew the students in her new class were just like the others she had taught to read. They simply needed the proper teaching. So she set to work developing a phonetic system based on songs—a fun departure from the sometimes monotonous drills used in earlier phonics teaching. Her class did so well that other parents began to request her for a teacher.

Eventually, she gave up teaching completely and began to work with CBN University on developing a program called Sing, Spell, Read, and Write. Test trials were done in inner cities, and the method worked. Previously sidelined children began to astound everyone with their progress.

In 1985, Pittsburgh schoolchildren one or more grades behind in their reading tried Sing, Spell, Read, and Write in summer school. In less than three weeks, the twenty-six children had jumped an astonishing average of 1.6 grades in vocabulary and 1.8 grades in comprehension. Paul Clark, director of this Cities in Schools project, said that in his thirty-eight years of educational experience he had never seen anything like it. In 1987, children in Aberdeen, Mississippi, sang their way to a 42-percentile point increase in reading performance in one year. CBN is now funding a statewide effort to raise the state out of the nation's literacy cellar.

Sing, Spell, Read, and Write has also gone to jail. Although it is obviously more suited for children, adult inmates, desperate to find a way out of their cycle of an illiteracy-related criminal life, gave it a try. It worked. In 1988, Dickson and CBN developed an adult version called Winning that uses rap, rock, and country music.

In his book, Flesch listed five major providers of phonics materials. Despite the availability of workable materials, it is heartbreaking that so many believe that they are hopelessly inept at reading, destined to dead-end jobs or no jobs at all. Flesch wrote: "In the past twenty or thirty years, our schools have labeled hundreds of thousands of children 'dyslexic,' 'minimally brain-damaged,' 'learning disabled,' or what have you. They didn't learn to read by whatever standard was used, *therefore* there was something wrong with them. . . . I don't mean to say that there are no children with organic disorders, but they are few and far between. The vast majority of those unhappy, stigmatized children are simply the victims of look-and-say."

Kozol started Literacy Action, a national organization to recruit volunteer tutors and help people learn to read. He said that it was very difficult for an adult illiterate to come forward, and even when one did there were no volunteers to help him. In Illinois alone, he estimated that there were more than a hundred thousand people on the waiting list.

Illiterates need personal tutors in their own neighborhoods. Many cannot follow a bus schedule or pass a driving test. Often they are so embarrassed by their illiteracy that they won't admit it to anyone or ask for help. Churches should be in the forefront of this outreach. Many are starting to get involved.

"Love your neighbor," Jesus said. Loving neighbors means to get them out of the ditch. If you are willing to be that Good Samaritan whom Jesus commended, there are several routes open to you:

- Contact Kozol at Literacy Action in Byfield, Massachusetts
- Obtain Sing, Spell, Read, and Write materials from CBN
- Contact a local literacy group that uses phonics
- Get together with parents and concerned citizens and insist that your local schools replace their reading curriculum with something that does not give degrees in illiteracy.

Raise extra money if you have to, but get it changed. Speak up for those who have no advocates in the ghettoes. No one should be ignored. A few lone voices like Kozol, Flesch, and Dickson can't change the entire public school system, but an uprising by concerned citizens can.

MATHEMATICS MUMBO-JUMBO

Another group of schoolchildren who need rescuing are those hopelessly confused by mathematics. Math is so difficult for today's young people that a study by the National Assessment of Educational Progress found that "nearly one-third of eleventh graders say they generally do not understand what the math teacher is talking about." Overall, said the NAEP's *Mathematics Report Card* in 1986, the high school students' performance is "dismal."

This is a solvable problem, yet, like the illiteracy fiasco, the solution is not getting through. Math was much easier for their parents than it is for today's schoolchildren. What has happened to math education in one generation?

Just as Sue Dickson was shocked at her pupils' reading, John Saxon was appalled at his students' arithmetic. Unlike Dickson's grade-school experience, his students had already reached the junior college level.

After retirement from the Air Force, where he had been a decorated fighter pilot, test pilot, and instructor at the Air Force Academy, Saxon had taken a job teaching algebra at Oscar Rose Junior College in Midwest City, Oklahoma. Confronted with his students' math deficiencies, Saxon began to look into the high-school textbooks that should have prepared them. He couldn't make heads nor tails of the books. The lessons were disorganized, out of order, and full of useless concepts with impossible names. He decided to do something about it.

In spite of incredible opposition from entrenched educators, Saxon developed his own high-school textbooks and organized a program to test the results. The books followed a logical progression from simple to complex and relied on daily homework assignments that reviewed old material as they introduced the new. The results were astonishing. On 21 December 1981, *Time* magazine reported: "Students using Saxon's book showed an overall gain of 159 percent as compared with the control group. The tests also revealed that Saxon students in the lowest-ability group (classified on the basis of their scores on the California Achievement Tests, given in August 1980) outscored their control counterparts by a staggering 246 percent."

One of Saxon's success stories is Northwest Classen High School in Oklahoma City. Classen's students were predominately from minority groups, and many lived in housing projects—a group many educators write off as uneducable. According to Barbara Keith, Classen's math department chairwoman, since the adoption of the Saxon series, an amazing 80 percent of the students have enrolled in mathematics.

None of the other schools in her district used the Saxon books, so Classen's students consistently outscored the other schools in math competitions by large margins—until the year the schools voted to hold the contest there. According to the rules of the competition, no school could enter contestants when it served as host.

The Classen students' math drills made them champions outside their school as well. When they weren't winning competitions, they were over on the other side tutoring the opposition, whose principals steadfastly refused to change textbooks.

Traditional learning methods like Saxon's were abandoned by the professional educators, not because they didn't work, but because according to John Dewey's philosophy they were not good for the children. Dewey contended that drills stifled creativity and destroyed one's ability to make decisions. He wrote in *Experience and Education:* "How many acquired special skills by means of automatic drill so that their power of judgment and capacity to act intelligently in new situations was limited?"

If Americans had been literate in the Bible, they would have known that anything Dewey proposed should be suspect because the same philosophy that destroyed America's math and science was staunchly against God. Literacy and math cannot be separated from God's world. He is the one who created order. He has also been known to confuse the language of those who insist on shutting Him out (Gen. 11:1–13).

Math teachers who accept Dewey's reasoning ought to talk to their school football coaches. If the coach wanted his team to win, he wouldn't say, "From now on during practice we won't run drills on our plays. Just get here a few minutes before the game, and we will think about how we can win." Instead, coaches usually tell their players to get their cleats on and run up and down some muddy field until they get the plays right.

Children learn by repetition. There is no way around it. There are ways of making drills more interesting, but there is no way to eliminate them wholesale. "Precept must be upon precept, precept upon precept; line upon line, line upon line; here a little, and there a little" (Isa. 28:10, KJV).

Children like the satisfaction of learning, even if they complain about the methods of getting there. John Saxon has become something of a hero to the children who use his books. Wherever he goes, he is treated like a celebrity. "It's humbling," he said in an interview, because "these kids don't con."

At one school, four or five children heard he was in the principal's office and came running in. "I'm having so much fun in math this year," one girl blurted out.

"Math is easy, isn't it?" Saxon asked her.

"It is if you have the right book," she said.

After years of steady determination, Saxon's books and methods are used in 10 percent of the American market, but 90 percent of the schools are closed to him. Like the phonics advocates, he has faced insurmountable opposition from the establishment.

The attacks have only strengthened his resolve. "I know I'm right," he said. "For some reason I've been selected and given the opportunity. All by myself I am going to kill the dragon and rescue the princess."

WHAT HAS GONE WRONG WITH SCIENCE?

On 4 October 1957, the American scientific community was shocked to hear that the Soviet Union had successfully launched the first satellite into space. A mad scramble began to improve America's space program, but despite the determination behind the task, Yuri Gagarin was the first man to orbit the earth.

Many American scientists responded to this "humiliation" by demanding an increase in funding for public school science programs. They also wanted to ditch those pesky theories of creation and concentrate on evolution (like their Soviet counterparts). They were successful on both counts, but the effort failed. Thirty years later, American science students finished dead last in a comparison with other nations. God is not mocked (Gal. 6:7, KJV).

American kids don't like science. They can't understand it. Christians are warned to avoid it. Classes in basic science are becoming unpopular electives in the nation's high schools. It just doesn't seem like any fun any more. Science without God is a drag.

Back when the modern scientific era began, scientists were excited about their discoveries because their findings confirmed the existence of the Creator and Sustainer and showed them practical ways to love their neighbors. Every time another mystery was solved, mankind was the beneficiary.

Robert Boyle, the seventeenth-century scientist behind Boyle's Law, was so cognizant of God's wisdom and power that he never mentioned God's name without a reverent pause in his speech. His scientific writings were precise, diligently documented, and full of the wonder of the Lord. He marveled in his *Usefulness of Natural Philosophy:*

> How boundless a power, or rather what an almightiness is eminently displayed in God's making out of nothing all things, and without materials or instruments constructing this immense fabrick of the world, whose vastness is such, that even what may be proved of it, can scarcely be conceived.
>
> *How manifold are thy works, O Lord: in wisdom hast thou made them all.* And therefore I shall content myself to observe in general, that, as highly as some naturalists are pleased to value their own knowledge, it can at best attain but to understand and applaud, not emulate the productions of God.

In 1979, the Pulitzer Prize for general nonfiction went to Edward O. Wilson for his book *On Human Nature.* Wilson built on the concept of sociobiology he introduced in 1975—a science that assumes there is a biological basis for all social behavior in animals, including man. There is no God, no personal relationship between man and his Maker, no joy in the wonder of His works. To Wilson, all thought, all religion, all action can be accounted for materialistically, as an inevitable outgrowth of evolutionary progress. "Religions," he wrote, "like other human institutions, evolve so as to enhance the persistence and influence of their practitioners."

Enhancing one's influence is not the true purpose of a relationship with Jesus Christ, of course, but it may sound plausible to members of a scientific community increasingly driven to self-promotion. With no God to watch at work, scientists may feel some reward for helping mankind (not only by their work but also by making regular attacks on the dangerous "myth" of creation). Nevertheless, they also anticipate their own advancement. The research trail is littered with "paper"—scholarly articles in journals that prove one's worth among his colleagues. So intense is the competition for this status-seeking that scandals are beginning to surface about scientists signing on as coauthors with little or no participation in the findings.

SCIENCE AS A MISSION FIELD

Concerned Christian parents often discourage their children from entering such an environment. Many Christian educators believe that this is unfortunate. Instead of avoiding careers in science, Christian young people should view it as an opportunity to examine and understand the intricate workings of God's creation and to use their knowledge to help their world.

In the centuries preceding the Reformation, those who wanted to live close to God were usually directed to the contemplative life, away from the temptations and deceptions of worldly living. In some ways this is representative of the modern Christian's attempt to avoid the faith-threatening atmosphere of science.

Even in the sixteenth century John Calvin urged a turnaround in this attitude. He wrote in his *Institutes,* "There is need of art and more exacting toil in order to investigate the motion of the stars, to determine their assigned stations, to measure their intervals, to note their properties."

Likewise, the Puritans had no sympathy with the infidels and atheists, but they still participated in scientific inquiry. Nineteenth-century historian N. Porter wrote, "The Puritan has that confidence in the foundations of his faith, which leads him to give to science an independent activity, and to prosecute every kind of study in a fearless spirit. His motto is—if religion will not endure the searching test of free thought, she is not worth retaining; if science can annihilate the claims of faith, or invalidate her records, let science do her utmost."

One of the keys to their strength in the face of unbelievers was their firm position on basic truths. Robert Boyle wrote, "The truths of theology are things, which I need not bring arguments for, but am allowed to draw arguments from them." Boyle reasoned deductively from what was known. Modern scientists reason inductively from what is unknown.

Boyle refused to accept a definition of God as an ethereal Force or a Divine Mind. He recognized that God was personal and also infinite. He was Creator and Sustainer. The continuity of the world He created was evidence not of a silent force but of an active, all-powerful will. Thus, as it pleased Him, God could sustain everything as it was from the beginning or He could suspend His own laws of nature for the intervention of a miracle.

Scientists have a problem with miracles. Since they can't understand them with their minds, they dismiss them as nonexistent. God sets a high premium on miracles. Over and over again throughout the Bible —and the Christian walk—He performs miracles as evidence of His power and His love. For centuries He continued to remind the Israelites that He had brought them out of Egypt with signs and wonders. Jesus was constantly working miracles. When the Jewish leaders demanded to know if He were the Messiah he responded, "I have already told you, and you don't believe me. The proof is in the miracles I do in the name of my Father" (John 10:25, LB). The Jewish leaders were so angry at Jesus that they were prepared to stone him. Men who pride themselves on their great minds are no less incensed today. Acceptance of miracles is an admission that our reason is not so complete after all. It is a humble acceptance of Someone greater than oneself.

To believe in miracles is to believe in a God who is more powerful than sickness, who is mightier than the elements of nature. Ultimately, it is to accept that a man who was killed by crucifixion two thousand years ago could rise from the grave to die no more. It is to believe the good news that God became a man so none need feel abandoned on the earth.

Those who deride Christianity as the enemy of science usually point to Galileo's difficulties in persuading the church to accept the statement of Copernicus that the earth revolves around the sun. The Copernican revolution, however, did not overthrow the Bible; it deposed the church's mistaken adherence to the rational idealism of Aristotle. The clergy were so bound to tradition that they misinterpreted certain passages from the Bible to support their belief that the sun revolved around a flat earth. The medieval clergy have no monopoly on scientific ignorance. In a 1988 survey, 21 percent of the American public revealed that they still think the sun revolves around the earth. It was human error, not biblical error.

When Clarence Darrow used the Scopes trial to ridicule biblical miracles, he revealed an ignorance common to many. He did not understand the way language was used in those documents. Events are described not in full scientific detail but as they would have looked to an ordinary person who happened to be watching. John C. Munday of CBN University observed, "With respect to the natural world, the Bible . . . can be expected to be plain and brief, using clear terms and concepts, not esoteric language, nor complex and detailed scientific ideas. As the purpose of the Bible is spiritual, references to the natural order are for the purpose of illustrations, or as a context for the history being presented and the message being conveyed. In sum, the parts and processes of creation are referred to as they would appear to ordinary people."

Scientists who limit themselves to their five senses and whatever knowledge has lodged in their brains over the years are leaving inoperative a major tool for the comprehension of truth—the spirit that reaches out to God. The Apostle Paul said: "The unspiritual man simply cannot accept the matters which the Spirit deals with—they just don't make sense to him, for, after all, you must be spiritual to see spiritual things. The spiritual man, on the other hand, has an insight into the meaning of everything, though his insight may baffle the man of the world. This is because the former is sharing in God's wisdom" (1 Cor. 2:14–15, PHILLIPS).

Some might call it arrogance to say that a believer can know more than an unbeliever, but Paul didn't apologize for his statement. Instead of arrogance, it is a statement of humility to acknowledge the existence of a real world beyond our senses.

To be truthful, however, Christians often are arrogant toward the scientific community, shouting insults at their evolutionary faith. Unfortunately, because so few Christians have entered the field of science themselves, their attacks often lack substance and make them look ridiculous. Nathan Hatch of the University of Notre Dame said, "It reinforces the view of secular academics that Christians have nothing to say that is intellectually coherent and compelling."

From the time of Francis Bacon, scientists have believed they were reasoning objectively, beginning with a collection of brute facts or data and inductively formulating their hypotheses. In 1962, however, Thomas Kuhn challenged that belief in "The Structure of Scientific Revolutions." He said, "Research on specific problems always [takes] place against the background of assumptions and convictions produced by previously existing science." That is why Einstein's theory of relativity was so devastating to the scientific community when it was proposed. Scientists had been building on presuppositions that Einstein proved were wrong.

Every scientist and every nonscientist has certain presuppositions, whether they are acknowledged or not. No one enters an investigation with a blank slate for a mind.

If Christians want to communicate with the scientific community and alter the course of science teaching in their schools, they will have to know the field of science, understand how scientists think, and challenge them to admit their presuppositions. Only one faith can survive that challenge. It may not happen immediately, but a praying, informed Christian need fear no defeat by a person of the world.

Christians who want to serve God need to ask if He wants them to enter a career in science. From medicine to meteorology, "The modern intellectual world is adrift," Hatch said, "incapable or unwilling to allow any claim of certainty to set the coordinates by which others are to be judged." Someone needs to show them the way to the dock.

Standards of Achievement

Although only three areas of basic education have been touched on in this chapter, the evidence is overwhelming, from every measuring device, that America's public schools are failing. For more than two decades national scores on the Scholastic Aptitude Test (SAT) have shown a steady decline. This tragedy has been ascribed mostly to insufficient funding, large classes, lack of parental involvement, limited abilities of minorities, and poor teacher salaries that don't attract qualified people. Some experts, however, say that none of those are the real reason.

Certainly, American educational institutions desperately need to improve in very practical ways. If teachers can't teach children to read, they should find another occupation. If a school gives diplomas to illiterates, it has no right to call itself a school. If textbooks are poorly conceived and written, their publishers should find new authors. Unfortunately, all of these common failings are safeguarded against reform.

America simply cannot allow this failed system to perpetuate itself any longer. Every school district should establish minimum standards of accomplishment that are absolutely necessary for promotion from grade to grade and for graduation from high school. The preparation of teachers needs to be revised drastically. Future educators need to be prepared with academic majors and theory minors. Older teachers should apprentice younger ones. Empty teaching positions should not be filled with substandard teachers but with qualified part-time people who would be an asset to the school. Unions need to be confronted with the need for schools to have more flexibility in hiring. Women with young children should be fitted into part-time schedules. Retirees who love children and know how to handle them should be welcomed. Those active within their profession should be recruited for specialty classes by arranging with employers for release time.

Even these suggestions, however, will not work unless the One who sustains all of life is granted the honor He deserves in the classroom. Pat Robertson noted that the decline in SAT scores began right after prayer was removed from the schools. All those years the children and their teachers helped keep the schools from disaster, and no one knew it.

School prayer will not resume until family prayer does. Parents already expect school teachers to do jobs that God has assigned to them. They cannot add prayer on top of everything else. Prayer in school should be a supplement to what is happening in homes.

It is time for the people most affected by the schools—the local citizens—to take the wheel of this wayward school bus. What happens in the schools and colleges of America is everybody's business.

Paul wrote to Timothy, "Study to shew thyself approved unto God, a workman that needeth not to be ashamed" (2 Tim. 2:15, KJV). Many public school dropouts, and even those who make it to graduation, are ashamed. They can't read. They can't do simple computations. They have been told it is unscientific to believe in a Creator and unnecessary to study science at all. Some of these are our own children, and others are not, but we are all in this together.

Remember what happened when a man asked Jesus, "Who is my neighbor?" Jesus told him about all the religious people who passed by an injured man lying in the road. Finally, a despised Samaritan came by. Jesus concluded: "'He went to him and bandaged his wound, pouring on oil and wine. Then he put the man on his own donkey, took him to an inn and took care of him. The next day he took out two silver coins and gave them to the innkeeper. "Look after him," he said, "and when I return, I will reimburse you for any extra expense you may have." Which of these three do you think was a neighbor to the man who fell into the hands of robbers?' The expert in the law replied, 'The one who had mercy on him.' Jesus told him, 'Go and do likewise'" (Luke 10:29–37).

For Further Reading

Rudolf Flesch. *Why Johnny Still Can't Read.* New York: Harper & Row, 1981.

Eugene M. Klaaren. *Religious Origins of Modern Science.* Grand Rapids, Mich.: William B. Eerdmans, 1977.

Jonathan Kozol. *Illiterate America.* Garden City, N.Y.: Anchor Press/ Doubleday, 1985.

Henry M. Morris. *The Biblical Basis for Modern Science.* Grand Rapids, Mich.: Baker Book House, 1984.

John C. Munday, Jr., and Judith B. Munday. "Helping the Child Think through Science." *Family Resources* (Spring 1988).

N. Porter. *The Educational Systems of the Puritans and the Jesuits Compared.* Library of American Civilization 40011. New York: M. W. Dodd, 1851.

Bernard Ramm. *The Christian View of Science and Scripture.* Grand Rapids, Mich.: William B. Eerdmans, 1954.

Charles B. Thaxton, Walter L. Bradley, and Dean H. Olson. *The Mystery of Life's Origin: Reassessing Current Theories.* New York: Philosophical Library, 1984.

Edward O. Wilson. *On Human Nature.* Cambridge, Mass.: Harvard University Press, 1978.

4

What about Values?

Mark Twain said, "In statesmanship, get the formalities right, never mind about the moralities." In 1986, that advice, in not so many words, was given to parents in Pennsylvania's Norwin School District. Some of them had asked the school board to excuse their teenagers from a health course they found offensive. Since a health course was required for graduation, they requested a substitute course that would be more appropriate for their conservative community.

On 18 August 1986, the school board announced its intention "to proceed with the current Health Education Curriculum as mandatory for graduation; to deny the right to opt-out; and to deny the right to alternative health education curriculum." The parents were stunned. They felt that the concerns they had expressed went to the heart of their Christian beliefs, their authority as parents, and their standards of moral decency. They decided to fight the board's decision.

For several months these parents exhausted every local, state, and federal complaint procedure. They attended school board meetings en masse. They repeatedly requested access to the course materials. Nothing they tried, however, seemed to work.

Finally, on 24 March 1987, thirty-one parents filed suit. In a complaint drafted by their attorney, Roxanne Sakoian Eichler of North Versailles, Pennsylvania, the parents insisted there was no justification under either state or federal law to make such a course mandatory. They also noted that the curriculum was so deficient of health "content" that, according to a physician, it omitted such basics as hygiene, first aid, and nutrition. It was filled instead, the complaint stated, with exhortations to disregard moral standards and to engage in whatever sexual practices the children found to their liking. The complaint stated, concerning the textbook: "Self-discipline and abstinence in sexual activity until marriage are cast as an improper value choice. Homosexuality is taught as a natural stage in sexual development. . . . Gang masturbation and masturbation as early as 14 years of age are recommended. . . . Transsexuality is condoned and statements are made that the transsexual is happier as a result of the sex change."

The complaint also stated: "The text promotes humanism and denies the sinful nature of man. Page 9 contains the diary of a 14-year-old girl which states, 'Religion has little place in my life. . . . I think Jesus is a phoney, set up by men only to scare men into being slaves of the church. Eventually, I think he will be denounced.'" Eichler observed wryly, "You are allowed to say things like that in a textbook, but you aren't allowed to say that Jesus isn't [a phoney]."

The textbook not only sought to erode the children's morals and religious beliefs, the complaint said, it also interfered with the parent-child relationship. In the book, parental strictness was blamed for adolescent neurosis. Parents were portrayed as confused about their own values and self-identity. Whatever standards parents had set for their children were devalued because they had not been chosen "freely" by the adolescent.

When families have a dispute with a school district, in many cases they can rely on the federal government to assist them because of the Hatch Amendment. Eichler, however, uncovered a stumbling block. The school board had informed the Department of Education that no federal funds had been used for the health curriculum, thus derailing any action by the agency.

By the time Eichler brought the complaint before a judge, she had assembled more than fifty pages of documentation. Although the judge was not initially impressed with the parents' viewpoint, he finally asked the school board to grant their request.

On 8 June 1988 the parents signed an agreement with the school board stating that an alternative health course would be provided. The offensive text would be excluded, and, in addition, the parents would be allowed to review the new curriculum.

Promiscuity and Personal Values

Like the Norwin parents, Jesus was also told more than once to abide by the formalities. According to the Ten Commandments, the Jews had one day a week when they were exempted from work, but the scribes and Pharisees had made this Sabbath blessing into a bondage. It became a day when the scribes and Pharisees exercised absolute control over the personal lives of the people.

On one occasion, Jesus saw a man with a deformed hand in the synagogue and had pity on him. The authorities were watching his every move. Would Jesus have the nerve to defy their absolute rule and heal a man on the Sabbath day? If so, they would surely have him arrested. Mark wrote: "Jesus asked the man to come and stand in front of the congregation. Then turning to his enemies he asked, 'Is it all right to do kind deeds on Sabbath days? Or is this a day for doing harm? Is it a day to save lives or to destroy them?' But they wouldn't answer him. Looking around at them angrily, for he was deeply disturbed by their indifference to human need, he said to the man, 'Reach out your hand.' He did, and instantly his hand was healed." (Mark 3:3–5, LB).

Like the entrenched authorities Jesus encountered, those with jurisdiction over America's school districts often reveal a stubborn adherence to formality and a deep indifference to human need. The Sabbath was made for man, Jesus said, and not man for the Sabbath. The public schools were made for children, not children for the schools. School boards are delegated with the responsibility of meeting the needs of the particular children in their community, not preserving their pet ideas of truth.

Sex education was introduced into the schools as an attempt to decrease promiscuity and teenage pregnancy. Through the efforts of Planned Parenthood, Swedish sex-ed advocates, and others, the country convinced itself that America was in the midst of an unprecedented epidemic of teenage pregnancy and that the only way to stop it was through better sex education in the schools.

Since the early days of America's public schools, education has always been promoted as a cure-all for society. It was supposed to elevate the poor to equal status, solve illiteracy, unify the nation, and train children in the duties of good citizenship. None of these goals has been met. Instead, we have a large population of poor people, one-third of which is functionally illiterate, and an apathetic voter pool that just stays home.

What happened when this cure-all philosophy of education was applied to teenage pregnancy? By 1985, 70 percent of all high school seniors had taken sex education courses, but during the period from 1960 to 1980, these well-informed teenagers contributed to a birth rate increase of 200 percent, despite an average of 500,000 abortions per year. Observed Larry Cuban of Stanford University, "In the arsenal of weapons to combat teenage pregnancy, school-based programs are but a bent arrow."

What happened? Because of the school's entrenched secularism, educators thought they had to teach the process of sexual intercourse without reference to America's dominant moral code. Since nature abhors a vacuum, the empty vessel of value-free sex education attracted all the immoral practices it was supposed to prevent. Since chastity was considered "religious," it was excluded; since promiscuity was not, it was allowed.

Teachers stood aside while their students debated something called "personal values," which teenagers were encouraged to make up on their own, without reference to any external code. Seven out of ten American adults want these courses to teach children that premarital sexual activity is wrong. Yet, said former Secretary of Education William Bennett, one gets the feeling from reading the sex education texts "that being 'comfortable' with one's decision is the sum and substance of the responsible life." In an article entitled "Truth in Sex: Why Johnny Can't Abstain," Bennett called the tendency for such "value-neutral" sex education "a very odd kind of teaching—very odd because it does not teach."

Societies have always regulated the sexual behavior of their citizens, said Bennett, because it is universally recognized that intercourse is a significant experience that extends far beyond the physical contact. "It is not just something you like to do or don't like to do," he said. "Far from being value-neutral, sex may be among the most value-loaded of human activities."

The Bible endorses sex for marriage partners, but it contains page after page of admonition against lust, adultery, and lewdness. Jesus said, "All such vile things come from within; they are what pollute you and make you unfit for God" (Mark 7:23, LB).

The question is, why are schools increasingly militant in pushing curricula opposed by their own citizens and contrary to traditional Judeo-Christian morality? The answer is found in the way these people think.

In the days when almost everyone could recite the Westminster Catechism, Americans agreed that "man's chief end is to glorify God, and enjoy Him forever." Times have changed. Thomas Emerson expressed the humanist perspective that "the proper end of man is the realization of his character and potentialities as a human being."

Abraham Maslow, a major influence in twentieth-century philosophy and education, developed the concept of man's "self-actualization," which he placed at the top of his "hierarchy of needs" theory. He described it as the desire to "become everything that one is capable of becoming." In a certain sense, Maslow was right that each of us has an unalienable right to develop our own peculiar talents and interests. However, Maslow didn't believe in the necessity for God to be involved in this process. Without the covering of God's law, self-actualization becomes a license for people to do what seems right in their own eyes. For many, that means irresponsible sexual license.

Until the time of Darwin, most people agreed that sex outside of marriage was wrong and that civilized people didn't give in to the "lusts of the flesh." Darwin gave people an excuse to act like animals, and Freud made the excuse into a command. "Don't repress your sexual tendencies," Freud said, "or you could become mentally ill." Satisfaction of one's "libido" became the route to happiness.

Alfred Kinsey, in his controversial 1948 study, chastised those who tried to restrict others' sexual expression as uninformed and undersexed. He blamed mothers and female schoolteachers for imposing standards that he said reflected only their own limited sexual needs. A typical ninth- or tenth-grade boy, said Kinsey, "has a higher rate of outlet and has already had a wider variety of sexual experience than most of his female teachers ever will have."

To prove his case, Kinsey allowed researchers to fondle baby boys as young as five months during the course of an hour. He said the babies responded with "convulsive action, often with violent arm and leg movements, sometimes with weeping at the moment of climax." This was then reported as documented evidence that boys need frequent orgasmic outlets. All his researchers did their work, Kinsey said, "without social or moral evaluation."

The picture of researchers engaged in such behavior "without moral evaluation" is not unlike the atmosphere in a sex-education classroom where the teacher stands objectively aside while the students discuss their rights to sexual freedom. No one realizes that for all the talk of freedom, they are all slaves. As the Apostle Peter said, "A man is a slave to whatever controls him" (2 Pet. 2:19, LB).

ADOLESCENT HEALTH

About the time the nation became concerned about the pregnancies resulting from this "freedom," legislators in Washington who were committed to the value-neutral approach to sexuality set out to end the epidemic of teenage pregnancy. Their motto was "Never mind about the moralities."

Thus, since the inception of Title X of the federal Public Health Service Act in 1970, word has spread that it is basically healthy for adolescents to engage in sexual intercourse but unhealthy for them to get pregnant. As a result, millions of taxpayers have been forced to support programs to help these promiscuous children with "family planning," a procedure that detaches them from their families and sets them up as "planners" of new ones—all at the ripe old age of thirteen or fourteen.

One result was the school health clinic, something that provides an opportunity for practical application of what is learned in sex education; namely, how to use contraceptives and condoms. All of this takes place away from the prying eyes of parents, who foot the bill—through taxes—for behavior they have tried to forbid.

In these school clinics, "failure" doesn't mean an "F" on the report card. It denotes the creation of a life. Health clinics, like sex education, were touted as a solution to promiscuity, "unwanted" pregnancy, and abortion; however, statistics haven't cooperated with this assumption. Douglas Kirby, Director of Research for the Center for Population Options (CPO), admitted as much to the pro-clinic National Family Planning and Reproductive Health Association at its 1988 annual meeting. He said that the health clinics could show no measurable impact on the teenage use of birth control nor on the pregnancy or birth rates.

CPO, the leading promoter of school-based health clinics, had spent an enormous amount of time and money trying to reduce teenage pregnancies. The organization established a national support center for clinic personnel and set up training programs for service providers. Along with organizations like Planned Parenthood, it mobilized millions of dollars in local, state, and federal funds, as well as coordinating large grants from private foundations. These efforts essentially skirted around community standards and provided all that the eager teenager desired for so-called responsible sex, all to no avail.

On 25 July 1988, Senator Jesse Helms (R-N.C.) told his colleagues in the Senate, "federally funded Family Planning Programs have not—and I repeat for emphasis, have not—reduced teenage pregnancy." Quoting a study of the Institute for Research and Evaluation, Helms added, "Greater teenage involvement in family planning programs appears to be associated with higher rather than lower teenage pregnancy rates."

This report found "a net increase of about 120 pregnancies among all 15-19-year-old women for every 1,000 family planning clients." Its results confirmed what other researchers had been finding: formalities without moralities were failing to meet human needs.

School Days and Abortion

One of the symptoms of the sex education and health clinic fever has been the urge to inform young girls of the "option" of abortion should her federally funded contraceptives fail to prevent pregnancy. Adolescents are notoriously inconsistent about protecting themselves, but even when they do they still seem to get pregnant. *U.S. News & World Report* found that among women of all ages, half of those who had abortions in 1987 were practicing contraception when they became pregnant.

Since the onset of the Family Planning debate, abortion has been a part of the battle. Abortion advocates have tried everything to cast doubt on pro-life efforts.

Beginning in the 1970s, Rep. Henry J. Hyde of Illinois participated in an effort to prohibit federal funding for abortion. In 1980, he proposed an amendment to block Medicaid payments for abortion except to save the life of the mother. Hyde is a Roman Catholic. The American Civil Liberties Union therefore contended that his efforts to control abortion were nothing more than an attempt to enact religious dogma into law. In spite of the attention that was focused on his religion, the Hyde Amendment passed.

Contrary to ACLU beliefs, opposition to abortion is not confined to sectarian religion. Pro-life activist Bernard Nathanson is an atheist. Nor is it confined to Democrats or Republicans. Opponents of abortion are deeply concerned not only with the death of the unborn child but also with the physical, emotional, and spiritual trauma to the adolescent mother.

Adolescence is a time of upheaval and uncertainty. James Dobson says in his book *Preparing for Adolescence:* "There is a tendency during the adolescent years to feel that 'today is forever'—that present circumstances will never change—that the problems you face this moment will continue for the rest of your life." Adolescents who can't see beyond today often make quick, irrational decisions based on the present moment.

Parents, when given the chance, are supposed to provide the sense of perspective these children lack. One teenage girl told Dobson, "We don't talk to our parents enough; we keep everything inside and we never talk to anybody who could help us. We talk to our friends who are having the same problems, but they don't have the answers and they don't know what to tell us." Adolescence is a time of breaking ties, of learning to be independent. The growing-up process always produces conflict, even in the best of families, but these conflicts are necessary for the maturing process, just as iron sharpens iron.

Abortion-rights advocates want the freedom to take somebody else's children, grant them instant adult status, and give them what their today-is-forever minds tell them they need. Nearly half a million abortions a year are performed on these ill-informed adolescents.

In their immaturity, teenagers will do almost anything to help them avoid ridicule. They are extremely conscious of their appearance, especially in the revealing bareness of gym showers. Yet these naturally modest young people have sacrificed themselves on the altar of shame and lust. Thanks to the barrage of propaganda from school and the media, they expect to enter a new dimension if they strip down and "go all the way." Once the act is done, there is no way to recapture their virginity or their dignity. Chances are, they will wonder afterward what has happened to them. They will discover that what was done in secret will be shouted from the housetops, and the romantic liaison will end in ignominious rejection. Many will never try it again before marriage. That seems to say something about the experience.

When a girl becomes pregnant, she is faced with the prospect of walking the corridors of her school under the critical gaze of her classmates, displaying a rapidly expanding abdomen. Is it any wonder that she takes the recommended route of abortion? It seems so simple, just a few minutes to remove that "extra tissue," and her disgrace is over.

Escorted by the thousands to profitable abortion clinics around the country, blushing girls disrobe, climb awkwardly onto paper-covered tables, and trustingly wait. Former clinic nurse Sallie Tisdale, who believes in abortion, couldn't help observing what happens next:

> I watch the shadows that creep up unnoticed and suddenly darken her face as she screws up her features and pushes a tear out each side to slide down her cheeks. I have learned to anticipate the quiver of chin, the rapid intake of breath and the surprising sobs that rise soon after the machine starts to drum. I know this is when the cramp deepens, and the tears are partly the tears that follow pain—the sharp, childish crying when one bumps one's head on a cabinet door. But a well of woe seems to open beneath many women when they hear that thumping sound. The anticipation of the moment has finally come to fruit; the moment has arrived when the loss is no longer an imagined one. It has come true.

There she is, a premature graduate of the school of "value-free sex," no longer wearing the mask of a sex-hungry, pseudo-adult. She is once again a child, lying on a cold table, without her mother and without her child.

Someone needs to give this girl some answers.

How to Help Them Say No

America's young people cannot survive much longer on "values." They need God, and they need that for which He stands.

Ted Koppel, moderator of ABC television's "Nightline," described this need to Duke University's 1987 graduating class:

> We have actually convinced ourselves that slogans will save us. Shoot up if you must, but use a clean needle. Enjoy sex whenever and with whomever you wish, but wear a condom.
>
> "No!" The answer is "No." Not because it isn't cool or smart or because you might end up in jail or dying in an AIDS ward, but "no" because it's wrong. . . .
>
> In the place of truth, we have discovered facts. For moral absolutes, we have substituted moral ambiguity. . . .
>
> In its purest form, truth is not a polite tap on the shoulder. It is a howling reproach. What Moses brought down from Mount Sinai were not the Ten Suggestions. They are commandments. Are, not were. The sheer brilliance of the Ten Commandments is that they codify in a handful of words acceptable human behavior, not just for then or now, but for all time.

Morality is not the invention of prudish women. It is an absolute standard, a gift from God by which we can judge all our actions. No teenagers should be abandoned and told to figure out their own personal values. They should be informed about the blessing of moral law and encouraged to listen to their parents, who can help them graduate to adulthood.

Consistently, those who have taken control of American "values" education have set low moral standards for teenagers and blocked parental intervention. When Senators Jeremiah Denton of Alabama and Orrin Hatch of Utah proposed that family planning centers promote self-discipline and chastity, they were sharply criticized by both liberals and conservatives. According to Maris Vinovskis, a consultant to Presidents Jimmy Carter and Ronald Reagan, Senator Edward Kennedy said he "did not want to be associated with anything harshly condemning the sexual activity of teenagers." The *New York Times* of 29 July 1981 reported that Representative Toby Moffet (D-Conn.) referred to the centers as "storefront chastity centers" and predicted that they would be laughed out of every junior high school in America.

When a provision for parental notification was requested by the Reagan administration as part of Family Planning legislation, the *New York Times* labeled it a "squeal rule," and the *Los Angeles Times* editorialized about a "snitch regulation." They argued that no one could stop adolescent sexual activity. Interference by the biological parents "would only mean more unwed mothers, abortions, school dropouts, welfare dependencies, and heartaches." With no factual evidence whatever, the media served as handmaiden to Congress in scoring another victory for the U.S. Government vs. Parents.

At a press conference on 18 February 1982, President Reagan

expressed his dismay at the relentless crusade against parental notification in Congress and the press. He said, "Those young people couldn't get their appendix taken out without their parents' permission. . . . I think the government has no business injecting itself between parent and child in a family relationship and where it is very definitely a problem of concern to parents who are responsible for the children."

For some reason, congressmen, journalists, educators, and jurists have the idea that parents (with the possible exception of themselves) are unfit to understand the best interests of their children. In 1976, the Supreme Court felt it necessary to rule against parental notification for abortions because of "the State's interests in protection of the mental and physical health of the pregnant minor." These decision makers seem to have construed all parents as monsters and their children as victims. The threat of the parent-monster's deviltry is then invoked as an excuse to block family communication.

When Jesus encountered scribes who had interfered in the family He told them:

> "You have a fine way of setting aside the commands of God in order to observe your own traditions! For Moses said, 'Honor your father and your mother,' and, 'Anyone who curses his father or mother must be put to death.' But you say that if a man says to his father or mother: 'Whatever help you might otherwise have received from me is Corban' (that is, a gift devoted to God), then you no longer let him do anything for his father or mother. Thus you nullify the word of God by your tradition" (Mark 7:9–13).

Neither scribes nor Supreme Court justices have the authority to nullify God's order for parents. Wherever parental notification has been required, pregnancy and abortion rates have dropped dramatically. Even if the intention is to decrease pregnancy, it is only logical to eliminate that which fails and legislate that which works.

Chastity is not some mean trick parents play on their children. It is a blessing of life and a way to find peace. James said, "Blessed is the man who perseveres under trial, because when he has stood the test, he will receive the crown of life" (James 1:12). This crown isn't something for the dim, unknown future, but a crown available now for a rich, full life.

The best rich, full life for a teenager is not one dominated by thoughts of sex. Those who "experiment" should be told that early experiences can be painful and can damage delicate body parts. Doctors have known for a long time that AIDS and various venereal diseases are spread by intimate contact. Now researchers say that cervical cancer increases greatly with promiscuity. The human body simply was not created to withstand such abuse.

Pregnancy that ends in childbirth, instead of abortion, is the only proper course to take. Pregnancy isn't a girl's punishment for sin, nor is the insistence that the father support his child, even if he is a mere boy himself. It is the tough love that says, "As you sow, so shall you reap" (Gal. 6:7). Every act has consequences, and the sooner children learn it the better.

If adoption is the choice, there are a multitude of fine homes awaiting a child. Partly because of America's fascination with dangerous contraceptives and abortions, approximately one-sixth of American couples struggle with infertility problems. No child need be "unwanted." Children are a blessing, a heritage, even under the worst circumstances.

Premarital sex is a choice, and it is up to the parents to ensure that their children understand all that it involves. Parents must start teaching their pre-teen children at home about their sexuality, while they are still young enough to listen to God's wonderful plan. If the church gets involved, parents must still be included in teaching sessions. Teaching about sexuality belongs in the family, where it can include intercessory prayer.

If a girl becomes pregnant, there must be a plan in place for what is to be done. If the option of abortion has been ruled out in advance, there will be no chance of considering it.

Premarital sex is a sin, but it is a forgivable sin. Oswald Chambers, in his book *Biblical Ethics,* said, "God holds us responsible for the way we judge a young life; if we judge it by the standards by which we would judge a mature life, we will be grossly unjust. Much misjudgment of young life goes on in the religious domain. . . . Be as merciless as God can make you towards the vices of a mature life, but be very gentle and patient with the defects of a growing life." Jesus is compassionate. He will not break a bruised reed (Isa. 42:3, KJV).

THE HOPE OF AMERICA'S YOUTH

In the end, the only real hope we have for ending the epidemic of teenage pregnancy is not education, in or out of the home. We can try to educate the mind, but until we reach the heart there is just so much we can do.

In each of the first three centuries of our history our forefathers also experienced epidemics of adolescent pregnancy, but, contrary to current experience, each of those crises was resolved. According to Maris Vinovskis, the only effective solution was always spiritual revival. Only a personal relationship with Jesus Christ could reveal the slavery of immorality and the liberty of righteousness.

The first American moral crisis involved the Puritan settlers. When they were still in England they faced not only religious persecution but also rampant immorality all around them. Pregnancy out of wedlock was a common occurrence. When they came to the New World, they convenanted together to follow a strict moral code and empowered both ministers and civil magistrates to enforce it. As a result, pregnancy was returned to marriage.

When humanism stepped up its attack on New England Calvinism, however, many of the clergy made adjustments in their doctrine to center it on people, not God. Everything that God did, they said, was directed toward a person's happiness. Instead of reasserting God's sovereignty and His right to rule as He pleased, they backed off from their absolutism and tried to use mere reason. They became so intent on defending the faith, that they forgot about the God who gave it. Like David in Saul's armor, they became unfit to fight the giant.

Parishioners began to make excuses to avoid the strident sermons and loveless attitudes that resulted from this verbal sparring. Without the fear of God, they began to say that they probably weren't converted anyway, so they might as well stay home from church. Without an awareness of God's love and sovereignty over all of life, they were easy candidates for immorality. By the early eighteenth century, said Vinovskis, about 30 percent of the pregnancies in New England were conceived out of wedlock.

The American people might have lost track of God, but He had not forgotten about them. A few men were concerned enough about their countrymen that they heard the call when God summoned them to lead a spiritual revival.

David Brainerd concentrated on converting the Indians. He drove himself unmercifully until he died at the age of twenty-nine. Clyde S. Kilby in his book *Heroic Colonial Christians* wrote, "Brainerd . . . saw the working of the Spirit as 'the irresistible force of a mighty torrent or swelling deluge' which bore down everything before it."

William Tennent, later called one of the "New Lights," founded what became Princeton University as a school to inspire evangelists with enthusiasm for the Christian faith. The "Log Cabin" school was so powerful that its graduates preached throughout the colonies and founded school after school along the frontier.

Tennent's son, Gilbert, lit revival fires throughout New Jersey, New York, Pennsylvania, and later New England. He also befriended the man who is remembered above all as the key to America's Great Awakening, George Whitefield.

Whitefield's preaching was so powerful that entire towns turned out to see him. On horseback, on foot, running, or walking, thousands at a time heard him tell about Jesus Christ, God made flesh, who had come to die for their sins. No one went away unchanged. Thousands gave their hearts to the Lord, and changed the direction of their lives. Even skeptical Benjamin Franklin said, "It was wonderful to see the change soon made in the manners of our inhabitants. From being thoughtless or indifferent about religion, it seemed as if all the world were growing religious, so that one could not walk through the town in an evening without hearing psalms sung in different families of every street."

The Great Awakening didn't produce quiet, closet conversions. It produced men and women who wanted to act on what they believed. They built the foundation for the American Revolution and One Nation Under God. Once again, they began to live like moral people.

By the waning days of the eighteenth century, however, complacency and lack of zeal once again plagued the new nation. Peace and freedom had brought with them a temptation to forget the God who had purchased it. It would take another spiritual firebrand to rekindle the embers.

The man responsible for the third and last great American revival was Charles Finney. Essentially ignorant of the Bible, Finney had set himself up at the age of twenty-six to study law. His first task was to read what every lawyer in the American colonies studied, the remarkable commentaries of William Blackstone. First published in England in 1769, the volumes quickly became the backbone of American law.

Finney found that Blackstone always described the law in terms of adherence to a higher law, the Bible. He bought a Bible and suddenly began to see that God had created an entire world with an incredible orderliness that applied to all areas of human affairs. Although he had been a sporadic church attender, he then began to attend in earnest. The only problem he encountered was that his studies in Blackstone and the Bible were far more dynamic than the preachers he heard. Before long, Finney became a preacher himself.

Like the men of the Great Awakening, Finney drew enormous crowds wherever he went. He confronted the sweating multitudes with a choice: Choose Jesus Christ and find peace with God or reject Christ and be eternally damned. Finney talked about a personal God, one who wanted each individual, no matter how insignificant in the world's eyes, to turn away from sin and follow Him. He was not afraid to preach judgment and the awful consequences of unbelief. His wife, Lydia, once told him, "though I know you love me, yet you are terrifying when the power of God comes upon you. You stand there like a mighty angel, shouting the Gospel and wielding the flashing sword of judgment."

There was sin in the land, and everybody knew it, but few attacked it like Finney, and few proclaimed the power of God to do something about it. Finney's converts began to sweep across America with a fiery zeal of their own. They attacked slavery and brought it to an end. They attacked immorality, and it came crashing down.

In 1984, for every 1,000 young women ages fifteen to nineteen, there were 109 pregnancies. Ninety-nine years earlier, with Victorian morals and no abortion or oral contraceptives, that rate was 18 births per thousand. The difference between the present and the past: spiritual revival.

Charles Finney said, "When the next great awakening comes, the ghastly spirits of lawlessness, unbelief, immorality, divorce, corruption, mammon, tyranny and selfishness, which now eat at the life of the world, will die as if smitten by a plague. Law, education, culture, science, ethics have failed. But one hope remains—a mighty revival of Christian faith. Austin Phelps never penetrated more deeply into the ways of God than when he said, 'If the secret connection of revivals with the destiny of nations be disclosed, they would appear more critical evolutions of history than the Gothic invasions.'"

Recapturing the Land

It is amazing, once one looks at history, to understand how the American people could allow the elimination of the one factor that has always saved them in the past—America's faith in God. Educators and legislators will try anything, no matter how fraught with error and compromise, to avoid God.

Sex education and health clinics are helpless. God is all powerful. If we believe in His ability to change people's lives, we must begin to recapture the land.

The public schools will never be a forum for conversion to Jesus Christ, but neither should they be the place where children are taught that there is no God and no moral law. America will regain its moral standards when children and teachers alike regain their constitutional rights to free speech and free exercise of religion.

When a California court ruled in 1987 that public school graduations could not include an invocation, the ACLU warned that its monitors would be checking all graduations for compliance. If anyone were found praying, the ACLU would file suit against the school board and against individual school board members. That was too much for the free citizens of California. They made up their minds to demonstrate that God is not subject to invented law nor the ACLU.

One school district in Quincy, which hadn't planned an invocation, suddenly decided to include one in its program. Other districts dramatized the prohibition in numerous ways. The *Education Reporter* noted the following:

> In one school district, parents rented a plane which flew overhead carrying a "God Bless Grads" sign. In another, a large group of students organized to put masking tape crosses on their mortar boards and, at one point during the ceremony, knelt down as a group for a moment of silence.
>
> In another ceremony, parents emphasized "under God" during the pledge of allegiance, followed by a long pause. Pickets, with signs such as "Russia can now pray in public—why can't we?" and "Pharoah—Let our people go," appeared in several districts up until graduation day and during the ceremonies.

Christians have begun to take a stand, not for "personal values" but for God and His Word. They are fighting against Goliaths of litigation, and it is costing them more than five smooth stones, but they have decided it is worth it.

A few are winning. The Christian Legal Society and the National Legal Foundation can help, but the main soldiers in this battle are the Christian parents. With God, nothing shall be impossible for them.

For Further Reading

William J. Bennett. "Truth in Sex: Why Johnny Can't Abstain." *Education* (Winter 1987).

Oswald Chambers. *Biblical Ethics.* Fort Washington, Pa.: Christian Literature Crusade; Oswald Chambers Publications Association, 1975.

Richard Ellsworth Day. *Man of Like Passions: A Dramatic Biography of Charles Grandison Finney.* Grand Rapids, Mich.: Zondervan, 1942.

James Dobson. *Preparing for Adolescence.* New York: Bantam Books, 1984.

William A. Donohue. *The Politics of the American Civil Liberties Union.* New Brunswick, N.J.: Transaction Books, 1985.

Thomas I. Emerson. *Toward a General Theory of the First Amendment.* New York: Vintage Books, 1967.

Alfred Kinsey, Wardell B. Pomeroy, and Clyde E. Martin. *Sexual Behavior in the Human Male.* Philadelphia: W. B. Saunders Company, 1948.

Peter Marshall and David Manuel. *The Light and the Glory.* Old Tappan, N.J.: Fleming H. Revell Co., 1977.

Erin O'Keefe. "Abraham H. Maslow: A Critical Analysis of His World View." M.A. thesis, CBN University, 1987.

Sallie Tisdale. "We Do Abortions Here." *Harper's Magazine* (October 1987).

Maris A. Vinovskis. *An "Epidemic" of Adolescent Pregnancy?* New York: Oxford University Press, 1988.

Part 2

The Family

These commandments that I give you today
are to be upon your hearts.
Impress them on your children.
Talk about them when you sit at home
and when you walk along the road,
when you lie down
and when you get up.

5

Perversions of Sexuality

Linda Boreman was an attractive young woman ready to start a business in New York when she barely escaped death in an auto accident. The crash almost destroyed her liver, but events that were to follow launched her on an even greater trauma. It was an experience that savaged her life and damaged millions of American men and women. In a matter of months, the pretty ingénue became Linda Lovelace, porn queen of *Deep Throat.*

Because of the seriousness of her automobile injuries, Linda left New York to recuperate at her parents' home in Florida. Raised in the pleasant, protected environment of a Roman Catholic family, she knew nothing of the world of violence and sexual perversion that she would soon enter.

Linda began to date a nice "all-American type of guy" named Chuck. He said he sympathized with the twenty-one-year-old's resentment of her parents' 11 P.M. curfew and issued an invitation for her to move in with him. She accepted.

Linda didn't consider it a compromising situation until she decided to return to New York. Enraged, her formerly platonic companion beat her savagely, and suddenly the stunned young woman was the captive of a sex maniac. Chuck began forcing her to perform perverted sexual acts at gunpoint and coerced her into prostitution. He was responsible for the degrading acting "career" that lasted seventeen days and never paid her a cent.

Deep Throat was the first hard-core porn film to break the neighborhood theater barrier, the first widespread perpetrator of the myth that women are sexually excited by sodomy, debasement, and intense pain.

Reporter Lesley Wilson said, "Playing a movie character that had her source of sexual stimulation genetically lodged in her throat, Linda was beaten, raped, and hypnotized into 'doing anything while feeling nothing,' she says. Linda says, 'women suffocated, were actually asphyxiated,' trying to emulate her unnatural sexual example."

This "unnatural sexual example," the sodomizing and sadomasochism of "Linda Lovelace," became a tremendously popular film in theaters coast to coast. Why was this depiction so successful (gross receipts over $600 million), and why should the act it popularized remain illegal in twenty-four states?

The answer to the first question rests with one of the current American myths promoted by journalists, filmmakers, and now many of our children's public school teachers: "Goodness has nothing to do with it. Don't worry about being good, just be careful." Nothing related to the genitals that two "consenting" adults can dream up can be considered taboo any more, according to an increasing chorus of advocates. America is having a love affair with lust. Like volcanic ash from Mount St. Helens, it covers everything with a layer of dirt.

Why is sodomy illegal? There are state and federal officials who contend that no search through centuries of jurisprudence can establish anything but abhorrence and censure for such practices. Sodomy—abnormal sexual practices such as bestiality and oral or anal intercourse—has become vigorously politicized ever since homosexuals rioted at New York's Stonewall Bar in 1969.

Sexual practices like sodomy are regulated because they spread disease. AIDS is only the latest in a series of infections spread almost exclusively by sexual contact, predominantly that practiced by male homosexuals with multiple partners. Penicillin and other drugs are increasingly helpless against these diseases. Because of the free-sex movement, only a few segments of society remain relatively untouched: celibate singles and monogamous mates.

The major reason for regulating sexual practices by moral code and legal precedent, however, is the theme that forms the basis of this book. The Creator has taken a stand that is clear, uncompromising, and just. Even lustful thinking is a sin. Any sex act outside of marriage or outside the created functions of the body is unconscionable. Sex is a gift with its own special ribbon, the inviolable bond of matrimony.

SOCIETY AND SEXUALITY

America was not always the land of free sex. In stirring tribute to its Puritan roots, Chief Justice Warren Burger and Justice Byron White declared that it is still possible to legislate morality. The occasion was the 1986 Supreme Court case *Bowers v. Hardwick.*

Michael Hardwick, a homosexual bartender, was sodomizing a male partner when police officers, acting on an unrelated matter, were directed to his room by a houseguest. Since sodomy is illegal in Georgia, they charged him, but the charges were later dropped.

Hardwick, however, decided to sue the attorney general of Georgia and push his case to the Supreme Court. In a five-to-four decision, the justices refused to find a right to consensual sodomy embedded in the main body of the Constitution, in the due process clauses of the Fifth and Fourteenth Amendments, or in any previous court precedent.

One problem free-sex advocates face is that they have come to believe their own rhetoric that the Constitution guarantees libertarianism. They have accepted textbook versions of America's origins as classical and secular, liberated during the Renaissance from the authoritarian, myth-dominated church, and released by Freud from Puritan and Victorian straitjackets. This view is false.

Instead of springing from classical Greece, our nation seems to be regressing to it. The Greeks, contrary to the Judeo-Christian tradition, encouraged public nudity, not only in their art, but also in athletics and religion. Homosexuality and indiscriminate sex were not matters of prohibition, only caution. Even their gods engaged in rape.

Across the world spectrum, sexual practices encouraged by other religions include worship of the phallus, prostitution, and mass ritualization. America, however, was settled and built up by people who took the Bible literally, with its commandments against fornication, adultery, rape, prostitution, and homosexuality. Far from causing impossible strictures that took all the fun out of life, their moral standards released them to concentrate on other matters, like staying healthy and building a nation.

One of the most insistent strategies for ending public censure of certain sexual practices is the bizarre practice of linking free sex with free speech. Instead of tracing unalienable rights to the Creator, as John Locke and the Founders did, these strategies rely on some of the following philosophies:

- Protagoras: Man is the measure of all things.
- Jean Jacques Rousseau: Do what comes naturally.
- Jeremy Bentham: Rights are determined by what will provide the greatest good for the greatest number.

- John Stuart Mill: Do whatever you please as long as you don't interfere with others' rights.
- John Dewey: Whatever can be justified as a contribution to society should be a right.

Most of the legal profession today also subscribes to the granting of rights from man to man, not from God to man. Thomas Emerson, law professor at Yale and legal scholar on First Amendment issues, suggests the following advantages of free speech:

- finding individual self-fulfillment
- attaining truth
- encouraging participation in decision making
- maintaining a balance between stability and change

The Founders' view of free expression was based on their common understanding of Scripture. In spite of denominational differences, there was a general consensus that Truth came from God, that people were fulfilled by glorifying Him and loving their neighbors, and that government was a God-ordained institution to encourage good works and punish evil (Rom. 13:1–4). As created in the image of God, each person should be given the right to speak, but as a sinner each was expected to abide by the common moral standards of the culture.

The First Amendment affirmed the right of minority factions to have their say about government, not to say what they pleased on any subject. The Founders never relinquished the right of the majority to decide in favor of these freely spoken minority recommendations or to overrule them.

Today, not only biblical principles but also the majority-rule principle are constantly under fire. As Allan Bloom wrote in *The Closing of the American Mind:*

> Much of the intellectual machinery of twentieth-century American political thought and social science was constructed for the purposes of making an assault on that majority. . . . Where this leads is apparent in, for example, Robert Dahl's *A Preface to Democratic Theory.* Groups or individuals who really care, as opposed to those who have lukewarm feelings, deserve special attention or special rights for their "intensity" or "commitment," the new political validation, which replaces reason. The Founding Fathers wished to reduce and defang fanaticism, whereas Dahl encourages it.

AND THEN THERE WAS *PLAYBOY*

In 1953, a first-rate, glossy magazine appeared on the market that was to set a standard for professional, engaging interviews by writers who commanded four-figure checks. It immediately became a hit on college campuses—not, perhaps, among the intelligentsia, but among fraternity brothers eager for a look at the centerfold.

Hugh Hefner's *Playboy* was the first pornographic magazine to emphasize the sweetness and innocence of its naked women. The Playboy Clubs that eventually sprang up around the world had strict standards for the behavior of their bunnies, and also for their physical endowments. In *The Mind Polluters,* Jerry Kirk mused, "Everybody recognizes ugly evil as evil, but pretty, innocent-looking evil? It was a marketing technique, and it worked. America bought pornography when it was wrapped in beautiful, healthy packaging."

Hefner's agenda was not simply to make money. He also wanted to make a statement, the so-called Playboy Philosophy. His goal was to replace the "repressive" Puritan heritage with his idea of unbridled pleasure. Although he flourished for a season, what Hefner hadn't counted on was the number of people who didn't feel at all repressed by the moral standards of their ancestors. In a growing wave of activism in the 1980s, Christian standard-bearers have recently influenced one store chain after another to eliminate this thinly veiled pornography placed within easy access of their children.

The Eckerd drugstores are one dramatic example. Jack Eckerd, president and chairman of the board for this chain of seventeen hundred retail stores, had spent most of his life resisting religion. When he enlisted the help of Prison Fellowship's Charles Colson on a Florida prison reform project, he said, "I realized his Christianity was real." Before long, he realized that he needed Christ and made his profession of faith.

Shortly after his conversion, Eckerd walked by the magazine racks in one of his stores. Something caught his eye. With shock and amazement he noticed for the first time that his "family" stores carried pornographic magazines. Calling the company chief executive officer, Eckerd insisted on the removal of the magazines, even though they were bringing in several million dollars a year. It was done. He said afterward, he had no choice in the matter: "The Lord wouldn't let me off the hook."

Naturally, Hefner and the other entrepreneurs who market these publications have had no warm, fuzzy feelings about such actions. Words and phrases like "censorship" and "free speech" infringement have become common fare. Producers and distributors of pornography, however, have no recourse to free speech claims. Frederick Schauer of William and

Mary noted that the First Amendment guaranteed communication of political or ideological opinions, but pornography "shares more of the characteristics of sexual activity than of the communicative process. The pornographic item is in a real sense a sexual surrogate."

Hugh Hefner notwithstanding, pornography addicts have little interest in philosophy and reason. As Reo M. Christenson said, "They want raw meat, and that's what they get."

THE FOURTEENTH AMENDMENT

Pornographers and those seeking legitimacy for sodomy, prostitution, and other illicit sexual activity appeal not only to the Bill of Rights but also to the Fourteenth Amendment. Ratified after the Civil War to reinforce the rights of the newly freed slaves, it reads in part: "No State shall make or enforce any law which shall abridge the privileges or immunities of citizens of the United States; nor shall any State deprive any person of life, liberty, or property, without due process of law."

Hardwick had argued that the Fifth and Fourteenth Amendments guaranteed his right to sodomy in Georgia. His claims, however, sound rather hollow upon closer examination. In 1868, when the Fourteenth Amendment was ratified, all but five of the thirty-seven states had criminal sodomy laws.

Free-sex advocates, who are not just dirty old men in bookstores but highly financed, professional people, insist that America must never return to the repressive sexual atmosphere of the Puritans and Victorians. It is unfortunate that so many of our citizens, including sincere Christians, believe these fabrications.

As mentioned in earlier chapters, throughout history morality by biblical standards was not a liability, but an asset. During the Victorian era sexual practices may have been kept discreetly secret, but they were a significant part of matrimony. The double bed was considered a necessity for every married couple. Novels omitted explicit sexuality, but this did not quench the ardor of marital relations. Normal sex wasn't dependent on artificial stimulation like the illicit animal passions.

The Victorian era, with a popular, highly ethical queen reigning in England, was not characterized by inhibited men rushing off to prostitutes, as some have charged, but by the family Bible and strong family identities. As mentioned earlier, the rate of unwed pregnancies was a fraction of what it is now.

It was a "conspicuously religious" era, but unfortunately it had become a time of taking God for granted. He was acknowledged, and everyone assumed He was out there somewhere making sure that everything would turn out right, but Jesus was not a close personal Lord and Savior. Thus, when loud voices declared that society's sexual mores and its Judeo-Christian religion were the source of evil, there were insufficient biblical weapons ready for the challenge.

There was the voice of Darwin saying that God did not create people. Man was nothing but an advanced animal descended from the lower primate forms. There was the voice of Marx saying that history proves that people are helpless before the forces of dialectical materialism. There was the voice of Freud saying that since sexual forces dominate human life, their repression can no longer be tolerated. Then Einstein, in a brilliant discovery, proved that space and time are relative. If the universe did not operate by absolutes, should not traditional mores, as well, be brought into question? It didn't matter that Einstein himself rejected this analogy; society decided to rewrite the book on morality.

THE ACLU

The free-speech/free-sex movement gained momentum with the radicals' outcry over the 1917 Espionage Act. As a wartime measure, the act provided heavy fines and imprisonment of those who made false statements intended to interfere with the success of the war effort, to undermine recruitment, or to promote disloyalty among the armed forces. Although socialist and German-language publishers were mostly affected, the act became a rallying cry for all free-speech advocates.

One of the people involved in that struggle was Roger Baldwin, founder of the organization that is today one of the strongest advocates for an absolutist interpretation of the Bill of Rights—the American Civil Liberties Union. This organization, which in 1988 stood nearly alone in its public demands that child pornographers be allowed to distribute their wares, began primarily as a crusader for labor rights and free-speech issues. Baldwin himself had grown up in the social action environment of a Boston Unitarian home and naturally gravitated toward reaching out to the underdog. He did this in typical twentieth-century "objective" fashion, ostensibly avoiding value judgments on who was demanding rights. He explained his "Voltairian doctrine" this way: "If the person you hate has no rights, then the person you like may have no rights either. And in order to defend the people you like, you have to defend the people you hate."

The trouble, however, with using a man-made document like the Bill of Rights as one's holy scripture, as the ACLU essentially does, is that it can become a tyrant, demanding ever greater sacrifices at its altar. One absolutist stand on free speech inevitably leads to another, until the train is out of control and running wildly down the track.

The Bill of Rights isn't an isolated rule of life. It is a corollary of the Declaration of Independence doctrine that all men are created equal, endowed by their Creator with *certain* unalienable rights. The same God who granted rights, however, also declared wrongs. His justice is not blind.

Baldwin and others correctly observed that their supposedly Christian society was not living up to its promise of equal rights. Yet America's greatest shame is not that it didn't honor the Bill of Rights, but that it didn't honor God and respect its own people, who are created in God's image.

Baldwin saw these injustices as proof that the Bible is not true. That was one reason why the ACLU was determined to overthrow the Tennessee creation law at the Scopes Trial. As was earlier noted, Baldwin said that the Scopes trial was "the Good Book against Darwin, bigotry against science."

Scopes also represented a new strategy for adding to the list of rights. ACLU litigants sought to take their cases beyond the jurisdiction of their local courts into the more secularized, powerful court machinery of distant federal courts. Rather than dealing with friends and neighbors among the local authorities (who might even be "religious"), they would seek an audience with the higher powers and demand their rights on lofty constitutional grounds. The 1925 Supreme Court ruling in *Gitlow v. New York*, as well as *Near v. Minnesota* in 1931, gave visible evidence that the Supreme Court was expanding its jurisdiction beyond that allotted to it by Article III of the Constitution and by the Tenth Amendment, which reserved most powers to the states. Instead of proving to be a bonanza for the free-sex advocates, however, Supreme Court activism denied certain rights to obscenity. Even though the Court's reasoning was frequently faulty, as will be discussed later, the cases did give anti-porn groups some ammunition for their battles.

In the previously mentioned *Near v. Minnesota* (1931), the Court ruled that in certain circumstances "the primary requirements of decency may be enforced against obscene publications." In *Roth v. United States* (1957), the justices stated that "obscenity is not within the area of constitutionally protected speech or press." The *Roth* tests for obscenity included (1) "whether to the average person, applying contemporary community standards, the dominant theme of the material taken as a whole appeals to the prurient interest"; (2) it is "utterly without redeeming social importance" and "deals with sex in a manner appealing to the prurient interest" (tending to excite lustful thoughts). The Court also used the Model Penal Code definition for obscenity: "a shameful or morbid interest in nudity, sex, or excretion."

The Court's ruling in *Ginzburg v. United States* (1966), defined "obscenity," as that which is "titillating," "erotically arousing," and sexual stimulation is stressed to the exclusion of other aspects. In *Stanley v. Georgia* (1969), the High Court prescribed that possession of obscene materials in one's home is not a crime, but that did not imply the right to buy, distribute, and display it. The Court's ruling in *Paris Adult Theater I v. Slayton* (1973), announced that the exclusion of minors from a theater did not release the proprietor from legal action. The Court said, "We categorically disapprove the theory . . . that obscene, pornographic films acquire constitutional immunity from state regulation simply because they are exhibited to consenting adults only."

The 1973 decision in *Miller v. California* said that "obscene material is unprotected by the First Amendment" and "as a whole" has no "serious literary, artistic, political, or scientific value." In 1978, the justices ruled in *FCC v. Pacifica Foundation* that the Federal Communications Commission may take action against a radio broadcast that contains indecent language demonstrating "nonconformance with accepted standards of morality." The Supreme Court ruled in 1986 in *Renton v. Playtime Theaters, Inc.*, that cities had the right to set ordinances regarding the location of adult theaters. The emphasis was not on the definition of obscenity but on its negative effects and on the citizens' right to preserve the quality of life.

Errors in the Court's Thinking

The pornography industry perceived these decisions as little more than a slap on its wrist. It continued its trade unmolested by the law. The Supreme Court failed to restore moral order to the country, even with these negative ratings for obscenity, because it relied on inconsistent and erroneous thinking concerning the obscenity issue. Some constitutional scholars have said that first and foremost the Court erred in assuming that obscenity was a First Amendment issue at all. The First Amendment only guarantees the right to criticize the government. Likewise, the Court erred in assuming that the Fourteenth Amendment gave it the right to act as a national board of censorship. The Court no longer limited itself to judgments on the constitutionality of statutes but actually viewed obscene materials to see if the local community that forbade them was too harsh.

Although in *Miller* Chief Justice Earl Warren said national standards were inappropriate for every town and hamlet in a country as diverse as the United States, the Court reversed itself in *Jenkins v. Georgia.* The Court said Georgia towns and cities could not ban the film *Carnal Knowledge* because it was not "patently offensive" to the justices.

In *Roth,* Justice Brennan had stated that the First Amendment did not protect obscenity because obscenity was "utterly without redeeming social importance." He contended that the Founders would also have made that distinction. His thinking, however, was not derived from eighteenth-century documents but from twentieth-century jurisprudence.

These days, speech is allowed or disallowed depending on how various rights balance out as the justices evaluate what is best for society. This was the utilitarian standard promoted by John Stuart Mill. The Founders, however, were not men who balanced truth. Nor did they consider it a role of civil government to provide a totally unregulated marketplace of ideas, as modern jurists do, so that everyone could find truth. They didn't believe truth was missing.

The Founders forbade obscenity not because certain members of the community didn't like it and would be offended by it, but because it was morally wrong. God's law forbade it, and community laws were modeled after God's. They didn't have to justify their actions by utilitarian balancing. It was an absolute that did not need to be questioned. No matter how hard legal experts try to justify a position for or against obscenity by juggling rights, they will never convince each other. The only appeal is to God's law.

As will be discussed further in chapter nine, the Founders recognized three major areas of speech, two regarding free speech and one with respect to its being regulated:

- Free speech (by unalienable right):
  - criticism of the civil government
  - personal matters of the mind and heart
- Regulated speech (because of laws of nature and of nature's God):
  - matters involving the moral and physical order in the community

God's standards are absolute. They are fixed, uniform, and universal. Human laws should be likewise. When justices of the Supreme Court interpret the constitutionality of a law in isolation from a moral absolute, they are making personal judgments on which laws should be enforced and which should not. They are relying on changing values instead of unchanging standards.

In most instances, when the justices set themselves up as qualified judges of pornography, they remove biblical standards from consideration and ignore the wishes of the neighborhoods involved. As a result, improper decisions are made and precedents are set that will bring about deterioration of the community in the future. To correct this injustice, communities must insist on their sovereign right to enforce moral standards of their own choosing. They must be allowed to base their laws on fixed, uniform, and universal laws that grant no free speech rights to pornographers. American society will make no dramatic improvements in this realm until the legal system returns its thinking to the teachings of Scripture.

Notorious Commission Endorses Porn

One governmental commission stands out in glaring contrast to the anti-obscenity rulings by the Supreme Court. In 1970, a prestigious panel, which had been appointed by President Lyndon Johnson, reported to President Richard Nixon that pornography was a blessing and not a curse on America. Chaired by a member of the ACLU, the commission's majority concluded that pornography helped society by improving marriages, reducing sexual inhibitions, acting as a catharsis, and decreasing the incidence of rape and child abuse. The commission noted that sexually related crimes declined in countries where pornography is legalized. It postulated that pornography was not harmful, but rather educational, providing an opportunity for open discussions of sexuality and releasing inhibitions. Pornography could not be construed as contributing to criminal behavior. This study also concluded that child pornography was almost nonexistent.

The report was gleefully greeted by the pornography industry, which immediately launched a full-scale expansion into new depths of depravity. At the same time, it was rejected by Nixon, Congress, and the minority group on the commission itself. Reports have since surfaced on the shoddy investigative methods of the commission.

Since 1970, evidence has surfaced that contradicts the conclusions of this commission. Researchers who questioned imprisoned rapists and serial killers found that a large percentage admitted that violent pornography stimulated their search for victims. Ted Bundy was responsible for as many as seventy or eighty murders and sexual attacks. Before his execution in January 1989, he told James Dobson that he was willing to "take full responsibility for what I've done," but Americans must stop the evil force of violent pornography "loose in their towns and communities," ready to entice those like him with "dangerous impulses."

Researchers also found that subjects who view a steady diet of violent pornography develop a greater tolerance for sexual excitement and require increasingly stronger depictions in order to react. Some women conjectured that rape might not be a criminal act since the story characters appeared to enjoy it. Excessive exposure to pornography caused diminished satisfaction with the physical appearance of one's sexual partner. Sex itself became isolated from emotional involvement and commitment. Any repression of sexual urges was considered abnormal.

The absence of so-called kiddie porn was questioned in a study that found an increasing number of depictions of children and young women dressed as children in the pornography of magazines like *Playboy.* Child/adult sex was implied to be glamorous and harmless.

CONDEMNING EVIDENCE

The next official commission, chosen by Attorney General Edwin Meese, reached a far different conclusion. Commission hearings in various cities frequently were extended to twelve hours a day just to accommodate the witnesses. Members of the commission were shocked by what they heard and saw. Some visited adult theaters and found either live or filmed depictions of every act possible to heterosexuals, homosexuals, and lesbians. These on-site visitors were repulsed by the sites themselves. Often the walls were equipped with access holes for anonymous sexual encounters.

Since the release of the Meese Commission's report in 1986, the media have virtually ignored it, but an army of decent citizens has begun to do something. One of the leaders in this march is Jerry Kirk of Cincinnati. As a Presbyterian pastor, he realized that members of his congregation were deeply troubled by America's changing moral climate. In his book, *The Mind Polluters,* he said: "My people were crying out for guidance and, while I knew the answer for any situation was God's grace and healing in Jesus Christ, I didn't understand the source of the problem. I found that I had no answer for the avalanche of immorality that was crushing my people. I wasn't sure where the real problem was."

Beginning with prayer meetings and expanding to church classes on how to fight pornography, his church members were ready to act when the Warner Amex Cable Company announced the introduction of the Playboy Channel to their locality. "It was at this time that we chose our name, Citizens Concerned for Community Values, and began to surface as an organized group," Kirk said. With the help of others in the community, they succeeded in blocking the new channel.

Since that time, Kirk has put together a team called the National Coalition Against Pornography. This nondenominational group owes its success to several tactics, such as the following:

- prayer and fasting for America
- education and literature distribution
- letter-writing campaigns
- campaigns uniting sympathizers for local action
- lobbying Congress

Their motto was expressed first by Edmund Burke in 1795, "The only thing necessary for the triumph of evil is for good men to do nothing."

Leaders like Kirk and the growing number of concerned and caring people are doing something now, and they are seeing results like those in 1988, when Congress took strong action against Dial-a-Porn and child pornography.

God Speaks Clearly

The first chapter of Romans is God's Bill of Rights for regulating the sexual conduct of His creation. He declares that everyone will be judged for ungodly and unrighteous behavior because God's truth is built into the fabric of our being, but we suppress it.

The first step into sexual immorality is rejection of God, a refusal to honor Him and follow His Word. In place of God, people erect their own idols and proclaim their own standards of rights, freedoms, and morality.

Ultimately, according to this passage in Romans, men and women exchange the natural attraction they have for the opposite sex for an unnatural desire for the same sex. Men "burn out" from their deeds, "receiving in their own persons the due penalty of their error" (Rom. 1:27, NASB). They not only practice these deeds, but also give hearty approval to others.

God's judgment in these matters is not arbitrary, nor is it imaginary. He sits as a righteous Judge whom all people must satisfy or else spend eternity in hell. Some feel that such a view is old fashioned and harsh. They would prefer a god who can be controlled, someone who would weigh good deeds in the balance and find them acceptable. Yet God says, "I am the Lord," and gives us the commandments.

If people know Jesus Christ as their Lord and Savior they will escape God's wrath. They will have the ability to overcome their insistent lusts or, if they fall, to receive God's forgiveness and cleansing. It is not fair for Christians to keep this news to themselves. They must go to these sleazy districts and speak to their denizens about the holiness and love of God.

They must also learn to "walk the walk," not just "talk the talk." In 1776, Edward Gibbon, in *The Decline and Fall of the Roman Empire,* attributed the rapid spread of Christianity "to the convincing evidence of the doctrine itself, and to the ruling providence of its great Author." In addition, he said, Christians themselves attracted multitudes because of their outstanding moral character. He wrote: "The primitive Christian demonstrated his faith by his virtues; and it was very justly supposed that the Divine persuasion, which enlightened or subdued the understanding, must at the same time purify the heart and direct the actions of the believer."

Gibbon, although somewhat skeptical, attributed Christian morality to a great extent on the fear of Christ's imminent return. It is true that Christians should live in expectation of the Second Coming, but there is another element that Gibbon missed, as explained by Paul. Believers demonstrate by their obedience that God gives His people *power* to overcome their natural sinfulness and live righteous lives. Otherwise, if they are no different from anyone else, "the name of God is blasphemed among the Gentiles because of you" (Rom. 2:24, NASB).

Christian obedience to the Law also shows the world that there is a standard. Unbelievers need to see that there is a difference between right and wrong and realize that they need a Savior.

Christians understand that they did not win God's favor by obedience to the Law. Rather, God justified them by their faith in Christ's atonement for sins. God dispensed justification as a free gift, without partiality. None can look down their noses at those in bondage to immorality and say, "I was never a prostitute (or homosexual, or adulterer, or porn queen), therefore I am acceptable to God." As Paul said in his first letter to the Corinthians, "Such were some of you, but you were washed, you were sanctified, you were justified in the name of the Lord Jesus Christ and in the Spirit of our God" (1 Cor. 6:11, RSV).

Neither can the Christian say by perverted reasoning, "Since I am not justified by the Law, all things are lawful for me." As Paul said, the body is the temple of the Holy Spirit. It is not right to use it for immoral purposes, because it is joined to the Lord (1 Cor. 6:12–19).

If Christians want to change the way America thinks about sexual perversions, they will have to start in their own homes. They must be that "city on a hill" that gives light to all so that they, too, can break free from the bondage of licentiousness.

If they start in their own bedrooms, they will not only be able to change America, they will refresh and revitalize their own marriages, using God's success plan for intimacy with holiness.

For Further Reading

Allan Bloom. *The Closing of the American Mind.* New York: Simon and Schuster, 1987.

Reo M. Christenson. *Challenge and Decision: Political Issues of Our Time.* 6th ed. New York: Harper & Row, 1982.

Thomas I. Emerson, *Toward a General Theory of the First Amendment.* New York: Vintage Books, 1967.

Jerry Kirk. *The Mind Polluters.* Nashville: Thomas Nelson Publishers, 1985.

Peggy Lamson. *Roger Baldwin, Founder of the American Civil Liberties Union.* Boston: Houghton Mifflin Co., 1976.

Tom Minnery, ed. *Pornography: A Human Tragedy.* Wheaton, Ill.: Tyndale House, 1986.

Christine Pierce and Donald Van De Veer. *AIDS: Ethics and Public Policy.* Belmont, Calif.: Wadsworth Publishing Co., 1988.

6

Marriage: The Way It Can Be

Scenes from America's daytime soap operas are full of propaganda for the latest national ethic: In marriage, the old rules don't apply anymore. America, it seems, has regressed into an age of perpetual puberty. Like Peter Pan, men and women who should know better seem determined never to grow up. Brainwashed for generations that change is the only constant, they see no point in taking on the permanent responsibility of stable homes and families. It's playtime every day. If an opportunity comes along, take it.

Adultery as Entertainment

A few years ago, media researchers Stanley Rothman and S. Robert Lichter surveyed Hollywood's foremost writers, producers, and directors to determine their attitudes on social issues and their plans to institute social change. Like their counterparts in television, the movie elite "enthusiastically support certain aspects of the new morality that emerged in the 1960s," they said. In addition, both groups felt so strongly that their liberated opinions were correct that they intended to use their medium to bring about social change. Their goal was to remove religion from its position of influence and replace it with their own views.

One of the items on their agenda was to discard the old-fashioned religious idea that adultery is wrong. As soap opera scene after soap opera scene demonstrate, they have no problem with a husband or wife who keeps his or her eyes open for greener pastures. When questioned about their opinion of adultery, more than half of the movie elite said that there was nothing wrong with it. Only 13 percent strongly agreed with the statement that adultery is wrong.

In God's reality, a man is in command of a situation not when his tongue hangs out over another man's wife but when he has the strength of character to put his lusts under subjection. A woman embraces a man not when he wants to use her for an evening's entertainment but when he becomes her helpmate. When a man treats his wife as Christ treats him, she knows he has staked his life on their happiness together.

According to some hedonistic standards, marriage is no fun because it requires the participants to do more than just share a bed together and say good-bye in the morning. It requires that a husband and wife occasionally show how much they care for each other in ways other than physical means.

A man and woman marry when they grow up, after they have realized that true happiness does not come with a rewriting of the rules but in honoring old ones. Every time a swaggering adulterer on television toys with someone's spouse and gets away with it, the message is communicated that this behavior is nothing to be concerned about. The entertainment community has been very successful in its effort to change the way America thinks, but it can't change the way they are.

Because of the way God created men and women, in real life adultery is a crushing blow. It hurts the victim and the perpetrator. Like premarital sex, it is an unnatural act that flies in the face of God's natural order.

In January 1989, CBN's "700 Club" had a two-week telethon based on the Ten Commandments. As soon as the program reached the seventh commandment—Thou shalt not commit adultery—so many callers jammed the toll-free phone lines that as many as eight hundred people at a time received busy signals. Those who got through poured their hearts out to the counselors. Many wept. Should America change the way it thinks about marriage? Are couples ready to fight for their marriages or those of their friends and relatives? How important is marriage for the survival of a nation?

A Dead End for Marriage?

The advertisements appear in every newspaper and on billboards along the nation's highways: "Divorce (uncontested) $130 + court costs, lowest fee in area." Everyone knows the divorce statistics. Is it hopeless? Has the value of a marriage been reduced to "$130 + court costs"?

Americans can change those statistics, but first they have to change the way they think about marriage, premarriage, and lifetime commitments. They have to make it conform to the Creator's plan.

In ancient times, when a prospective husband found someone to be his wife, he had to earn her. He was required to serve an internship with her father to prove his intentions and demonstrate his worthiness to be brought into the family. The Bible tells us that Jacob served seven years with Laban before he earned the right to marry into Laban's family.

Even in recent times, a young man asked permission of his prospective bride's parents for their daughter's hand in marriage. A period of courtship then ensued so that the future mates could confirm that they wanted to spend the rest of their lives together.

During this waiting period, both parties had the opportunity to become acquainted and also to practice restraint against the physical attraction between them. An *opportunity?* To a liberated man and woman it sounded more like the unjust regimen of a puritanical society. They dispensed with it. They reasoned that whatever happened naturally must be good. These "old-fashioned" restraints, however, were not some desperate ploy to prevent premature pregnancy, although it was considered logical to keep childbearing in the safety of a family. A chaste courtship was considered the final stage in the maturing process that prepared a man and woman to show respect for each other's dignity. Chastity was also excellent training for the responsibility of a home, where a husband and wife could ill afford to be captives of their passions.

When the Christian husband-to-be controls his temptation to violate his future wife's virginity, it is an act of obedience to the Lordship of Christ and a practical opportunity to learn holiness. As the Apostle Paul wrote to the church in Thessalonica: "God's plan is to make you holy, and that means a clean cut with sexual immorality. Every one of you should learn to control his body, keeping it pure and treating it with respect, and never allowing it to fall victim to lust, as do pagans with no knowledge of God. . . . The calling of God is not to impurity but to the most thorough purity, and anyone who makes light of the matter is not making light of a man's ruling but of God's command. It is not for nothing that the Spirit God gives us is called the *Holy* Spirit" (1 Thess. 4:3–5, 7–8, PHILLIPS).

When the future wife refused to be seduced, she asserted her right to retain control over her body and share herself only with the man who would take care of her for life. On her wedding night, the wife gave her husband the greatest gift she could offer, her virginity. According to the Old Testament, this gift was so significant that the bride's parents kept a record of it. If the husband later defamed her, saying he did not find her a virgin, they could vindicate their daughter's good name. (See Deut. 22:13–19.)

When Americans lost their respect for premarital chastity, they didn't escape the jail built by a few celibate churchmen. They played hooky from God's basic training camp, and now they can't fight the war to recapture their marriages.

THE "ENEMY" OF FREEDOM

In the twentieth century, promiscuous Americans have openly fraternized with two of God's enemies, a man and a woman who spent their lives labeling God and the church as enemies to be defeated. These Goliaths of the sexual revolution are Sigmund Freud and Margaret Sanger.

Freud offered a "succulent variety" of gnosticism, wrote historian Paul Johnson; namely, a secret society of sexuality. Intellectuals and novelists found it tantalizing and were soon promoting his philosophy. Freud seemed able to explain anything with his sexually rooted theories, and he was willing to take a stand against something the intellectuals had no use for anyway—the Christian church.

Religion, to Freud, was man-made, and its influence could be destroyed. Once rid of this delusion, people could go about the real business of solving their problems. He wrote, "The religions of mankind must be classed among the mass-delusions of this kind. No one, needless to say, who shares a delusion ever recognizes it as such."

Thus was the church dismissed as a problem creator and its members as incapable of rational thought. The church said courtship and marriage should be modest and restrained. That was too restrictive. Sexual restraints (morals) had almost destroyed modern society, he said, and the world's only hope was to set itself free. Whoever would eradicate mental illness and world war must find the sexual secrets imprisoned within each person and let them out.

The woman who claimed to know the secret to women's sexual freedom was an unsuccessful wife and mother named Margaret Sanger, the founder and inspiration of Planned Parenthood.

When Pat Robertson ran for the presidency in 1988, he said Sanger was a eugenicist who promoted forced sterilization and advocated the creation of a master race. The media were delighted and immediately obtained an angry denial from Planned Parenthood's president, Faye Wattleton. "All the charges are unfounded and, frankly, ridiculous," she told reporters.

Wattleton is at best misinformed if she truly believes what she said about her organization's founder. Sanger herself made no attempts to cover up her positions.

In her 1922 book, *The Pivot of Civilization,* Sanger wrote of "the lack of balance between the birth rate of the 'unfit' and the 'fit,' admittedly the greatest menace to civilization." Throughout her life's work she made repeated references to different grades of people, as if they were cattle on the way to market. In post-Darwinian language, she placed human beings in the barnyard with all the other animals instead of in the place where God put them—loved and created for a divine and unique purpose, no matter how lowly their circumstances.

Births to inferior humans were the greatest menace to society, she said. Its greatest hope, however, was sexual intercourse, carefully controlled by women through contraception. She wrote, "Through sex, mankind may attain the great spiritual illumination which will transform the world, which will light up the only path to an earthly paradise."

Sanger called on individuals to stop practicing "self-sacrifice" and begin "self-development." She said that a person "does his best for the world not by dying for it . . . but by increasing his own stature." The main way for a woman to increase her stature, Sanger said, was to control reproduction. Birth control was the "pivot of civilization," the declaration of independence by women of the world.

In her first newspaper, *The Woman Rebel,* Sanger shouted from the masthead "No Gods! No Masters!" No God. No submission to one's husband. No cooperation with him in producing and raising a family. No family at all if a couple were judged "unfit."

With so many couples mating under the auspices of Planned Parenthood and imbibing the sex potions of Freud and Sanger, is it any wonder that no one knows what normal married life means any more? Those who know God must talk to Him about marriage and read His Word. In an age of chaos there are time-tested methods that work. Marriage in America is not dead. Americans must not think that way. God has the answers. Legitimized lust must be stopped by people who are willing to take a stand for sexual dignity and God's definitions of pleasure and sin. America needs people who believe in standards of moral purity and appreciate the quality of lovemaking that only marriage brings.

RESPECT FOR MARRIAGE

Marriage is a reenactment of one of the oldest themes in human history. As the Bible teacher, Derek Prince, wrote in *God Is a Matchmaker,* "From Genesis to Revelation, from the first act in Eden to the last act in the heavenlies, the central theme of human history is marriage."

When God instituted marriage, He called it becoming "one flesh" (Gen. 2:24). Unity replaced division. He used it as a model for the way humans relate to Him. Divorce is devastating because it is the tearing apart of a single unit. That is why God said, "I hate divorce" (Mal. 2:16, NASB).

The Anglican Book of Common Prayer (1549) said marriage was "instituted of God in the time of man's innocency . . . . [not] to satisfy man's carnal lusts and appetites, like brute beasts that have no understanding." If marriage were nothing but a transient sexual partnership, it would not hurt so much when it was over. But marriage is not "sanctioned lust," it is a new, sovereign unit of society, a "miniature body politic," as Allan Bloom called it.

Man and woman have a natural attraction to one another (Gen. 2:18–25), but even in marriage they are not to lust after each other but to respect each other's dignity. Each is created in the image of God. Self-control is no longer necessary for abstinence, but even on the marriage bed their actions should honor the Lord. God created sex and He made it good, but He didn't create it so that one partner's actions might defile the other.

Unnatural Marriage

The story is not all that uncommon. A wife may discover her husband satisfying his own sexual urges with the assistance of pornography. Usually the excuse is that he had just been doing it to "help" the marriage.

Sexual problems in marriage have many causes, but, according to James Dobson, pornography will not solve any of them. Pornography is not a help to a marriage because no one's wife could measure up to the artificial voluptuousness depicted by it. Realistically, no one can be too comfortable with the poses and procedures dreamed up by photographers. Sodomy is frequently depicted, and, as was noted earlier, it is illegal in many states, even between married partners. Leather, whips, and chains belong in torture chambers rather than the bedchamber.

Husbands who abuse their spouses in this manner are abusing the natural tendency toward submission that God gave to women. Women are not required to obey their husbands when their husbands disobey God. The Father takes precedence. Women may submit for a time to these degrading practices discovered by their husbands, but only fear or a demoralized self-image convinces them to continue. None of this is the basis for a healthy marriage.

For those who need outside help with their problems, Dobson recommends that couples either see a Christian counselor with specific experience in sexuality counseling or visit a physician. Christian bookstores also carry helpful books and tapes. Sexual problems may be caused by such things as hormone imbalances, certain foods, smoking, medications, previous experience with sexual abuse, premarital sex, poor self-image, and lack of sex education from parents.

There is no greater marriage killer than the tyranny of the urgent. Couples need quantities of time to share their lives, to sit and talk, to walk together. Couples today suffer from the false impressions presented in romance novels, films, and television that intimacy is almost exclusively a by-product of a physical act. They are told that if there is no glamorous sex life—no constant, richly varied, thrilling physical excitement—there is no marriage.

This is simply not true. A fulfilling sex life is the product of a good marriage, not the source. Intimacy comes from a sincere commitment, the "knowing" of the biblical description. The marriages that thrive for decades involve two people who have come to know each other, not only in body, but also in soul and spirit. That is the reason why godly marriages have the greatest potential for success, because they include the spiritual element.

In 1968, Pope Paul VI released his encyclical *Humanae Vitae* on the subject of natural family planning. There was such a furor in this country over his prohibition of contraception that few noticed his gentle insistence that a husband honor his wife's biological timetables. He wrote, "A man who grows accustomed to the use of a woman [disregards] her physical and emotional equilibrium." A husband was not to use his wife as a sex object, but to be sensitive to her as a human being who experienced specific monthly changes. Recent findings on the physical and emotional effects of premenstrual syndrome (PMS) confirm his counsel. The pope also recommended that couples use their understanding of these cycles as a natural method of contraception.

IS SEXUAL INTERCOURSE EVIL?

If television were the only standard of life in the United States, one might think that sex is everything. If the only barometer of the American lifestyle were church sermons, one might think sex didn't exist. How can the church change the way America thinks about sex if pastors rarely talk about it?

Derek Prince observed, "Sex has been treated as an unfortunate necessity, almost an aberration of the Creator, which requires some kind of apology." The Bible, especially books like Song of Solomon, is not silent on human sexuality; however, God's Word makes it abundantly clear that His only sanction for intercourse is in marriage.

Even within marriage, the early church fathers had problems with it. Augustine, for example, kept a mistress during his years of dissolute living. When he became a Christian and eventually accepted a life of celibacy, he began to identify intercourse with the Fall, reasoning that Adam and Eve's first action had been to cover their genitals. Even marriage couldn't completely dismiss the evil nature of sexual intercourse, he said. The best it could do was to divert the practice to the one positive purpose—conception.

The Middle Ages was the time of Dante and Beatrice, troubadours with their romantic ballads, and of Chaucer's ribald tales, but it was also a time when certain church fathers took a grim stand against sexual intercourse. They adopted pagan dualism, such as that of Plato, which considered the body a hindrance to the soul. Some even demanded that intercourse occur only on certain days of the week. Procreation was the only excuse for any such behavior.

The Apostle Paul, however, told married couples in Corinth that they had an ongoing duty to one another, and he didn't even mention procreation. He wrote: "The husband should give his wife what is due to her as his wife, and the wife should be as fair to her husband. The wife has no longer full rights over her own person, but shares them with her husband. In the same way the husband shares his personal rights with his wife. Do not cheat each other of normal sexual intercourse, unless of course you both decide to abstain temporarily to make special opportunity for prayer. But afterwards you should resume relations as before, or you will expose yourselves to the obvious temptation of Satan" (1 Cor. 7:3–5, PHILLIPS).

COMMITMENT, THE GOLDEN CHORD

When Satan tempts men and women to abandon their mates and find sexual gratification elsewhere, he is tempting them to treason and unadulterated self-interest. Marriage is a covenant relationship involving three parties: the husband, the wife, and God. David asks in Psalm 15, "O Lord, who may abide in Thy tent?" and then answers, the man who "swears to his own hurt, and does not change" (Ps. 15:1, 4, NASB). Marriage vows are not to be entered into without counting the cost, but once taken, the righteous person does not break them.

Jesus commanded us to love others as we love ourselves. The world tells us to love ourselves. The drum beat of "me first, me first, me first" began in the Garden of Eden and has grown louder and louder through the centuries. Now it is almost deafening in its intensity, drowning the music of love.

During the sixties, everyone liked to quote Polonius: "This above all: to thine own self be true." Richard John Neuhaus observed dryly, "This is taken to be great wisdom, but it is in fact the most tragic folly. It is too often forgotten that Shakespeare intended Polonius as the fool."

Adultery and premarital sex are self-centered, but they also destroy the self. They engender what psychiatrist Raymond Vath called "pseudointimacy." Both partners realize underneath that it is "a temporary illusion of devotion and closeness." By contrast, true intimacy marks the relationship between a man and woman who have committed their lives to one another for life. These are the partners who not only say they are married, but also work out every conflict so they can stay married.

SUBMISSION: SLAVERY OR FREEDOM?

Daniel C. Maguire of Marquette University represents those in America who, like Margaret Sanger, are appalled by the thought of submission in marriage. He called it "a macho and oppressive solution." He contended, "The New Right would strip women of their sense of dignity and of their rights, make them more submissive, and in that way restore peace to the family scene."

Those who want to eliminate headship and submission from marriage say it destroys women, making them little more than slaves. Their position is not only unbiblical but also destructive to the future stability of the American family. Instead of saving marriages, the refusal to follow this biblical model is ending them.

The automatic assumption that all of today's wives, especially those in Christian homes, need liberation from oppression is simply not true. Most women, even in the church, are suffering from *lack* of male authority in the home, not its abundance. Desiring to grant everyone equal rights (which are not ours to give, since God has already created us equal), we have ended up with households where no one is in charge, where everyone does what is right in his own eyes (Judg. 21:25). Lack of leadership has been the downfall of every empire, and it is killing our families and our nation.

God specifically said that the husband was to be the head of the wife. That means someone has to have the last word, because someone has to take the ultimate responsibility for providing for the family's needs and receiving the rap when a bad decision is made. As Harry Truman said, "The buck stops here."

God never said the husband could be a tyrant. In fact, He set aside all man's potential excuses for tyrannizing his family by saying the man must love his wife as himself, and he must submit all his decisions to Christ, who is head over him (Eph. 5:21–33). God shows no partiality to men and women and has made them joint heirs of the kingdom (1 Pet. 3:7).

As Dee Jepsen wrote in *Women: Beyond Equal Rights,* no company can function with two CEOs, and a family cannot function with two heads.

Submission does not mean inferiority, it means protection and nurture. Alexis de Tocqueville, observing American women in the early nineteenth century, said that even though most of them limited themselves to domestic life, he had never seen women in a loftier place. To him, they far excelled those on the European continent who were continually engaged in battles for rights. He attributed the strength and prosperity of America to the superiority of its women.

During the much-maligned Victorian era, Victoria willingly submitted to her beloved Albert. Victorian women gave their husbands a place of refuge, but they were not doormats. They insisted that their men be sober and respectful. Far from an inferior, servile breed, said historian Esmé Wingfield-Stratford, these women were "the most brilliant galaxy of feminine genius that has adorned any age or country." There were women such as Elizabeth Barrett Browning, Charlotte and Emily Bronte, George Eliot, Florence Nightingale, Louisa May Alcott, and Harriet Beecher Stowe.

When a wife is fulfilled, active, and free to care for her husband and children, her husband is blessed at home and at work (Prov. 31:10–31). Most wives function best when their husbands take the primary responsibility for feeding the family, although many women need an outlet of at least part-time work in a field that interests them. Some can even handle full-time work, but they need to beware of divided loyalties and diminished strength.

According to the U.S. Bureau of Labor Statistics, when mothers of young children hold outside employment, they spend as much as eighty-five hours a week at those two full-time jobs. They have more headaches, stomach aches, and menstrual pain than full-time homemakers. Sometimes 75 percent of the paycheck disappears into taxes and child care.

In *The Christian Couple,* Larry and Nordis Christenson wrote:

If a husband abdicates his responsibility as head, he strikes at the very core of the relationship which God has established between him and his wife.

The relationship is designed to build up both husband and wife, according to the divine model. The Father exalts the Son. He delights to lift Him up, to honor Him. This is the way headship behaves when it is grounded in love. The courtesy which a husband shows toward his wife, the way he honors her before the children, his open and evident esteem for her, is the foundation upon which the wife's respect and trust in her husband is built. And then she, in turn, will acknowledge and exalt her husband, gladly submitting to his authority—as Jesus exalts the Father and submits to His authority.

Every marriage will experience conflict. The only ones that survive are those where couples establish their own healthy system for resolving these conflicts. What they learn in the family they can then apply to their community and society.

In the New Testament church, a man who would serve as bishop or deacon must first prove himself a good husband and father. Likewise, the nation needs the leadership of stable family men who love God, love their wives and children, and are committed to them for life. In the vagaries of politics, adultery is still one sin the majority of voters will not tolerate. It is one last thread of logic in a diminishing sensitivity to truth.

James Russell Lowell wrote in *The Present Crisis:*

> Though the cause of Evil prosper, yet
> 't is Truth alone is strong,
> And, albeit she wander outcast now, I see
> around her throne
> Troops of beautiful, tall angels, to
> enshield her from all wrong.

We can do it. We can change the way America thinks about marriage because God's truth is strong. If we are strong in the Lord and the strength of His might, we may even save our children.

For Further Reading

Larry and Nordis Christenson. *The Christian Couple.* Minneapolis: Bethany Fellowship, 1977.

Esmé Wingfield-Stratford. *Those Earnest Victorians.* New York: William Morrow & Co., 1930.

George Grant. *Grand Illusions: The Legacy of Planned Parenthood.* Brentwood, Tenn.: Wolgemuth & Hyatt, 1988.

Paul Johnson. *Modern Times.* New York: Harper Colophon Books, 1983.
Geoffrey Parrinder. *Sex in the World's Religions.* New York: Simon and Schuster, 1987.
John Paul II. *Reflections on* Humanae Vitae. Boston: Daughters of St. Paul, 1984.
Derek Prince, with Ruth Prince. *God Is a Matchmaker.* Old Tappan, N.J.: Fleming H. Revell, 1986.
Margaret Sanger. *The Pivot of Civilization.* New York: Brentano's, 1922.
Raymond E. Vath and Daniel W. O'Neill. *Marrying for Life: A Handbook for Marriage Survival.* Minneapolis: Winston Press, 1982.

7

War on Children

On Friday afternoon, 6 March 1987, the ferry *Herald of Free Enterprise* left the Belgian port town of Zeebrugge on a routine crossing of the English Channel. The 460 passengers included servicemen on leave, families on holiday, and couples making a new start in life. Before they reached Dover 190 of them would die. They were victims of "the worst British peacetime marine tragedy since the sinking of the *Titanic.*"

The ship's captain was a veteran of many crossings. Members of the crew could always be depended upon to follow their routine. This time, through a tragic combination of crew negligence and faulty ship design, the ferry's twelve-ton hydraulically operated bow doors were left open. The cargo of people was headed for destruction. As the ferry picked up speed, a wave of water built up before it. Soon, like a caged lion loosed upon its keeper, it attacked the car deck with two hundred tons of water per minute.

Susan Hames and Robert Heard were seated in the ship's restaurant when suddenly dishes and silverware began flying off the tables. Within seconds terrified passengers were falling, smashing hard against tables and walls. As the tide of water surged toward them, the lights flickered and went out.

Susan clawed her way to the top of what was once the bar, by then turned sideways with the list of the sinking ship. Dim figures surfaced beneath her, illumined by twilight from the window-turned-skylight above her. She called out to Rob, but there was no response.

She saw a man, bleeding, holding onto a girl waist-deep in water.

Reaching down, she pulled the girl up onto the more shallow water of the ledge. Soon she was also holding the girl's infant brother.

Above Susan, a young man crash-landed on a ledge, and they worked together to lift the children even farther up. Lawrence Elliott described what happened next:

> Other voices called out:
>
> "Can you take my child, please?"
>
> "My baby is in the water . . ."
>
> Children, one at a time, were handed along to Susan; she lifted three of them up to the man on the ledge. Suddenly her eye was caught by lights and movement overhead. Someone had come to get them! . . .
>
> "Please," Susan called, "there are small children here. Can you lower something to take them out?"
>
> What came down was a large wicker basket. People called for it—"Send it over here!"—but Susan had hold of the basket and she said firmly, "The children are going up first."

Children as Enemies

Susan's contribution to saving the children's lives would be heroic in any age, but in the twentieth century it symbolizes what life was like before society declared war on children.

War on children. Is that an exaggeration? Couples contemplating marriage today have one priority: how to keep babies from coming. To accomplish this they ignore warning labels on pills and horror stories on the news. Corporations solicit employee participation in community-wide fund drives that provide drugs and abortions in order to control the size of the poor population. From the time children enter public school, they are taught not only the ABCs but also the XYZs—explicit information on how babies are born and how to prevent conception when they grow up. When children become adolescents, the information is so prevalent that a boy and girl can copulate without "complications."

The war on children is more methodical than any American military actions were against Vietnam, Grenada, or Libya. In German, it is called *kinderfeindschaft:* children as enemies. Many, many people today think of children as enemies, especially the women who might conceive them.

In 1988, when actress Kathryn Hepburn was honored for her decades of work with Planned Parenthood, she told the press, "Abortion is necessary unless women are going to be absolute slaves." Abortion is the "only practical way to handle a situation where the population would go mad otherwise," she said. "There are too many of us, anyway. It seems so obvious."

Is it obvious that "there are too many of us"? Mother Teresa of Calcutta says no. "Every child," she said, "has been created for greater things, to love and be loved, in the image of God. That's why people must decide beforehand if they really want to have a child. Once a child is conceived there is life, God's life. That child has a right to live and be cared for."

Two irresolute sides in a war—one to prevent live births and one to ensure them. Both are convinced in their thinking that they are right.

HOW AMERICA THINKS ABOUT CHILDREN

Remember these innocent little rhymes:

What are little boys made of?
Snips and snails, and puppy-dogs' tails;
That's what little boys are made of.

What are little girls made of?
Sugar and spice, and everything nice;
That's what little girls are made of.

Either children have changed or the way America *thinks* about them has changed. Many adults no longer think of them as bundles of joy. Why? Here are some common arguments used for continuing the war on children:

"There are too many of us."

Kathryn Hepburn's argument traces back to Thomas Malthus (1766–1834) who said that the earth's population was increasing too quickly for available resources to support it. Malthus has been discredited, but his theory lives on. Americans use it to justify abortions in their ghettoes and around the world. It is a prime example of the panic that sets in when people forget they have a Creator who has promised to provide food, clothing, and every other resource for those who trust in Him.

"Children should not bear children."

If a teenage girl becomes pregnant, her pregnancy should be terminated because she would not be a fit mother, the argument goes. There is no question that it is tremendously difficult for an immature girl to raise a child, but with God all things are possible. Grandparents, pro-life counselors, and church women are often eager to help. Adoptive children are desperately wanted all over America. No perceived ill consequences can possibly justify killing an unborn child. Two thousand years ago, Mary was a young teenage girl when Jesus was born to her. God never questioned the propriety of allowing her to bear His Son.

"The weak are a drain on family and society."

Following Charles Darwin's revival of the theory of evolution, Herbert Spencer coined the term "survival of the fittest." In order to perpetuate healthy human "stock," it became one's duty to discourage the reproduction and maintenance of "unfit" human babies because their care would divert resources from the strong members of society. As Margaret Sanger wrote in *The Pivot of Civilization,* philanthropic efforts toward this "dead weight of human waste" were dangerous: "Instead of decreasing and aiming to eliminate the stocks that are most detrimental to the future of the race and the world," she said, "it tends to render them to a menacing degree dominant."

Many Americans have accepted some form of this reasoning, considering it a favor to kill a fetus or newborn child who shows signs of a handicap, but it is opposed to the teaching of Scripture. Jesus said, "When you give a banquet, invite the poor, the crippled, the lame, the blind, and you will be blessed. Although they cannot repay you, you will be repaid at the resurrection of the righteous" (Luke 14:13–14).

Friedrich Nietzsche (1844–1900) advocated a return to the noble ancients who were motivated by power, self-affirmation, health, and beauty. He said the weak, the insecure, and the ugly offered nothing to a person on the move and to show pity on them was to destroy society. His advice was taken by Adolph Hitler.

"Prevent child abuse by preventing unwanted children."

In a monochromatic world where people see only themselves, it seems impossible to imagine that an unwanted pregnancy might result in a happy mother-child relationship. Thus the bizarre solution to preventing abuse of an unwanted child is death before birth.

The fallacy of this reasoning is exhibited in the high incidence of child abuse to children who were *wanted,* not to those who were not. The most hardened heart can be softened by a child, and the most selfish desire for a child can be turned to hate. Most parents abuse their children because they don't know how to handle them. Perhaps they were abused themselves or never had a good model of parental behavior. Most of them don't know how to love because they don't know God's love.

When the House of Representatives prepared a report on child abuse in 1987, the committee said that child abuse would drop significantly if certain measures were taken. They recommended parent education, support and training for pregnant women and teens, programs to increase parental self-esteem, and efforts to maintain the family unit. Most states, however, neglected these preventive and treatment measures and dealt only with offenders.

There is an army of people who could help these potential child abusers, but they never try. They are the people of God. There is a desperate need for a number of them to get involved and help those who are helpless against their own rage and frustration.

The prophet Malachi said that when Elijah returned he would "turn the hearts of the fathers to their children, and the hearts of the children to their fathers." That day began when John the Baptist proclaimed the coming of the Messiah, Jesus Christ. Help is available through Him, but if the people will not love their children and parents, God said, "I will come and strike the land with a curse" (Mal. 4:6).

"A fetus is not a person."

In the 1973 *Roe v. Wade* decision, the Supreme Court declared that a fetus was not a person. It was a dramatic step in a movement that had already begun to change the way America thought about children—not as God's little miracles but as adversaries.

Once upon a time, movie children like Shirley Temple giggled and frolicked their way into adult hearts. Increasingly, however, children are now portrayed in literature and the media as exploiters of adults and one another.

According to the Bible—and common sense—a child, born or unborn, is a delicate, dependent creature who needs the nurture, love, and guidance of the parents who conceived him. In awe before the God who made him, David wrote: "You made all the delicate, inner parts of my body, and knit them together in my mother's womb. Thank you for making me so wonderfully complex! It is amazing to think about. Your workmanship is marvelous—and how well I know it. You were there while I was being formed in utter seclusion! You saw me before I was born and scheduled each day of my life before I began to breathe. Every day was recorded in your Book!" (Ps. 139:13–16).

David's own children were no less a miracle to him. From hard experience, he knew their lives depended on the mercy of God. When his son, Solomon, grew up, he became a king renowned for his wisdom. In a dispute over a child that erupted between two prostitutes, Solomon determined which woman was the child's mother by finding out who would refuse to have him killed (1 Kings 3:16–28). To everyone present, the willingness of one woman to kill the child was evidence that she could not possibly be the mother. How drastically thinking has changed since those days.

"If abortion is outlawed, women will die."

Pro-abortion protesters heckle pro-life activists with the words, "You don't care if women die!" They scream that if abortion becomes illegal, women will resort once again to coat hangers and dirty back-alley abortions.

Legal abortions, however, are not so safe after all. During the recent crusade for international acceptance of the French drug RU486, which causes the death of a fertilized egg in the womb, the researcher who developed it made a startling admission in the process of trying to promote it. Etienne-Emile Baulieu said, "Almost 50 million women have abortions each year, and some 150,000 women die annually from botched abortions." If he is right, that means death for one in every 333 abortion attempts worldwide.

Abortion not only kills children, it also kills their mothers. Childbirth is painful, but it is almost never fatal. For those willing to forego the coat hanger and allow God to have His way, the fruit of the womb is God's reward (Ps. 127:3), not a punishment. Jesus said: "A woman giving birth to a child has pain because her time has come; but when her baby is born she forgets the anguish because of her joy that a child is born into the world" (John 16:21).

It is almost impossible in an age of situation ethics to communicate to the hecklers that you can't cover over a sin by making it less dangerous. What those women are doing is wrong, and no sterilized amphitheater for their crime makes it any less bloody.

It is also impossible to function in an environment where information about God is suppressed and secular solutions are funded for worldwide problems. Americans are compassionate and want to help Third World women as well as the poor among us here in our own country, but the militant feminists who demand contraception and abortion for these people will never solve the problem. It will only get worse. The problem is a spiritual one. The only ones who can help are missionaries of the Gospel, and they don't have the money to do it. Something needs to be done about our priorities.

"I need the backup of abortion for the liberated life."

Even pagan cults worshiped gods of fertility, but today American men worship at the altar of barren woman, properly sterilized, awaiting their pleasure. The liberated woman, free from "enslavement" to children, is now enslaved to a man who will make no commitment to the offspring of her body.

In moments of weakness, when all the clamor of "liberation" seems like slavery, she may yearn to hold an infant in her arms. Hardened as she is, she must suppress this weakness and find solace in her freedom. When she is old, it will be all that she has.

"A child would ruin all my fun."

Some couples may make the decision to remain childless for a variety of reasons, but once a child is conceived—even by "accident"—they have lost that option. When God has intervened in the process, there is no turning back.

The idea of avoiding anything painful in life is not only unbiblical but also unrealistic. Ever since avoidance of pain was promoted by people like Jeremy Bentham (1748–1832), it has been a popular idea. In *An Introduction to the Principles of Morals and Legislation,* he wrote: "Nature has placed mankind under the governance of two sovereign masters, *pain* and *pleasure.* It is for them alone to point out what we ought to do, as well as to determine what we shall do."

Having a child who keeps you up at night, throws up on your couch, messes diapers, and requires constant babysitting can be a pain. But is the only pleasure in life a child-free home? There must be something good hidden there, because God repeatedly promised children as a blessing to the people of Israel. People do not need to live under the tyranny of pain and pleasure. They can turn their lives over to Jesus Christ and have a Lord and Master who loves them. As Paul wrote, "God causes all things to work together for good to those who love God" (Rom. 8:28, NASB).

"A woman has a right to her own body."

Philosopher John Stuart Mill (1806–73) is the granddaddy of those who say a woman's right over her own body should be absolute. In his *Treatise on Liberty* he wrote: "The only part of the conduct of anyone for which he is amenable to society is that which concerns others. In the part which merely concerns himself, his independence is, of right, absolute. Over himself, over his own body and mind, the individual is sovereign."

Mill is right that each person is a unique entity, but he is wrong that no one is answerable to a higher law. Even things that people do to their own bodies will be judged by God and also judged by their fellow man. Society not only legislates what is necessary for interaction with others but also enforces laws that protect the individual from himself, such as drug abuse, for example. There is a sense in which we are all our brother's keeper.

The main fallacy in the statement "A woman has a right to her own body" is that an unborn child is not part of the woman's body. The mother is the temporary life-bearer, but the child is a separate entity from the very beginning. Not even the mother has the right to take its life.

"I have a right to live my life the way I want."

Self-actualization mania is on the loose in America. Bookstores are crammed with the latest methods of self-centered living. Seminars costing hundreds of dollars and attracting thousands of inquiring minds teach people how to make themselves successful. Self-actualization is a phenomenon full of sound and fury signifying nothing. It is a false god demanding ever greater sacrifices at its altar.

Some people demand their right to a self-centered life for materialistic reasons. Some see it as a matter of survival. Existentialist Jean-Paul Sartre made affirming the self a necessity because he saw people as being adrift in a meaningless universe. The only way to put meaning into life was for these people to find something that was important to them and then do it. All acts were neutral, he said. Nothing was intrinsically good or intrinsically evil, so individuals had a right to try anything in an effort to authenticate their existence.

Sartre's authentication doctrine and all-American "selfishness" are the opposite of the truth. They represent the same gullibility that trapped Eve when the serpent told her, "You can be a god."

The universe is not meaningless. It is created and sustained by God. People have worth not on the basis of accomplishment but rather in realizing that they are loved by God, created in His image, and redeemed by Jesus Christ. Nor are actions morally neutral. Everyone is accountable to the Supreme Judge who established a universal moral code and made it known to all people.

"Abortion must be allowed in cases of rape, incest, and danger to the life of the mother."

This is a topic that many sincere pro-lifers struggle with, but once again God has given answers. There is not a single incidence in Scripture where God condones deliberately taking the life of an unborn child for any purpose. God determines the span of life; He determines when it begins and when it ends. The elderly person past his prime is still under His care, as is the unborn infant who has not yet seen the light of day.

According to Old Testament law, the one who caused even an accidental miscarriage was punished (Exod. 21:22). How much more severely will God deal with those who methodically enter a mother's womb and destroy her living child!

Rape. The father, not the child, is to be punished for his sins. The child is innocent. "The soul who sins is the one who will die. The son will not share the guilt of the father, nor will the father share the guilt of the son" (Ezek. 18:20). To be raped and bear a child is a terrible price to pay for someone else's sin, but Jesus paid an even greater price for ours. Many women who have killed the rare child conceived by rape have lived to regret it. They later saw that the destruction of an innocent victim compounded the first violent act with another one, and the second act was one of their own choosing.

Incest. God prohibited incest, but He did not destroy any child conceived by it. Consider Lot and his daughters after the destruction of Sodom and Gomorrah (Gen. 19:30–38). A popular Scripture even among nonreligious people is Micah 6:8: "And what does the Lord require of you? To act justly and to love mercy and to walk humbly with your God." Almost everyone fails to notice the previous verse that defines what kind of action is unjust and lacking in mercy: "Shall I offer my firstborn for my transgression, the fruit of my body for the sin of my soul?" The answer is no. No child should be condemned to die for another's sin.

Life of the mother. In a widely publicized case in February 1989, Martin Klein of Manhasset, New York, became legal guardian for his comatose wife in order to terminate her pregnancy. Doctors had told him an abortion could increase her chances of recovery. In a dramatic and widely criticized move, pro-life activists John Short and John Broderick of New York tried to intervene on behalf of the unborn child and the emotional needs of the mother who would lose him. They were defeated in court and the child died. The same week that Klein's wife had an abortion to "save her life" a news story appeared about Barbara Blodgett of Yakima, Washington, who had miraculously emerged from a coma after eight months. In June 1988, when an auto accident plunged her into "cerebral death" she, too, had been pregnant, but the baby was left alone. On 9 December 1988, still in the coma, she gave birth to a healthy baby boy. Shortly thereafter she began reaching for her children, and started communicating by pointing to letters on a board. The confounded doctors theorized that hormonal changes associated with the birth triggered her recovery.

Only God determines the time to live and the time to die.

"Abortion and contraception are a boon for females."

The Pill. When the oral contraceptive hit the market thirty years ago, it quickly became the most widely prescribed drug in history. Although it was initially limited to married women, court cases quickly disposed of such "discrimination." Now anyone, from adolescence to menopause, can easily stop babies from coming.

Unfortunately, the pill causes some nasty side effects that didn't show up immediately. Women who would never contract for an abortion should know that occasionally an egg is produced and fertilized even while a woman is taking oral contraceptives, especially if she misses one or more doses. Since the lining of the uterus is not equipped to support it, the new life dies. Birth control pills cause abortions.

The pill can cause permanent sterility and even death. A 1988 study linked prolonged use of oral contraceptives to an increase in breast cancer, which was added to the known risk for a rare kind of liver tumor, two or three times the normal rate of heart attack, and blood clots, which are sometimes fatal.

Women liberated for recreational sex often find another unpleasant effect. As the pill dulls their senses, irritates their breasts, promotes infections, and leaves them tired and depressed, they no longer have an appetite for casual sex.

The Intrauterine Device (IUD). The primary function of the IUD is the instant abortion of a fertilized egg. It sits like a barbed-wire fence around the pleasant pastures of the womb where the newly conceived child needs to rest. In recent years, numerous stories have surfaced that not only the child but also the woman is at risk. Side effects include infection, permanent sterility, and even death from perforation or an ectopic pregnancy.

The Condom. Condoms to prevent conception and block the transmission of disease are doled out to children in public school classrooms and sold in vending machines. For those so inclined, they come in a variety of colors and flavors. They also leak, without warning, and are difficult to handle without touching the secretions one is trying to avoid. When condoms are used in combination with a spermicide and conception still occurs, the resulting child may be deformed.

Abortion and the little boy preference. Abortion may be seen as a boon for women, but it is definitely not a blessing for little girls who are destroyed in utero at a far greater rate than boys. In India, abortions of girl babies are openly advertised as a means of avoiding dowries. In China, where couples are forced to abort any pregnancy after the first child, some couples consent to kill an infant daughter in hopes of later conceiving a son. In civilized America, 20 percent of geneticists in a 1989 poll approved of abortion to achieve the preferred sex.

Each new development in the birth-control drama is heralded as the breakthrough that everyone has been waiting for. There are voices echoing Margaret Sanger, who wrote that birth control is "the pivotal factor in the problems confronting the world today." Thus, the war on children continues.

"Abortion helps the poor."

One of the problems that birth control was supposed to solve was the high rate of infant mortality, especially among the poor. Sanger contended that babies died because their parents had too many children, but in the time since her Planned Parenthood clinics attacked the ghetto birthrate, the infant mortality rate has been skyrocketing.

By 1964, babies had a better chance of surviving their first year if they lived in any one of fourteen nations other than the United States. By 1988, the United States had dropped to an appalling twentieth.

Ever since society singled out poor children as unworthy of being born, ghetto women have been exposed to the mass marketing of contraceptives and abortion. As a result, they seem to have lost the ability to distinguish between the disposable babies in the womb and the keepable ones who actually make it to delivery. Since they have no access to information contrary to this war effort, they are held captive to the message about devaluation of children. Once they are brainwashed, they seem to lose their normal instincts to protect their offspring. Life in the ghetto has become cheap. Murder, violence, drugs, and pornography are everywhere. Even young children witness atrocities.

Jesus said that the gates of hell could not prevail against His church. The ghetto has become Satan's territory, yet hardly anybody in the church is trying to break down those doors any more. The church could take down the devil's barricades and rebuild the ruined city with God's love, but it stays away. The only steady visitors to the ruins are those engaged in the ongoing war on children.

"Criminalizing abortion would discriminate against Blacks."

Jesse Jackson is alive today because his mother refused to have an abortion, but he crusades for the right for other black women and girls to abort their children. One of the effects of this "right" has been a disproportionate decline in the population of African Americans. George Grant noted in *Grand Illusions: The Legacy of Planned Parent-*

hood that "according to a Health and Human Services Administration report, as many as forty-three percent of all abortions are performed on blacks and another ten percent on Hispanics. This, despite the fact that blacks only make up eleven percent of the total U.S. population and Hispanics only about eight Percent. . . . In most black communities today abortions outstrip births by as much as three-to-one."

The American people are beginning to take notice of this discrepancy. In Chicago in 1987, a lawsuit filed by Black ministers, parents, and educators "charged that the city's school-based clinics not only violated state fornication laws, but that they also were a form of discrimination against blacks."

"Puritanical taboos are out of date. The old rules don't work any more."

For two centuries, the protective wall of biblical thinking that once guarded the lives of innocent children has been crumbling. Philosophers and scientists, aided by the cooperation of misguided church people, have changed the way America thinks about the value of life and the authority of God's law.

Georg Wilhelm Friedrich Hegel (1770–1831) described everything as engaged in a process of dialectic. Everything that seems permanent actually has an opposite with which it is constantly interacting. During a process of synthesis, the "thesis" and its "antithesis" produce something entirely new. As each new order arises, the old order is gone. Auguste Comte (1798–1857) stated that belief in the supernatural had become outdated. People long since evolved beyond the primitive "theological" stage when they believed in God. They also abandoned the "metaphysical" stage, claiming to have graduated to the "positive" stage where everything can be explained scientifically.

Charles Darwin (1809–82) hypothesized that human beings are animals continually undergoing change due to evolutionary forces. The old myths of Creation and a God-imposed moral order are no longer valid. Karl Marx (1818–83) interpreted the course of history as ruled by economic forces that irresistibly propel people and nations from one stage to another. Moral codes are invented by the ruling class and changed inexorably as society changes. Albert Einstein (1879–1955) revolutionized the understanding of the universe with his finding that space and time are relative terms of measurement, not absolute ones. Einstein's theory was applied by others—over his objections—to moral law, launching an era of moral relativism.

Sigmund Freud (1856–1939) propounded that knowledge is hidden, revealed only to those with special understanding—none of whom could be tainted by religion. Persons are not responsible for their actions but are victims of the forces at work within them.

Charles Sanders Peirce (1839–1914) and William James (1842–1910) stipulated that pragmatism is the only logical way to deal with the vacuum left by the necessary abandonment of moral absolutes. New rules of behavior are determined by trying them out to see if they work. The test of truth is success. John Dewey (1859–1952) built on this philosophy the theorem that experience leads to ever-newer truths. "God" means an ideal for which one strives.

The current New Age movement preaches that god is within every individual. Modernist churches confuse the issue with the belief that God speaks differently to everyone with His own inner witness.

Finding a Way Through the Wilderness

In the mid seventies, as an editor of *The National Courier,* I remember with sadness my efforts as a Christian newsman to find my way through this wilderness of philosophies. So many voices were raised that questioned the reliability of the Bible as a moral standard. When I wrestled editorially with the question of abortion, unhappily I followed the trend of much Christian thinking in that period. I couldn't see how it was possible to take an absolute position on an issue on which so many disagreed, so I declared *The Courier* to be firmly opposed to abortion, which was a correct position as far as it went. I voiced a willingness to allow for abortion in cases of rape, incest, and danger to the mother. I was thoroughly wrong in that editorial. Murder is murder, no matter what the circumstances of conception are. I honestly knew that life begins in the womb, not on the delivery table. Thus I knew that a killing occurred with every abortion.

I have since repented and fully embraced the truth that God is the Creator of all life and that I have no right to murder His creatures. I have discovered that not only the Scriptures but also American life itself demonstrates the bad fruit of this wrong thinking.

Like the people of Israel, America's Founders made a covenant with God when they settled in this land, and I believe God will honor that covenant if we will turn to Him and repent of our sins. He told the Israelites that if they would keep His law, He would bless them and grant peace to their land, "so that you may lie down with no one making you tremble" (Lev. 26:6, NASB). Then He said: "You will chase your enemies, and they will fall before you by the sword; five of you will chase a hundred, and a hundred of you will chase ten thousand" (Lev. 26:7–8, NASB).

By the sword of the Spirit—the Word of God—that will happen and is beginning to happen in America.

NATURAL FAMILY PLANNING

In the last few years, Protestant evangelicals have awakened to the terrible nightmare of abortion and the war on children. Long before that, however, another group was engaged in its own worldwide peace initiative on behalf of children: the Roman Catholic Church.

In 1968, the world received the shocking news that Pope Paul VI had refused to endorse the prevailing pro-contraceptive philosophy of his time. He also refused to follow the recommendation of his fifty-eight-member commission that he rescind the church's traditional prohibition of contraception.

The previous ruling had been made by Pope Pius XI in 1931 when he released his encyclical *Casti Connubii.* In this message the pope had condemned birth control and criticized those who labeled offspring "the disagreeable burden of matrimony."

Thirty-seven years later, after much prayer and study, Pope Paul VI refused to yield to the pressure groups which said that the old rules didn't apply any more. He stated flatly in *Humanae Vitae* that a husband and wife are "not free to act as they choose in the service of transmitting life." It set off a shock wave around the world.

Charles E. Curran of Catholic University rallied the dissenters and held a press conference disassociating himself and others from the pope's position. Since the position paper was an encyclical, not claiming infallibility, there was room for discussion, but probably even the pope did not expect such an outpouring of antagonism when he called for a "lively debate."

The pope and other church leaders were accused of a "bachelor psychosis," with no concern for married couples. The church's proscriptions were antifeminist and impersonal and would drive youth from the church, critics said. "Fidelity to the divine law must be combined with solicitude for human problems," opponents said, adding that the pope had a static world-view, not one of evolving humanity.

The Roman Catholic Church did not completely close the door on family planning, however, nor did it recommend that couples use the inefficient "rhythm method" of birth control. The Lord had provided a better way. Natural family planning, or the "ovulation" method, is a team effort that relies on the woman's observation of natural changes in mucus that signal stages in the menstrual cycle. Abstinence is practiced briefly each month if conception is to be avoided. One of the developers of this method, Evelyn Billings, said that it works for couples who feel "fertility control is a joint responsibility and that, because of this, neither partner should be required to bear a health burden."

For the last decade, "natural family planning" has been used successfully by the World Health Organization in a number of Third World countries. Mother Teresa has recommended it successfully in India. Its effectiveness, when correctly practiced, rivals the best of the prescribed contraceptive methods without the side effects. It also builds desperately needed closeness between husband and wife.

ABOLITIONISTS VS. ABORTIONISTS

The war on children rages on, but God's people are beginning to take up arms. During the Democratic National Convention in Atlanta in the summer of 1988, Randall Terry of Operation Rescue organized sit-ins at local abortion centers. His intention was to draw attention to the Democratic party's pro-abortion platform and to the high rate of abortion among Atlanta's African-American population. One out of every two Black babies conceived in Atlanta was killed before birth.

With Terry's act, a civil rights movement was resurrected from the secularism and politicization that had replaced the biblical roots of the first one. Once again, Christians were being jailed for those whom God loved. From all across the country, White and Black alike came to Atlanta to go to jail. For a season they became "Baby Jane Doe" and "Baby John Doe" on behalf of those who had died without being named. For some it was their first attempt to stop the holocaust.

The tactics of Operation Rescue have come under fire from fellow pro-lifers who had been laboring for years to reverse *Roe v. Wade* through quieter means. It was inevitable that differences would arise. It happens in every major movement. Each time a crusade gets underway there are several distinct perspectives on the same problem. The abolition of slavery came about through everything from the fiery rhetoric of William Lloyd Garrison to the moving novel *Uncle Tom's Cabin.* As abolitionist Wendell Phillips said in 1859, "Truth is one forever absolute, but opinion is truth filtered through the moods, the blood, the disposition of the spectator."

The war on children will not be stopped by one method or one leader. It will take a move of God's Spirit all across America. Some who respond will be families who take in despairing pregnant women. Some will march. Some will fold diapers. Everyone will have to work on changing the way America thinks.

The most important goal for each group is to seek God and obey His commandments. Before criticizing each other, they must ask the

Lord who the real enemy is in this battle. Phillips said, "Revolutions are not made; they come. A revolution is as natural a growth as an oak."

For Further Reading

Evelyn Billings and Ann Westmore. *The Billings Method.* New York: Ballantine Books, 1980.

Elasah Drogin. *Margaret Sanger: Father of Modern Society.* Coarsegold, Calif.: CUL Publications, 1980.

George Grant. *Grand Illusions: The Legacy of Planned Parenthood.* Brentwood, Tenn.: Wolgemuth & Hyatt, 1988.

John F. Kippley. *Birth Control and the Marriage Covenant.* Collegeville, Minn.: Liturgical Press, 1976.

Jonathan Kozol. *The Night Is Dark and I Am Far from Home.* New York: Continuum, 1984.

Malcolm Muggeridge. *Something Beautiful for God* [Mother Teresa's story]. San Francisco: Harper & Row, 1971.

Geoffrey Parrinder. *Sex in the World's Religions.* New York: Oxford University Press, 1980.

Margaret Sanger. *The Pivot of Civilization.* New York: Brentano's, 1922.

Francis A. Schaeffer. *A Christian Manifesto.* Westchester, Ill.: Crossway Books, 1981.

William H. Shannon. *The Lively Debate: Response to* Humanae Vitae. New York: Sheed & Ward, 1970.

Maris A. Vinovskis. *An "Epidemic" of Adolescent Pregnancy?* New York: Oxford University Press, 1988.

8

A Future and a Hope

A popular children's book portrays a "typical" American family situation in these words:

> I don't think I'll ever get married. Why should I? All it does is make you miserable. Just look at Mrs. Singer. Last year she was Miss Pace and everybody loved her. I said I'd absolutely die if I didn't get her for sixth grade. But I did—and what happened? She got married over the summer and now she's a witch!
>
> Then there are my parents. They're always fighting. My father was late for dinner tonight and when he got home we were already at the table. Daddy said hello to me and Jeff. Then he turned to Mom. "Couldn't you have waited?" he asked her. "You knew I was coming home for dinner."

Nobody gets along in this portrait of American family (from Judy Blume's *It's Not the End of the World*). Family life is so miserable, according to Blume's writing, that after 174 pages of petty parental bickering, criticism, and lack of communication, the girl's parents are divorced, and she calmly teaches her best friend what to do when the inevitable happens to her. She says, "Even though Debbie says her mother and father are not going to get divorced it can't hurt her to know the facts. This way she will be prepared for anything!"

Contrary to the good intentions of the girl in Blume's story, the answer to America's family problem is not to teach children how to accept divorce. It is to admit that American homes have slammed the door in the face of God and all hell is breaking loose inside.

From the time the first couple met in the Garden of Eden, God said that the two would become "one flesh" (Gen. 2:24, KJV). From then on, every couple who started a family had these responsibilities:

- build a relationship with God and keep His laws
- learn how to get along with their partners
- become as one in conception and child rearing
- accept each other as individuals

That was, and is, the counsel of God. It is a wonderful plan for a family, and it always works. As the psalmist wrote, Blessed are those whose "delight is in the law of the Lord" (Ps. 1:2).

That is the way it once was in America, until children growing up to become parents began to listen to what the Bible calls the "counsel of the ungodly" (Ps. 1:1, KJV). In public schools, seminars, and even churches, they listened to teachers who taught them how to get the most out of life, without even mentioning the Author of Life. With scarcely a backward glance, they looked at the future pictured by the ungodly, and it looked wonderful. Instead of God at the center and a spouse and children alongside, this photo showed an enlarged, smiling self at the center with others lighted dimly behind.

The righteous, said the psalmist, are "like a tree planted by streams of water, which yields its fruit in season and whose leaf does not wither" (Ps. 1:3). The ungodly "are like chaff that the wind blows away" (Ps. 1:4). One family lasts. The other family perishes. It is as simple as that.

Promoters of the Broken Family

Years ago, Americans thought of the family as the one bond that could be trusted. Once a family, always a family. Whatever it took, the most important goal was to keep families together. Even people with no strong belief in God basically followed His commandments. Their families reaped the benefits. Today, that thinking has changed. According to many of the world's experts, family breakups are not only inevitable, but also healthy.

Psychiatrists (whom Allan Bloom labeled "the sworn enemies of guilt") encourage troubled clients to see divorce not as a defeat but as an opportunity for greater happiness for all concerned. No fault need be assigned to anyone. This decision is then followed by many hours with a therapist to help everyone adjust to the new reality.

Self-actualizers pursue divorce when they find that their families stifle their pursuit of the ultimate "meaning" of life. Abraham Maslow, who included self-actualization at the top of his "hierarchy of needs" philosophy, was happily married, but he saw the experience of love as only one preliminary stage on the way to self-actualization. He considered God as irrelevant and moral law as useless. "All externally-given value systems have proven to be failures," he said.

"Marriage constitutes slavery for women," wrote Sheila Cronan in *Radical Feminism,* so "it is clear that the Woman's Movement must concentrate on attacking this institution. Freedom for women cannot be won without the abolition of marriage." Karl Marx equated marriage with prostitution and child raising with exploitation. He wrote in the *Communist Manifesto* that to destroy the family was to do society a favor. Anthropologist Helen Fisher wrote in a 1988 piece for *U.S. News & World Report* that multiple sets of parents are helpful to children. "Children grow up with more adult role models and a larger network of relatives," she said, "increasing their range of power and influence within society."

A NATIONAL PLAGUE

A few years ago, it hardly seemed necessary to refute these experts with detailed scientific studies. That was before American society became so dominated by secularists like these who seek to explain and improve life without reference to God. To a secularist, moral questions involve only the well-being of mankind in this present life. Anything relating to belief in God, His Law, or expectation of a future life is automatically excluded.

That kind of thinking creates a serious problem, because the world, into which God sent His only begotten Son, is far too important to leave to those who have no profound understanding of it.

Researchers have uncovered several details on one of the most obvious failings of secularism, the high divorce rate.

Women on their own after divorce find they are not liberated after all, but often plunged into poverty. Divorced women and their children average a 73 percent decline in their standard of living. One-third of the homes headed by women are below the poverty line, compared to one in nineteen families with two parents.

While former husbands who once promised to love and cherish them are now off seeking happiness, single mothers frequently lack the time and energy even to maintain an orderly home. Their sons, who watched dad leave mom to fend for herself, often treat her with contempt, including physical and emotional abuse. Many of these boys also consider their fathers uncaring and have difficulty establishing normal gender roles.

Children most frequently in trouble for fighting, lying, and skipping out on school come from divorced homes. Broken homes also produce far more drug abusers than intact families.

Studies show that fathers and mothers make distinct, different contributions to their children's education. The best learners usually have two parents at home. Children with only one parent have consistently poorer academic records at all levels of schooling. They score lower on college entrance examinations and have more emotional problems once enrolled at universities. Allan Bloom, as a professor, observed of his students whose parents were divorced: "They are full of desperate platitudes about self-determination, respect for other people's rights and decisions, the need to work out one's individual values and commitments, etc. All this is a thin veneer over boundless seas of rage, doubt, and fear."

Divorce is the leading cause of childhood depression and increases the rate of mental illness among children. Even ten years after divorce, young adults still express sadness over the breakup of their families. The 50 percent increase in teen suicide since 1970 has been linked with the concurrent rise in family disintegration.

Boys whose parents are divorced sire twice the number of illegitimate children. Girls from divorced homes often expect to cohabitate before marriage, apparently because they have learned that male/female relationships tend to be short term and conditional. These premarital activities, plus the emotional scars from divorce and the lack of positive role models, all contribute to a higher rate of divorce than among children from intact families.

No matter how many years we put between us and Adam and Eve, no matter how many authorities arise to promote divorce, human beings are still naturally drawn to family life and are always damaged when it falls apart. The Creator has instilled that desire in His creation. God hates divorce (Mal. 2:16). Jesus called it "hard-hearted wickedness" (Mark 10:5, LB). Paul said it was forbidden for all but the most extreme cases of abandonment (1 Cor. 7:10–17).

Divorce is worse than death because it is the voluntary dissolution of a bond that God intended to be permanent. Those deserted by a spouse or parent feel humiliated and betrayed by someone they thought truly loved them. They become embittered with the knowledge that people live only for themselves. All of life suddenly becomes arbitrary and unsafe.

Jesus said, "The thief comes only to steal, and kill, and destroy; I came that they might have life, and have it abundantly" (John 10:10, NASB). I submit that secularism is that thief. By subtly changing America's thinking about the family, the secularists have robbed the people of true life, crippling them and denying recovery to them. They have no real answers, yet they continue to grasp at chaff with one hand while with the other they drive off the only ones who do have answers—the people of God. The time has come to put a stop to it.

WHAT GOD CAN DO

The First Commandment is to love God, and the Second is to love our neighbor as ourselves. The first prescription for healing the American family is to honor God and begin to understand what "true love" really means. I'm talking about *agape,* as Paul described it in 1 Corinthians 13: "Love is very patient and kind, never jealous or envious, never boastful or proud, never haughty or selfish or rude. Love does not demand its own way. It is not irritable or touchy. It does not hold grudges and will hardly even notice when others do it wrong. . . . If you love someone you will be loyal to him no matter what the cost. You will always believe in him, always expect the best of him, and always stand your ground in defending him" (1 Cor. 13:4–5,7, LB).

This kind of love—of husband for wife, wife for husband, parent for child, child for parent—is not just an emotional attraction. It is a stable kind of love that combines human effort with divine power. Nurturing this *agape* in families will require that family members make a commitment to stop finding fault and start finding good. As Paul advised the Philippians: "Fix your thoughts on what is true and good and right. Think about things that are pure and lovely, and dwell on the fine, good things in others. Think about all you can praise God for and be glad about" (Phil. 4:8, LB).

Since you are, or once were, part of a family, I want you to do a little exercise. Take a moment to list all the positive qualities you can think of for all the members of your immediate family, no matter how difficult they might be, and praise God for them.

DISCIPLINE: PUTTING THE SELF IN ITS PLACE

Did it take discipline for you to list those qualities for some members of your family? I suggested that exercise to make the point that love is closely linked to discipline. A happy family doesn't just happen. It is formed by a continual effort to make it work.

The family is the training ground for a successful life. From the time children are born they want to be the center of the universe. It is their parents' job to love them, certainly, but also to teach them day by day, year by year, that the world does not revolve around them. They learn external discipline first, by being subject to their parents, and then they gradually develop self-discipline. This is all greatly advanced if they have the help of God, because a fruit of the Spirit is self-control.

Ever since the breakup of the family became a national crisis, children have been growing up without learning the emotional controls they need as adults. When their parents are out of harmony with each other, children learn to manipulate them. When they are separated or divorced, children learn to dishonor them. When they have no godly rules, children learn to do as they please.

As a result, America has become overpopulated with self-centered, egotistical, immature people. Eventually their marriages end up hurting themselves and their mates as they constantly search for "happiness." The divorce epidemic will continue until parents reverse these trends in childrearing still infecting America's children.

THE FRUIT OF PERMISSIVENESS

After World War II, American families began to resume their childbearing. The war—with its appeasement of dictators, holocaust against the Jews, and promiscuity at home and abroad—had exacted a heavy toll on the country's already troubled Judeo-Christian consensus.

New parents weren't as certain of the guidelines for raising children as their parents had been, so they were delighted to discover that a hard-working pediatrician had compiled a thick volume of handy information on all aspects of child care. It contained symptoms of childhood diseases, tips for toilet training, and advice on discipline. The book was so popular that in the next fourteen years it sold 11 million copies and became, according to its publisher, the "best selling new title issued in the United States since 1895, when best-seller lists began." Eventually an entire generation was raised according to Benjamin Spock's *Baby and Child Care.*

Spock didn't try to take credit for all of his ideas. He drew on the work of men like Sigmund Freud, John Dewey, and others who said that traditional child-rearing attitudes were too "strict and inflexible." His critics have conceded that Spock was not completely wrong. He heightened parents' sensitivity to children, but in so doing he raised children to the point that they were worshiped by their parents.

Children, Spock wrote, are the "greatest satisfaction in life" and the parents' "visible immortality." Like Spock, John Dewey said that parents should intervene only rarely to bring order to a child's life. In most cases the situation would take care of itself. He saw the family as a democracy where the parent functioned as "the representative and agent of the interests of the group as a whole."

Since children knew what was in their best interests, Dewey said, they would cooperate if the parent or teacher did his job right. Children who seemed either rebellious or passive got that way by being "victims of injurious conditions"—like authoritarian rule. "Pitting one will against another in order to see which is strongest," he said, would never work.

Spock agreed. "We want to be kind and cooperative (most of the time)," he said, "because we like people and want them to like us." Childish rebellion showed that the child needed to release his hostilities. "Too harsh a repression of aggressive feelings and sexual interest may lead to neurosis," he wrote.

By the time Spock produced his 1957 edition, he had become a trifle worried about parents' wholesale application of his philosophy. Parents said their children still misbehaved when they showed love to them, and it frustrated them and made them angry. Many of them carried around guilt, blaming themselves for their children's sins. They had been led to believe that it was natural for children to cooperate and that it was the parents' fault when they didn't.

Spock wrote in his updated version, "Nowadays there seems to be more chance of a conscientious parent's getting into trouble with permissiveness than with strictness. So I have tried to give a more balanced view." By then, however, permissiveness had become deeply entrenched. Those who used the old-fashioned "authoritarian" method usually felt they should apologize to everyone, especially if they used spanking as a legitimate part of child rearing. (Spock admitted spanking could occasionally clear the air, but he was "not particularly advocating it.")

The permissive generation, raised according to Spock, came of age in the 1960s and early 1970s with a massive upheaval in American life. Yet the blame cannot be placed totally on people like Spock, Dewey, and Freud. The problem arose, just as in the days when Isaiah was prophesying to Judah, because parents were willing to abandon the principles of God. When "capricious children" rule, Isaiah wrote, "the people will be oppressed" (Isa. 3:4, 5, NASB). In America, students rioted on college campuses and staged takeovers of university buildings. They demanded equal status with the schools' faculty and administrators. Anti-war activists flouted the authority and the office of the president of the United States, visiting the city of Hanoi and ridiculing American POWs who said that they had been tortured. Most significant of all, these young people became the next generation of parents.

DARE TO DISCIPLINE

Into this fray stepped a preacher's kid who had been raised by "authoritarian" parents and lived to tell about it. In fact, he felt compelled to sound an alarm for parents who couldn't see what was happening. In a book entitled *Dare to Discipline,* psychologist James Dobson proclaimed in 1972, "Permissiveness has not just been a failure; it's been a disaster." Figuratively grabbing America by the lapels, he exclaimed, "Discipline works!" It doesn't squelch the tender nature of children or permanently damage their relationship with their parents. It is just the opposite: Discipline "permits the tender affection made possible by mutual respect between a parent and child," he said.

Dobson approached child rearing as his parents had practiced it on him: Assume the child has a sinful nature that must be trained by loving but firm discipline. His views are supported throughout Scripture. Consider this passage from Hebrews. It is an affirmation of parental authority and of the Higher Authority it represents:

> If you are not disciplined (and everyone undergoes discipline), then you are illegitimate children and not true sons. Moreover, we have all had human fathers who disciplined us and we respected them for it. How much more should we submit to the Father of our spirits and live! Our fathers disciplined us for a little while as they thought best; but God disciplines us for our good, that we may share in his holiness. No discipline seems pleasant at the time, but painful. Later on, however, it produces a harvest of righteousness and peace for those who have been trained by it (Heb. 12:8–11).

Permissive parenting has not only wrought havoc with children, parents, and society, but has also disrupted personal relationships with God. This trend can be reversed, but it will require that people recommit themselves to the Lordship of Christ in all areas of life. Here are a few ways we can change the way we think about training children.

We must understand that our children have a natural tendency toward sin, not goodness. In 1987, Dobson published *Parenting Isn't for Cowards,* in which he reported the results of a survey of 35,000 families. Only 3 percent of the parents surveyed said that they had a "very compliant" child, the only kind who might possibly be trainable by permissive parenting. There were fully twice as many whom parents labeled "very strong-willed," and the rest were in various degrees of rebellion.

It is no wonder parents who bypass biblical child raising are "near the breaking point," Dobson said. "Their sense of guilt is overwhelming, and yet they have typically carried their pain in silence. I would expect the incidences of child abuse, child abandonment, parental alcoholism and other evidences of family disintegration to be inordinately high in this category. And of course, it is not a category or a group at all. I'm talking about real *people*—living, breathing mothers and fathers who are going down for the count."

Parents need to make allowances for immature mistakes. However, unless they act swiftly against defiant disobedience, their troubles will never end, and they will be passing on to their child's future spouse an impossible mate. "Foolishness is bound up in the heart of a child," said Solomon, and "the rod of discipline will remove it far from him" (Prov. 22:15, NASB).

I will leave it to Dobson and others to give you specifics about "the rod" and other methods of correction. But I want you to remember that part of discipline is taking time afterward to talk about it. Let your children repent, then forgive them and pray about it. It is essential that you convince them that you don't stop loving them when they misbehave, any more than God stops loving us when we disobey Him.

Apply the Scriptures as much as possible to the process of discipline and training. The New Testament's love chapter quoted earlier and proverbs on rebellious children will do for starters. The basic principle is this: You must let your children know at an early age that they are to honor you, for your own sanity and for their future benefit. Along the way, you will also help them develop more fully their God-given talents.

Children who are required to follow a fixed, external standard of behavior are not stifled by it. In fact, according to a study of preschoolers, they evince more creativity and are able to adjust and function more independently in a new environment. It was the children whose parents followed the laissez-faire model of conflict resolution who were more inhibited and insecure.

The news about the benefits of discipline, including an occasional spanking, apparently hasn't impressed a national coalition of educators, lawyers, and doctors. They met in August 1988, to condemn corporal punishment in the schools, and, while they were at it, they also took a shot at parents. "A study several years back found that 90 percent of parents use corporal punishment in their homes," said Adrienne Hauser of the National Association of Social Workers. "That tells us we've got a lot of educating to do."

A children's television personality, Bob Keeshan, known as "Captain Kangaroo," pulled this observation about spanking out of his pocket: "It rates an 'F' because it does not meet its stated purpose of maintaining discipline, and because it treats the symptoms and not the cause of the underlying unruly behavior."

Spankings in school are one thing, but this group had no comprehension of the purpose of a correctly administered spanking in the home, done in love—and a little frustration, to be sure. Corporal punishment in the home is directed not at symptoms but at the root cause of the problem: rebellion against parents.

If schoolteachers were allowed to post the Ten Commandments, then everyone could read, "Honor thy father and thy mother: that thy days may be long upon the land which the Lord thy God giveth thee." Childish rebellion is a sin against God, and parents have been instructed to take appropriate action.

As Dobson said, it is not spanking that has hurt children but the insistence that it is wrong: "It is when parents are desperately trying to avoid punishment that their level of irritation reaches a dangerous level. By then, anything can happen. That is why I have contended that those who oppose corporal punishment on the grounds that it leads to child abuse are wrong. By stripping parents of the ability to handle frustrating behavior at an early age, they actually increase the possibility that harm will be done to children as tempers rise."

An Atmosphere for Growth

Once parents are released to maintain order in the home, they will also be released to enjoy their children and begin to recapture their minds. One of the blessings of parenthood is the opportunity to help children find out who they are and what they like to do. Each child is a unique individual, created just that way by God Himself. Parents can cause great harm by comparing one child with another or by ridiculing their attempts to express themselves. They can do much good with praise.

For centuries of child rearing, parents have quoted the verse, "Train up a child in the way he should go: and when he is old, he will not depart from it" (Prov. 22:6, KJV). It has given them assurance that sacrifices on their child's behalf are not in vain.

An even deeper meaning of this verse is revealed in the marginal rendering of the New American Standard Bible: "Train up a child according to his way." Each child marches to a different drummer, and parents need to listen to the beat. This is not only true in matters of interests and a career, but also in the area of correction. Some children are so sensitive to criticism that only a few words will make a difference. Others need something consistently stronger. God made each person for a purpose, and He can even use stubbornness, properly trained, to build His kingdom.

Living Out the Bible

The search for the inner self cannot be done on the purely human level, however, because we can never truly know ourselves until we know God and study His Word. Pastors, elders, Sunday school teachers, and youth leaders can teach children about the Bible, but they will never live it out before their eyes the way parents do. The home should be an ongoing school of applied theology, an opportunity for children to find out who they are in God's eyes and how the Bible applies to their personal lives.

Parents, although imperfect, can teach their children biblical truth every day as they interact with them. They teach reverence for God as they model His love, justice, and forgiveness. They teach His law as they refuse to gossip, lie, or covet what is their neighbor's.

Parents who live in obedience to the Word bring blessings to their families (Deut. 28:4; Prov. 20:7). They prepare the next generation to cope with adult life by giving their children a set of ethical standards for making decisions. No one can find reliable ethics without God's law. Few children find them without godly parents. The Bible says all of us are surrounded by a cloud of witnesses (Heb. 12:1). That is never more obvious than when we are in the home.

Children should know that for an hour a day, or maybe several hours, they can sit down with dad and mom to pray, read the Bible, talk about school, enjoy a read-aloud story, and learn how to think. Most children learn how to think from their schoolteachers, their television shows, and their friends, yet during their early years they are wide open to hear from their parents, too. It is an opportunity not to be missed.

During World War II, a number of stalwart European families, at great risk, refused to ignore the ignominious attacks on their Jewish neighbors. Some, like Anne Frank's benefactors, kept whole families in hiding; others, like Corrie ten Boom's family, facilitated their escapes. In a study on the "altruistic personality," a team led by Samuel and Pearl Oliver studied thousands of these rescuers to find out why they had done it. They discovered that these were people who honored eternal moral truths above their own self-interests. They held themselves accountable for their actions to their children, their neighbors, and God. They didn't select a few comfortable "values"; they accepted something outside of themselves for a standard. Our children will benefit as we do the same.

MOVING IN ON EVERY FRONT

Several years ago I was on the way home from attending the wedding of a young lady I had known most of her life. Driving along the highway with my own wife of thirty years, I thought about the bride, Elizabeth, with her red hair, lively freckles, and quick smile, and wondered how she and Charlie felt about their chances of staying married in secular America.

Although I had been a Christian for several years, I was battling a sense of hopelessness over the tremendous hold that the ungodly had on America. I knew God must have answers, but I didn't know what they were.

A short time later my wife, Gloria, and I were in the office of Terry Fullam, the rector of St. Paul's Church in Darien, Connecticut. Before I could ask for his help, I remember how he grabbed a big, hardcover study Bible and began to read aloud something he had been studying in Jeremiah 29. This is the gist of what he told me:

> We shouldn't be fearful of secular America. God's people survived when He sent them into the pagan environment of Babylon. While they were there, He expected them to continue to build houses, marry, and raise children.
>
> God gave His people a responsibility to improve the city where they lived and to pray for others' welfare, whether they believed in Him or not.
>
> They were to be in the world of the unbelievers, but not of it. They were to trust God, even if He required of them great patience and perseverance, not listen to dreamers and prophets who told them lies about the good life and offered their easy solutions.
>
> They should have hope for the future. Jeremiah wrote: "For I know the plans I have for you," declares the Lord, "plans for welfare and not for calamity to give you a future and a hope. Then you will call upon Me and come and pray to Me, and I will listen to you. And you will seek Me and find Me, when you search for Me with all your heart" (Jer. 29:11–13, NASB).

America has a family crisis because it has a faith crisis. People say they believe in God, but they don't follow Him. They don't trust that He has a plan for their good, but instead insist on making a plan of their own. Instead of welfare, they get calamity because they don't seek Him with all their hearts.

Those who don't believe marriages can be fixed don't believe in the power and goodness of God. They have been listening to the secular psychiatrists, self-actualizers, feminists, and social scientists, when they should have been listening to God. They don't know or don't practice the specific principles about family life that have been written down in the Bible. They have not sought the power of God that is able to help us love others as much as we love ourselves.

I think we have a task today that is just as important as what God called his people to do in Babylon. We have to build strong families in the church once again, and we must break through the barriers in our own families to begin working with the families around us. Whether we realize it or not, each of us leads a life that is a testimony to others—in our neighborhoods, our workplaces, our schools. Many of the people we meet have become hardened toward "religion," disgusted with "televangelists," and derisive of Christian literature. They desperately need relationships with real, flesh-and-blood Christians who live out their faith.

A few years ago, Joel Van Ornum, a Kirkland, Washington, businessman, enrolled his second-grade son, Andy, for his first soccer team. To Joel's dismay, he soon received a call saying, "We don't have a coach. It's either you or nothing."

Joel had never played soccer himself, let alone coached it, but he believed God wanted his son on a team. So he made some phone calls and invited all the soccer parents to his home to discuss their options. "I'd be willing to do it for one year," he told the mothers and fathers perched casually on his couches and chairs, "but I'll need your help."

"God made each of your children unique," he told them. "I think our goal in organizing this soccer team should not be winning but getting to know our children." That was a startling concept. Most parents looked at sports as a way to keep their children occupied when the schools were through with them. "I'd like to have as many parents as possible attend every practice," he said. Somewhat reluctantly, they agreed.

It turned out that the parents didn't know much more about soccer than Joel did, but seven or eight of them would show up every time he scheduled a practice. They took the boys aside in groups of two or three and worked on fundamentals. There wasn't an outstanding player in the group, but Joel told the boys, "You may not know how to kick the ball yet, but if you can at least keep the ball away from the other team they can't score."

Meeting on the grass-and-mud playing field day after day, the boys began to see their fathers in a new light. Joel encouraged the dads to keep pouring on praise. "Never say, 'He was terrible. Why did he do that?'" he advised them. When times were tough he'd tell everyone better times were coming.

It turned out that a few Christian parents were in the group, and they began sharing their faith with the others. Relationships were established. Whole soccer families, not just players, became a team. One couple on the verge of divorce received so much support from the group that they reconciled their marriage.

By the end of the season, the team with the members who cared about one another had won half its games against far more experienced coaches. The next year it added several boys whom other coaches had rejected. That season it came within one goal of the state championship.

"Winning has become so important in sports," Joel said, "that we have lost sight of relationships."

I wonder if "winning the world for Christ" has become so important in the church that we have lost sight of relationships with those around us.

We can't leave things in the hands of all those people who hold a negative and inadequate view of life. The world is fallen, but there is redemption and hope in the person of Jesus Christ, sent by God the Father, who loved the world and its people so very much.

Jesus spoke in a parable, "Can the blind lead the blind? Shall they not both fall into the ditch?" (Luke 6:39, KJV). How many families do you know who seem to be falling into the ditch? We must do everything we can as followers of Christ to make our families conform to the biblical model, and then reach out to rescue the world from its blind leaders. That means moving in on every front. Are you ready?

For Further Reading

Allan C. Carlson and Bryce J. Christensen. "Of Two Minds: The Educational and Cultural Effects of Family Dissolution." Paper presented to a conference on The Family and Education, sponsored in June 1988 by the Office of Educational Research and Improvement of the U.S. Department of Education.

John Dewey. *Experience and Education.* 1938; New York: Collier Books, Macmillan Publishing Co., 1963.

James Dobson. *Dare to Discipline.* Wheaton, Ill. Tyndale House Publishers, 1972.

———. *Parenting Isn't for Cowards.* Waco, Tex.: Word Books, 1987.

Abraham H. Maslow. *Toward a Psychology of Being.* 2d ed. New York: Van Nostrand Reinhold, 1968.

Benjamin Spock. *Baby and Child Care.* New York: Pocket Books, 1957.

Proverbs on Discipline (see esp. The Living Bible): 1:7–9; 6:20–24; 10:1; 12:1; 13:9, 18, 24; 15:5; 17:16, 25; 18:1–3, 6, 7, 17, 19; 19:13, 18, 26, 29; 20:3, 11; 22:5, 6, 15; 23:13–16; 24:9; 26:3–11, 18, 19; 27:11; 28:13, 24; 29:1, 14, 17, 19.

Part 3

The Nation

America! America!
God mend thine every flaw,
Confirm thy soul in self-control,
Thy liberty in law.
Katherine Lee Bates

9

Rights and the Law

The concrete plaza of the Chicago Federal Building became a cauldron of screaming humanity as Frank Collin and twenty of his fellow American Nazis emerged from the building's basement. A heavy police guard formed a human corridor for the brown-shirted, black-booted storm troopers. Bedecked with swastika armbands, the self-proclaimed haters of Jews, blacks, and other "non-whites" watched their leader raise a portable amplifier and begin to speak.

No one could hear a word Frank Collin said, but, incredibly, he had every right to say it. After fourteen months of litigation, at a cost of hundreds of thousands of dollars—paid for by everyone but himself—the Skokie villain had won the right to spout hatred.

On 24 June 1978, as Frank Collin spoke those fifteen minutes of inaudible rhetoric, the American Civil Liberties Union that had defended him lay in shambles. The ACLU had decided that even a Nazi like Collin had a right to speak in Chicago, or in the predominantly Jewish community of Skokie nearby, and it had cost them dearly. The ACLU's executive director at that time, Aryeh Neier, estimated that the controversy had cost the national organization 30,000 members and $500,000 in lost annual income. The Illinois state office alone had laid off five of its thirteen workers and lost 30 percent of its income. Collin's lawyer, David Goldberger, himself a Jew, had been the object of personal attacks. Like the state director, David Hamlin, he had received vicious threats and countless harassing phone calls. Why did they do it? They believed they had no choice. Neier, also a Jew, who had escaped with his family from Berlin in 1939, wrote in *Defending My Enemy:* "I supported free speech for Nazis when they wanted to march in Skokie in order to defeat Nazis. Defending my enemy is the only way to protect a free society against the enemies of freedom. . . . The Nazis . . . must be free to speak because Jews must be free to speak and because I must be free to speak."

Although I rarely find myself in agreement with the ACLU, Neier's restraint and commitment to principle are admirable. The ACLU's sacrificial defense of free speech puts many Christians to shame. Unfortunately, however, the ACLU lacks the one element that will restore full application of the First Amendment to American law: an understanding of the biblical basis of free speech, a free society, and the rights of one's enemies. As long as the ACLU and others in law, government, and education continue to view the Bible as a subversive document, none of their noble crusades for freedom will prevail.

Frank Collin gained his greatest renown in Skokie, the predominantly Jewish suburb of Chicago that made national headlines and nightly newscasts for months. America was convinced that a sinister army of American Nazis was on the verge of a hostile march past the quiet homes and synagogues of Holocaust survivors. A national campaign raised 2 million signatures and promises from 50,000 people to travel to Skokie for a counterdemonstration. Most of them had no idea of the nature of Collin and his band of malcontents or the principles at stake in his defense, but they knew what Hitler had done, and they were determined to keep it from happening again.

Few could understand why the ACLU would defend Nazis. Almost everyone agreed with Bonnie Pechter, national director of the Jewish Defense League, who said on 19 March 1978, "Nazis should have no rights. Jewish survival must come before the Constitution or the First Amendment." Little did they realize the holocaust that would come if such overrulings of the law were allowed to prevail.

When Collin had tried initially to speak in Chicago's Marquette Park, he was told he must post a $350,000 bond. A veteran of previous First Amendment wars, Collin knew the park department had no constitutional right to require the bond, but this time he craftily sought to draw attention to his cause by invading the suburbs. He told the "village" of Skokie (which actually had a population of nearly 70,000 and more than 1,000 businesses) that he was preparing to give a speech. They, too, demanded an exorbitant sum. Collin informed the village that he would bring his followers to the front of the Village Hall to protest this injustice in a brief statement.

When word reached the churches and the nine synagogues of Skokie, an uncontrollable brush fire of panic broke out all across the village and erupted into a national conflagration. The fact that Collin intended to spend only a few minutes speaking in one spot to a small group of followers was quickly lost. According to David Hamlin's account, journalists added fuel to the flames with inaccurate two-word definitions like "Nazi parade," "Neo-Nazi demonstration," and "Nazi rally." At one point a reporter called Collin's office and was told that the Nazis might rally on April 20, Hitler's birthday. Collin had no such plan, but the story made national news.

With the biblical basis for law and rights long buried in the ash heap of history, nobody understood the true issues involved in Collin's request to speak. Only the ACLU realized that something important was at stake.

Skokie's civil officials attempted every regulatory restriction they could think of to assert their authority and save the reputation of their village. The Illinois state legislature tried to pass a bill making it a crime to defame a group of people. Lawyers sought to charge Collin with incitement to riot, to forbid his swastika as "fighting words." They tried to invoke a "heckler's veto," saying that although they couldn't assume Collin would break the law, once he showed up, the law would surely be broken.

Everywhere the ACLU went, its representatives were reminded, "You can't yell fire in a crowded theater." Antagonists argued, "How can you defend someone on free speech grounds when he, if he had the power, would deny free speech to others?" The Jewish Defense League, which usually sided with the ACLU on First Amendment issues, decided this case was too sensitive and picketed the ACLU office.

In the end, it was not the people who decided the case but the ever-powerful court. In his opening argument on 28 April 1977, ACLU lawyer David Goldberger had told Cook County Chancery Judge Joseph Wosik: "This is a classic First Amendment case, your Honor. It tests the very foundations of democracy. The Village of Skokie moves for an order enjoining speech before it has occurred even though that speech is to occur in an orderly fashion in front of the Village Hall for a period of between twenty and thirty minutes on a Sunday afternoon, this Sunday afternoon. Such an order, whatever we might feel about the content of the speech, violates the very essence of the First Amendment."

On the basis of the First Amendment guarantee of free speech, Collin eventually won the right to speak in Skokie. Almost immediately, he decided he would not exercise that right.

Watching the ominous tidal wave of opposition cresting before him in Skokie, Collin turned back to his original goal, a speech in Chicago. With Chicago's gerry-rigged barricades crumbling before the court's First Amendment steamroller, Collin soon had a chance to speak in his own backyard. Thus he was escorted to the Federal Center Plaza in June and on 9 July 1978 to Marquette Park. Both audiences were huge, hostile, and roaring mad. He said his piece, and left.

DISRUPTION OF THE FREE SPEECH MANDATE

Today, in Chicago, as in the rest of America, many people are still full of anger, not just toward a small band of Nazis but against anyone not "of our own kind." Whites hate blacks, blacks hate whites, non-Jews hate Jews, and anyone who wants to say so is protected by the First Amendment. It all seems very legal.

There is only one problem: The First Amendment was never written to cover such speech. The ACLU was correct in arguing that Collin had a right to speak, but because it did not understand on biblical grounds *why* he could speak, it has been unable to extend the same courtesy to Christians and Jews. Collin could speak on federal property with a city police escort, yet Christians cannot speak about Christmas or Jews about Hanukkah under the same civil authorities' auspices.

The Skokie incident provoked the nation's rage, and this rage has not yet subsided. The ACLU has rebuilt most of its membership, but "Skokie" is still invoked as the symbol of their sin.

Part of the reason the Skokie attitudes were never resolved is that hardly anyone understands the true nature of evil. As Allan Bloom observed, evil has become personified in Hitler. Bloom wrote of his college students: "They have no idea of evil; they doubt its existence. Hitler is just another abstraction, an item to fill up an empty category. Although they live in a world in which the most terrible deeds are being performed and they see brutal crime in the streets, they turn aside."

Capitalizing on this near-universal antipathy toward "Hitler," radical political activists often label their more conservative opponents as "fascists." This is often the charge leveled against Christians who dare to set foot in the political arena. Jerry Falwell had this experience. He recounted, "At Harvard University, as I began my address, a well-organized group of students rose and began to chant in unison: 'Hitler rose, Hitler fell: racist Falwell, go to hell.'"

According to "heckler" reasoning, since Falwell was a "fascist," Falwell had no right to speak. Although it is doubtful if they had thought it through, they were assuming that constitutional rights could be abridged if the speaker were, to them, an evil person. Since the inept authorities wouldn't stop Falwell any more than they stopped Frank Collin, the crowd would just have to shout him down.

In this spirit of selectively granting rights, Randall Kennedy, a professor of law at Harvard University, gave a lecture advertised as "Hey, Hey, Ho, Ho, Free Speech Has Got to Go!" His lecture stated that free speech should be limited because "toleration has its limits." Kennedy, the people of Skokie, and others would like to be the ones to set those limits.

The free speech controversy cannot be resolved by granting certain persons jurisdiction over speech. Nor can it be resolved by making everything free in a libertarian free-for-all. It involves a deeper understanding of the First Amendment, an understanding of what constitutes "speech," which kinds are legally free, and why we have any rights at all.

To understand the true nature of rights it is necessary to look at a significant American document, one that preceded the Constitution, yet is an integral part of it. That source is the Declaration of Independence.

AMERICA'S GUARANTEE OF FREEDOM

The Declaration begins: "When in the Course of human Events, it becomes necessary for one People to dissolve the Political Bands which have connected them with another, and to assume among the Powers of the Earth, the separate and equal Station to which the Laws of Nature and of Nature's God entitle them, a decent Respect to the Opinions of Mankind requires that they should declare the causes which impel them to the Separation."

In those words, the representatives of the thirteen colonies announced to the civilized world that the "Political Bands" connecting them with the English king had been irreparably broken. George III had reneged on his part of the contract with the colonists, and they were exercising their right to break this political covenant. After decades of trying to resolve their differences with the king, lower magistrates—official representatives of the colonists—lawfully and without violence presented their case before the nations and the Supreme Judge of the world.

A significant factor in the colonists' freedom to write the Declaration was their knowledge that certain rights are "unalienable." Their rights were not dependent on the favor of the king of England but came directly from God, according to "the Laws of Nature and of Nature's God." Frank Collin's right to speak was not dependent on his favor with the Skokie authorities. It was his as a grant from the Creator.

Ever since the secularization of America took captive the thinking of our people, Christian and non-Christian alike have assumed from the language of the Declaration that Thomas Jefferson and the signers were Deists. Historians, including Christians, have stated that references such as "the Supreme Judge of the world" and "Divine Providence" prove that the Founders believed in a "watchmaker" God, one who had set the universe in motion and then let it run. Nothing could be further from the truth. It is vital that we correct our thinking on this issue, because disinformation about the faith of our Founders is destroying the rights for which they fought.

Rights in America are currently doled out by city councils, legislatures, and judges on the basis of a complex formula of presuppositions and conditions. As a result, each citizen is forced to comply with the whim of whoever is currently in power. That is not what our Founders intended and is not in accordance with the will of God. America was established as a nation ruled by law, and those laws were to conform to God's law.

When God created the universe, He gave Adam dominion over all the creatures of the earth (Gen. 1:26), but this does not imply that He also gave one person or nation the right to dominate others. As John Locke wrote in *Of Civil-Government* (1689), man has "in the State of Nature no Arbitrary Power over the Life, Liberty, or Possession of another, but only so much as the Law of Nature gave him for the preservation of himself."

Even after people have formed a society, individuals retain their "unalienable" rights because they are God-given and cannot be given away or usurped by another. The Declaration eloquently summed up these rights with the words, "We hold these Truths to be self-evident, that all Men are created equal, that they are endowed by their Creator with certain unalienable Rights, that among these are Life, Liberty, and the Pursuit of Happiness."

To avoid tyranny, Locke had written, those who form a society must specify what laws will rule all of them, from the highest civil ruler to the lowliest servant: "They shall be govern'd by *declared Laws,* or else their Peace, Quiet, and Property will still be at the same uncertainty, as it was in the state of Nature." A tyrant accepts no such restrictions, Locke said, and "makes not the Law, but his Will, the Rule." Only a tyrant refuses to be bound by the law and declares the law to be what he alone says it is.

In 1644, Samuel Rutherford, a Calvinist and scholar who, like Locke, believed in God's sovereignty, published *Lex Rex* ("the law is king"). In this document, for which he was eventually charged with treason, Rutherford proclaimed that everyone, including the king, must submit to the law. As the Magna Carta had established centuries earlier, there was no "divine right of kings."

Contrary to the theory that all law is man-made, or "positive" law, Rutherford argued that all laws, to be just, must conform to the "Laws of Nature and of Nature's God."

The Laws of Nature

As Rutherford, Locke, and the Founders used the term, the "Laws of Nature" did not have the same meaning as "Natural Law," which required the assent of human reason. Instead, it meant that God sovereignly reveals—by revelation to each individual—His standards of right and wrong. He is the Author of moral law, and He reveals it through nature as a model for man's law. Locke wrote, "The Rules that they make for other Men's Actions, must, as well as their own, and other Men's Actions, be conformable to the Law of Nature, *i.e.* to the Will of God."

The laws of nature are not dreamed up by people; they are imprinted on them by the Maker because everyone—believer and unbeliever—is made in the image of God, and thus capable of comprehending His will, of knowing in at least a primitive way the difference between right and wrong. Even without a Bible, individuals still have available to them the laws of nature, and God holds them accountable to these laws. Thus God could justly punish Cain for the murder of his brother (Gen. 4:1–15) even before He gave the commandment, "Thou shalt not kill" (Exod. 20:13).

As the psalmist wrote, "The heavens are telling the glory of God; they are a marvelous display of his craftsmanship. . . . Without a sound or word, silent in the skies, their message reaches out to all the world. . . . God's laws are pure, eternal, just. They are more desirable than gold" (Ps. 19:1, 3–4, 9–10, LB). And Paul said, "Since the creation of the world God's invisible qualities—his eternal power and divine nature—have been clearly seen, being understood from what has been made, so that men are without excuse" (Rom. 1:20).

The Laws of Nature's God

The second part of the phrase, "the Laws of . . . Nature's God," refers to the written revelation of God: the Bible. This written Word elaborates on creation law. Without the Bible, all people are still accountable to God, but they understand much less about His ways, and, although they have a sense of sin, they do not know about the Savior by knowing about sin.

The English subjects in the colonies knew the laws of nature and of nature's God, and they knew that their English king had broken them. They had fought a continual battle with the crown, as the Declaration documented, to claim the rights to which the laws of nature and of nature's God entitled them. After waiting for years and enduring "a long Train of Abuses and Usurpations," they became convinced it was time to appeal to the Supreme Judge to rectify the situation. They had confidence that He was a God of justice and would look favorably on their cause. As a last resort, they needed to "throw off such Government, and to provide new Guards for their future Security."

In order to secure the rights of the citizens of the colonies, even against their own revolutionary governments, representatives of the people in each colony wrote new state constitutions as soon as the Declaration was signed. Because they understood the sinful nature of people, they knew that only fixed, uniform, and universal laws would protect them from each other. The American Revolution succeeded in bringing about a permanent state of liberty. Uprisings in other nations only brought temporary freedoms that ebbed and flowed with the leaders in power. That is because they substituted one form of tyranny for another. Only a government based on a sound biblical foundation can guarantee unalienable rights. Only when God grants rights is someone prohibited from taking them away.

The Demise of Religious Liberties

When the Founders wrote the First Amendment, they said, in part: "Congress shall make no law respecting an establishment of religion, or prohibiting the free exercise thereof; or abridging the freedom of speech, or of the press." In so doing, they served notice on their elected representatives that the civil government was forbidden to usurp authority over the people's unalienable rights.

The framers chose to protect religion because, as James Madison wrote, "We hold it for a 'fundamental and undeniable truth,' that religion, or the duty which we owe to our creator, and the manner of discharging it, can be directed only by reason and conviction, not by force or violence. . . . In matters of religion no man's right is abridged by the institution of civil society." The jurisdiction of the legislative body is "both derivative and limited," Madison added. In no instance should it be allowed to "overleap the great barrier which defends the rights of the people. The rulers who are guilty of such an encroachment, exceed the commission from which they derive their authority, and are tyrants."

Religious liberty must never be taken captive by the civil rulers, said Madison, yet two centuries later that is exactly what has happened. Christians and Jews no longer have religious liberty in the public forum. Why don't more of them fight back? Those who submit to tyranny, said Madison, are slaves. It is time for the slaves to arise and demand their rights.

Nude Dancing and Free Speech

It is a commentary on modern American society that the most vocal proponents of free speech denounce expressions of Christianity and applaud expressions of nudity. The framers did not seek to protect free speech from congressional interference in order to let loose a flood of obscenity but rather to protect a citizen's unalienable right to criticize the government. In England and the early colonies, speech critical of the civil authorities had been severely restricted and even penalized. According to the situational ethic of English theory, British citizens were forbidden to express anything but favorable attitudes toward the civil ruler so that law and order could be maintained. They weren't even supposed to *think* negatively.

This is not the biblical model, and thus it was rejected by the framers. In the Bible, for example, David allowed Shimei to pour out a torrent of verbal abuse as David was fleeing from the treason of his son, Absalom. As the king and his entourage trudged dejectedly along the road, Shimei ran along the hillsides cursing David and throwing stones. Abishai implored David, "Let me go over now, and cut off his head!" (2 Sam. 16:9, NASB). But David said, "No! . . . Let him alone, for no doubt the Lord has told him to do it. And perhaps the Lord will see that I am being wronged and will bless me because of these curses" (2 Sam. 16:10–12, LB).

In recent years, the First Amendment protection of free criticism of one's rulers has been expanded beyond speeches against the government and also beyond speech itself. In most dictionaries, definitions of speech involve the use of verbal communication, yet the Supreme Court has been asked and has agreed to consider First Amendment cases that include categories like child pornography and nude dancing as issues of free speech.

Distortions like these have arisen from an abandonment of the framers' use of the term "speech" as covering three specific, independent categories. As defined by Herbert W. Titus of CBN University, they are as follows:

> *Free by the First Amendment: criticism of the civil government.* Criticism of the civil government (except for treason as defined in the Constitution) is the only speech protected by the First Amendment.
>
> *Free in Accordance with God's Grace: personal matters of the heart and mind.* The free-speech right that should have been invoked in the Skokie controversy is the freedom to speak about one's philosophy, religion, reason, and ideals. Frank Collin broke God's law of love when he attacked the Jews, but he broke no law of the land. Without repentance and forgiveness through the blood of Jesus Christ, Collin will pay dearly

for his transgressions before God, but the civil authorities had no jurisdiction over his speech.

Regulated by Law: matters involving the moral and physical order of the community. Every society eventually recognizes that it cannot survive long without maintaining moral and physical order. As a result, the Founders were consistent when they allowed unbridled criticism of the civil government but forbade libel, slander, fighting words, and obscenity.

JEFFERSON AND THE POWER OF GOD

Thomas Jefferson, whom many secularists erroneously count as an ally in the battle to destroy the influence of the church in society, explained why speeches ranging from expressions of hatred to a Christian's expression of love must not be regulated in a free society. In a profound document that is still on the books of the commonwealth of Virginia, he explained that matters of the heart and mind must never be regulated by the state because individuals are to follow the example of God.

Jefferson said that God, "the holy author of our religion," has the "Almighty power" to coerce His creation to accept His will, yet He refuses to exercise that power. Instead, God "created the mind free, and manifested his supreme will that free it should remain." Nevertheless, civil rulers continually and illegitimately do what God has refused to do. Jefferson wrote,

> [They,] fallible and uninspired men, have assumed dominion over the faith of others, setting up their own opinions and modes of thinking as the only true and infallible. . . . [Yet] the opinions of men are not the object of civil government, nor under its jurisdiction; that to suffer the civil magistrate to intrude his powers into the field of opinion and to restrain the profession or propagation of principles on supposition of their ill tendency is a dangerous fallacy, which at once destroys all religious liberty, because he being of course judge of that tendency will make his opinions the rule of judgment, and approve or condemn the sentiments of others only as they shall square with or differ from his own.

Whenever one man sets himself up as judge over another man's beliefs, he is interfering with that person's liberty, yet it happens all the time. Even within the church, factions regularly launch attacks against each other's doctrine. As the Apostle Paul said, instead of loving one another, those in the churches insist on "biting and devouring each other" (Gal. 5:15). This has become particularly evident since certain Christians became involved in matters of law and government.

Daniel C. Maguire of Marquette University, for example, opened his book *The New Subversives: Anti-Americanism of the Religious Right,* with the chapter title "Born Again Fascists." Under this heading he described the "New Right" as "a motley group of ultraconservative, self-defined 'Christian fundamentalists' who decided that the United States was losing its heritage, and so have roared into the political arena to make what they see as the law of God the law of the land."

Included in the "born again fascists," he said, are such groups as Christian Voice, the Heritage Foundation, Jerry Falwell, and the Moral Majority. Maguire, who is president of the Society of Christian Ethics, said, "They claim to be fundamentalists, but they miss the crucial fundamentals of the Bible and are fixated on biblical side issues. . . . They claim to be American patriots, but their spirit is fascistic and authoritarian."

To discredit what he assumed represented the heart and mind of New Rightists, Maguire quoted extensively from Virginia's Statute for Religious Freedom (quoted above). In the process, he deleted every reference to God. Jefferson's references to God are important because they demonstrate that God's dealings with individuals provide a model for their dealings with each other. References to God in an act currently in force in a commonwealth demonstrate that the law of God is already incorporated into the law of the land. Christians are not trying to force it in; they are trying to show others that it is already there.

Matters of the heart and mind can be freely spoken of in public forums of the United States because God would allow it if He were writing the law. God alone is qualified to judge the thoughts and intent of men's hearts, yet even He does not suppress that of which He disapproves. He never granted any one person jurisdiction over the minds of others because He knows that no one can truly know another's thoughts. As God told Samuel, "Man looks at the outward appearance, but the Lord looks at the heart" (1 Sam. 16:7, NASB). Even knowing the evil in a human heart and mind, God still refuses to stop it from coming out. There is no prior restraint with God.

If, in reality, the New Right had the tyrannical agenda described by Maguire, it would be a dangerous group indeed. Like so many others, he uses the familiar symbols of evil and suppression—Hitler and fascists—to arouse hostility. Yet the analogy is faulty. There is a difference between an effort by the New Right or anyone else to restore America's biblical heritage of liberty and Hitler's campaign for a rigid one-party dictatorship of anti-Semitism and obsessive nationalism.

America needs biblically based law and order to restore free speech to the nation. That is the solution to the suppression of free speech, not its cause. No judge, teacher, clergyman, or city council member has the ability to determine truth for every citizen. Each has the duty to promote a community where speech on matters of the heart and mind is truly free. The notion that "the civil magistrate is a competent judge of truth," wrote Madison, "is an arrogant pretension, falsified by the contradictory opinions of rulers in all ages."

"Truth . . . will prevail if left to herself," Jefferson wrote. Truth "has nothing to fear from the conflict, unless by human interposition [she is] disarmed of her natural weapons, free argument and debate; errors ceasing to be dangerous when it is permitted freely to contradict them."

Even after all the media access Frank Collin enjoyed, few bought his version of "the truth." In 1980, he was summarily dismissed from the party himself after he was convicted of a morals charge and sentenced to prison.

GOVERNMENT SUPPRESSION OF FREE SPEECH

For the last several years, the training ground for the unbiblical, unconstitutional restraint of free speech so prevalent now in America has not been the church, as its enemies claim, but the nation's public school system. Contrary to the Founders' determination that America would be a nation of unity *and* diversity, public school advocates sought to squelch differences. Inevitably, as Jefferson predicted, they began to make their own opinions the rule of judgment, approving or condemning others according to their own standards.

Consider these two examples of public school infringement on the First Amendment.

In Omaha, Nebraska, a group of high school students asked to organize a Bible club in a classroom after school at the same time as other club meetings were being held. Their request was denied on the basis that to do so would constitute an establishment of religion. Three years later the courts reversed that ruling.

In Berkeley Gardens Elementary School in suburban Denver, the principal ordered removed from the school's main library the only copy of the Bible. She justified her action by saying that the Bible's presence in the library violated the separation of church and state. She also demanded that a teacher remove two Bible story books from his classroom.

Contrary to the belief of these secular educators and thousands like them, the Bible is related to everything a child learns. It has played a prominent role throughout world history and continues to guide a significant segment of the American population. The public schools are anti-Christian; within their walls the state is the teacher, and state control over matters of the mind and heart is so pervasive that it acts as if it were a church itself. Jefferson denounced government control over matters of the heart and mind because the government is funded by private citizens, who have their own private opinions. He said it was "sinful and tyrannical [to] compel a man to furnish contributions of money for the propagation of opinions which he disbelieves and abhors." Most taxpayer-funded schools propagate the message that the Bible and God have no place in everyday life. Thus, those who believe in God are compelled to pay for a system that renounces Him and deletes God from history, science, mathematics, morality, and literature. Locke, Jefferson, and the founders of America would call that tyranny.

Until recently there were few complaints raised against such thought control. Because this kind of indoctrination crept in so slowly and so subtly, most of those who believe in God came to think that they had no right to express their faith in anything but the broadest terms. They bowed in homage before the royal throne of secularism, offering up their spiritual weapons at the feet of the state. While believers were surrendering, the secularists remained in the battle to squelch free speech and free exercise of religion, at least for Christians. Like the well-intentioned citizens of Skokie, they wanted to exercise some control over speeches which they didn't like, but in the process they did freedom a disservice.

The law can rightly forbid such categories of speech as obscenity, libel, slander, and fighting words, as well as that which is considered treason. Differences of a political or ideological nature, however, may be freely spoken.

"Greatest Good" Argument Is Bad Law

During the Skokie controversy, instead of enforcing Collin's right to free speech, U.S. District Court Judge Bernard M. Decker used a "balancing" argument. He ordered a cooling-off period during the Skokie controversy to allow time to "balance the likelihood of harm to the small local neo-Nazi group against the potential harm to the public interest."

The idea of balancing is a popular one. As a journalist, I was supposed to balance a news account by giving both sides of a story. It sounds like a good idea, but the underlying assumption is wrong. It rules out the existence of absolute truth. Balancing in terms of the law is utilitarian. Because it acknowledges no higher law, it says that the most moral thing society can do is to provide the greatest good for the greatest number. In every case this is determined by society, not God.

Utilitarianism was promoted in the nineteenth century by philosophers Jeremy Bentham, John Stuart Mill, and Herbert Spencer. Each one believed that individuals could make moral decisions based on personal pleasure and the best interests of society.

In recent years the courts have increasingly relied on an evolving law that looks not to fixed, uniform, and universal principles but rather to the utility of the present moment. In *Roth v. United States* (1957), for example, Supreme Court Justice William Brennan contended that the First Amendment's free speech and free press clauses were written because the framers wanted "to assure unfettered interchange of ideas for the bringing about of political and social change desired by the people." Instead of understanding that the framers were guided by biblical law in protecting certain kinds of free speech and not others, Brennan assumed that their thinking was just as utilitarian as his. He assumed that they granted a right to free speech because in their own minds it seemed likely to bring the greatest good to society.

Justice Brennan used his assumption of the framers' utilitarian reasoning to rule against obscenity. He said that the framers considered obscenity inappropriate for a marketplace of ideas. Brennan did not base his decision on the principle that free speech is an unalienable right. He did not say that laws against obscenity were necessary for the moral order of the community. He assumed that the framers operated under no predetermined laws, no preordained order from God that people should simply follow. He assumed that the framers believed that individuals used reason to decide which activities were good for society and which were not.

According to the utilitarian view of the law: If it is useful, do it. One of the most horrifying applications of this thinking is the use of living and aborted fetuses for research and "harvesting" for transplantation. There is no application of a higher law, only the lower law of a momentary need.

When Justice Brennan ruled against obscenity in *Roth,* opponents of pornography rejoiced. Yet because Brennan's thinking in that decision was utilitarian, the Supreme Court could just as likely rule in favor of obscenity another time if it seemed more useful to society. That, in fact, is just what has happened.

The only way for a nation's courts to rule consistently and fairly is for its judges to make decisions based on fixed, uniform, and universal laws. When they rule on the basis of each other's opinions, they have only each other to answer to. In the end, that kind of society is forced to accept human opinions for what is right and wrong. There is no safety and there is no freedom in that.

Warning: Tyranny Awaits

When judges and ordinary citizens reject God and His Word as the source of absolute truth, they also seem to assume it is the job of government to find truth. Justice Zechariah Chafee, to whom Brennan referred in the *Roth* decision, said, "One of the most important purposes of society and government is the discovery and spread of truth on subjects of general concern."

That is a dangerous and impossible proposition. When reason is used to balance good and evil, it is not possible for a new truth to emerge. That is a false, Hegelian dialectic. Instead, when a judge is allowed to balance rights and arbitrate truth, sacred human rights are destroyed. No laws or rights can survive such tampering.

Balancing relies heavily on the guesswork and whims of judges. It gives them a tremendous amount of power. After they are presented with a case, judges imagine the effect on society if a certain action were allowed to prevail. If they imagine a good result, the right is granted. If they imagine an ill result, the right is denied.

As Jefferson said, "To restrain the profession or propagation of principles on supposition of their ill tendency is a dangerous fallacy." It is wrong to suppress free speech solely on the assumption that evil will come of it. No matter how many potential problems the people of Skokie could envision if Frank Collin spoke, that did not justify the revocation of his right to free speech.

Some speech is limited for matters of national security or community order, but free speech regarding matters of the heart and mind is an unalienable right, granted by God. It is too important to be left to the arbitrary whim of those in authority who have their own standards of good and evil. America should be a nation of fixed laws, not personal tyranny.

Jesus said, "Do not judge according to appearances, but judge with righteous judgment" (John 7:24, NASB). When judges make decisions by balancing, they are judging by appearances, not by righteous laws. They have become arbitrary lawmakers. As a result, there are no longer any fixed rules, only judicial orders based on whatever collection of evidence is presented in each case. The Founders would have called that tyranny, and each new generation is just as deceived as the last.

Restoring a Biblical Basis for Law

Until the end of the nineteenth century, to "think like a lawyer" meant to understand the biblical basis of American law. Lawyers reasoned deductively, proceeding from absolute truth (the laws of nature and of nature's God) to applied truth (their particular cases). Future lawyers learned how to think this way by apprenticing themselves to practicing lawyers and studying William Blackstone's eighteenth-century *Commentaries on the Laws of England.*

Blackstone defined law as "a rule of action which is prescribed by some superior, and which the inferior is bound to obey." Moreover, obedience to God's law was considered essential to the "pursuit of happiness" that the Founders wrote into the Declaration of Independence. As the psalmist wrote, "How blessed are those whose way is blameless, who walk in the law of the Lord" (Ps. 119:1, NASB). Likewise, obedience to just laws, when they were patterned after God's law, brought blessings upon a nation's citizens. By contrast, one need only look at nations like the Soviet Union that have been subject to tyrants to find the curse of ungodly law.

The "Pursuit of Happiness," listed as a right in the Declaration of Independence, is not a license for unrestrained hedonism but a description taken from the English common law. Blackstone wrote, God has "inseparably interwoven the laws of eternal justice with the happiness of each individual." People have no sense of personal well-being unless they obey the laws of their Creator.

Our forefathers largely pursued happiness according to godly standards, but by the end of the nineteenth century, happiness had been divorced from obedience to God, and so had the law itself. Blackstone's *Commentaries* began to lose their esteemed place in American legal education simply because they did not fit the theory of evolution.

In 1870, Harvard's President Charles William Eliot chose Christopher Columbus Langdell as the first dean of the Harvard Law School. Langdell, like Eliot, was convinced that the traditional principles and practice of biblically based law must immediately be updated and replaced with evolutionary law. He set out with religious zeal to do just that. In "God, Evolution, Legal Education, and Law," Herbert Titus wrote, "Langdell did not just introduce a new method of teaching law, he introduced a new faith about law. He believed that man, led by the ablest scholars and judges, could discover and determine the laws governing human affairs; man did not need the aid of God and of the Holy Scriptures. Langdell dropped God out of legal education, not by default, but by design."

Blackstone and the Founders believed it was impossible for one to use unaided reason as the basis for establishing law. As biblically literate men, they knew that human nature, including reason, was fallen. Blackstone wrote that man's "reason is corrupt, and his understanding full of ignorance and error"; however, he did not recommend that one discard reason and govern by trancelike revelation. Human beings were to use their minds, but, as Blackstone wrote, they should look for guidance to "the revealed or divine law . . . found only in the Holy Scriptures. These precepts, when revealed, are found upon comparison to be really a part of the original law of nature."

People of all ages have tried to compile laws and ethical systems based on their perception of the laws of nature. Thus men like Hammurabi and Confucius could discover some elements of sound law. "Revealed law," wrote Blackstone, "is of infinitely more authenticity than that moral system which is framed by ethical writers, and denominated [by] natural law. Because one is the law of nature, expressly declared so to be by God himself; the other is only what, by the assistance of human reason, we imagine to be that law."

After a century of evolutionary law, members of the American legal profession are beginning to see that a great void has been created in the country's legal system. In "God, Man, and Law," Herbert Titus observed: "In 1971, Harvard law professor Harold J. Berman, in the Lowell Lectures on Theology at Boston University, suggested that the divorce of law from its historic religious base has precipitated a 'massive loss of confidence in the law—not only on the part of law consumers, but also on the part of the law makers and law distributors.'"

In 1974, fifty-three law professors and deans petitioned the American Association of Law Schools to establish a permanent section on Law and Religion. After decades of neglect, they felt it was time to acknowledge and study the theological roots of Western legal education. The grafted-on theories of evolutionary law were beginning to bear bad fruit.

As you will recall from the Prologue, Herbert Titus was on the faculty of the University of Oregon Law School when he had a remarkable encounter with Jesus Christ. The experience sent him searching through the Scriptures and the history of the law to understand how God could be sovereign over all creation. The students and faculty at Oregon, deeply committed to a belief in evolutionary law, strongly opposed what he discovered.

In 1979, Titus had an opportunity to assist in the founding of a Christian law school at Oral Roberts University. "I remember the day I left the University of Oregon," Titus said. "The man who had been dean of the law school there and had been active in the American Bar Association and the American Association of Law Schools said to me, 'Herb, I want you to know that I think you are throwing your life away. That law school will never be accredited.'" Eventually, the ABA did grant accreditation to ORU's law school, but only after a federal judge charged the foot-dragging organization with abridging the school's right to religious freedom.

Titus said, "We took a stand for righteousness. We said, 'We will not back down from our faith in the Lord Jesus Christ.' That was the issue. If we had simply said we do not require Jesus to be Lord of this law school, they would have said, 'You can have your accreditation.' But we said, 'No, we will not do that.'"

The ORU law school was moved to CBN University and once again the ABA rose up. Its evolutionary concept of law by precedent was entirely different from the biblical model established by the Founders and perpetuated by Christian legal scholars. Those who guard the den of the antibiblical creature of modern law may bare their teeth, but they must not be allowed to prevail.

America is a nation with a rich legal heritage, but the law has become a shabby transient, skulking from precedent to precedent, warily eying the wind. It is essential that we change the way we think about the law and that our schools once more train lawyers to think biblically. Jesus said, "Woe to you lawyers! For you have taken away the key of knowledge; you did not enter in yourselves, and those who were entering in you hindered" (Luke 11:52, NASB). For their own sake, as well as for the nation, we must tell lawyers, in love, what Jesus said.

For Further Reading

An Act for Religious Freedom, adopted by the Virginia General Assembly (16 January 1786), recited in Code of Virginia, Sec. 57-1, Code of Virginia 1950 (annotated). Charlottesville, Va.: Michil Co., 1986.

William Blackstone. *Commentaries on the Laws of England.* Edited by St. George Tucker. 1803. South Hackensack, N.J.: Rothman Reprints, 1969.

Jerry Falwell. *Strength for the Journey.* New York: Simon and Schuster, 1987.

David Hamlin. *The Nazi/Skokie Conflict: A Civil Liberties Battle.* Boston: Beacon Press, 1980.

John Locke. *Of Civil Government.* In *The Christian History of the Constitution of the United States of America.* Edited by Verna Hall. San Francisco: Foundation for American Christian Education, 1966.

Robert S. Alley, ed. *James Madison on Religious Liberty.* Buffalo, N.Y.: Prometheus Books, 1985.

Daniel C. Maguire. *The New Subversives: Anti-Americanism of the Religious Right.* New York: Continuum, 1982.

Aryeh Neier. *Defending My Enemy.* New York: E. P. Dutton, 1979.

Herbert W. Titus. "God, Evolution, Legal Education, and Law." *Journal of Christian Jurisprudence* (1980): 11.

———. "Religious Freedom: The War between Two Faiths." *Journal of Christian Jurisprudence* (1984/1985): 119–38.

———. "The United States Supreme Court and Obscenity: Reversed and Remanded." In *Pornography: Solutions through Law.* Edited by Carol A. Clancy. Washington, D.C.: National Forum Foundation, 1985.

10

The African-American Experience

Coretta Scott King had been a mother for only a few weeks. The firstborn child of Coretta and Martin Luther King, Jr., was a girl, Yolanda. For just over a year, Coretta and Martin had lived in the white-frame parsonage of the Dexter Avenue Church in Montgomery, Alabama, where twenty-seven-year-old Martin served as pastor. On the evening of 30 January 1956, Martin had another task, as well. He was speaking to a mass meeting of newly aroused Black people who had decided to stand up for their rights. Before the night was over, Martin's nonviolent Christian principles would be sorely tried, and he would be catapulted into a world of hate, imprisonment, and character assassination; eventually he died for the cause in which he believed.

Ever since King had taken the side of Rosa Parks, a forty-two-year-old Black seamstress who refused to give up her bus seat to a White person, he had been at the center of a whirlwind. Parks had boarded the bus after work nearly two months earlier, on 1 December 1955, tired and relieved at the chance to sit down. At the next stop, several Whites boarded the bus. The bus driver routinely ordered Parks to get up. She refused. As she said later, she had no idea of starting a revolution: "I was just plain tired, and my feet hurt." Her personal needs were the last thing on the mind of the bus driver, however. To him it was a blatant attempt by an inferior Negro to break the segregation laws of Alabama. He found a policeman who arrested her and took the weary lady to the courthouse. Coretta King described what happened next:

> From there Mrs. Parks called E. D. Nixon, who came down and signed a bail bond for her.
>
> Mr. Nixon was a fiery Alabamian. He was a Pullman porter who had been active in A. Philip Randolph's Brotherhood of Sleeping Car Porters, and in civil-rights activities. Suddenly he also had had enough; suddenly, it seemed, almost every Negro in Montgomery had had enough. It was spontaneous combustion. Phones began ringing all over the Negro section of the city. The Women's Political Council suggested a one-day boycott of the buses as a protest. E. D. Nixon courageously agreed to organize it.

In some ways Montgomery, the "Cradle of the Confederacy," was an unlikely place for an uprising of Blacks. Located on the banks of the Alabama River, the state capital was a thriving center of industry, education, and the arts. Blacks like the Kings lived in segregated neighborhoods and attended segregated schools, including higher education, but, except for occasional flareups, they rarely challenged their subordinate status. Out of thirty thousand Blacks in the county, only two thousand had challenged the limits of the system even to vote.

Martin's father and grandfather, pastor and former pastor of Ebenezer Baptist Church in Atlanta, had always refused to accept the Whites' scornful evaluation of Blacks and had passed on to Martin a sense of self-worth. Likewise, Coretta's father, a successful entrepreneur who had been frequently sabotaged by White competitors, taught her that she was a child of God who did not need to hate others in order to be strong.

Entering college at fifteen and earning a Ph.D. at twenty-five, Martin had studied under theologians and philosophers, gaining a biblical perspective on why people were full of despair and sin, and what he could do about it.

Even as a student he was eager to be involved in social change, but he was uneasy with Friedrich Nietzsche's contention that only power could change the world. Was love a strong enough force to compete with raw power? He decided it had to be, because of God.

Once Martin comprehended that a philosophy based on the Bible was the only practical foundation for social change, he became convinced that he must use only nonviolent methods to implement it. So he turned to Mohandas K. (Mahatma) Gandhi's technique of nonviolent resistance, a change from the passive acceptance that had governed the Blacks' affairs up to that time. As King would say in "An Experiment in Love," "Christ furnished the spirit and motivation, while Gandhi furnished the method."

On the night of January 30, the Blacks' one-day boycott of the Northern-owned Montgomery City Bus Lines had already extended into weeks of nonviolent protest, and no end was in sight. The loss of transportation was a genuine hardship on the Black citizens of Montgomery, many of whom had no other means of transportation. Yet they were enthralled with the possibility that they might never again be degraded on a bus.

Even though 70 percent of the bus passengers were Black, they were always treated with scorn. The front seats were reserved for Whites, who took seats from the front backward. The back seats were relegated to Blacks, who were seated back to front. Black passengers were not allowed even to walk past the seated Whites. Coretta King wrote,

> Negroes had to pay their fares at the front of the bus, get off, and walk to the rear door to board again. Sometimes the bus would drive off without them after they had paid their fare. This would happen to elderly people or pregnant women, in bad weather or good, and was considered a great joke by the drivers. Frequently the white bus drivers abused their passengers, called them niggers, black cows, or black apes. Imagine what it was like, for example, for a black man to get on a bus with his son and be subjected to such treatment.

As soon as the boycott caught on, volunteers, including Ralph Abernathy, King's close friend and the pastor of Montgomery's First Baptist Church, organized a veritable army of drivers, both Black and White, to take care of the transportation needs. Participants faced constant threats and intimidations, including every legal barrier the local authorities could erect.

One institution the authorities could not demolish was the Black church. Ever since Reconstruction, even if they owned no other property, Blacks would build themselves a church. Until the 1960s, few had any hope that the system could be changed, but, as Mrs. King wrote, "The preacher's role was to keep hope alive in nearly hopeless situations."

On that January night, Martin was presenting to the crowd a hope borne out of his own experience with God, and confirmed by principles he had discovered during his years of study. Although relatively soft-spoken in person, the conservatively dressed doctoral graduate with the slim mustache could stir an audience with all the fire of a traditional Baptist preacher. As one reporter for the *New York Times* would write a few months later, "He can build to his climax with a crescendo of impassioned pulpit-pounding that overwhelms the listener with the depth of his convictions."

In previous generations, Black preachers had usually emphasized freedom in the life to come and patient endurance in the here and now. Thus, when King promoted activism, some drew back, but others found themselves providentially well equipped for a siege.

When King stepped into the pulpit of Abernathy's church for that particular meeting, he knew that his wife and baby were at home alone with a church friend, Mary Lucy Williams. The previous weekend the Kings had received such a volume of obscene and threatening phone calls during the night that he had announced to his congregation that he would have to leave the phone off the hook during sleeping hours. "Often the woman callers raved on about sex," Coretta wrote, "accusing Martin and me of incredible degeneracies."

After one particularly nasty caller had hung up, King found himself overwhelmed with the floodtide of evil surging toward his family. Rolling out of bed, he slipped into the kitchen to pray. Mrs. King wrote later:

> With his head in his hands, Martin bowed over the table and prayed aloud to God, saying, "Lord, I am taking a stand for what I believe is right. The people are looking to me for leadership, and if I stand before them without strength and courage, they will falter. I am at the end of my powers. I have nothing left. I've come to the point where I can't face it alone."
>
> Martin said to me, "At that moment I experienced the presence of the Divine as I had never experienced Him before. It seemed as though I could hear the quiet assurance of an inner voice saying, 'Stand up for righteousness; stand up for truth; and God will be at your side forever.'"

King carried that inner serenity with him to the meeting. By the end of the evening, he would need it.

Coretta and her friend were in the sitting room when they heard a heavy thump on the concrete porch. Jumping up, they scattered to the back of the house just as a "thunderous blast" shook the house and smoke began to pour through broken windows. Mary Lucy began to scream. She grabbed hold of Coretta, but the young mother had only one thought in mind. She rushed to her baby's bedroom where, incredibly, she found little Yolanda fast asleep.

Within seconds, neighbors came flocking to the house, frightened and angry at this unconscionable attack. Coretta managed to contact someone at the church where Martin was speaking, but he said later, "Strangely enough, I accepted the word of the bombing calmly. My religious experience a few nights before had given me the strength to face it."

By the time King reached his house an angry crowd had gathered, scarcely held in check by the nervous police force. Many were trying to sing "My Country 'Tis of Thee," but tension filled the air. Several in the crowd were armed. After King checked on his family, and reminded his wife she was still in her robe, he stepped out on what was left of his bombed-out porch. As he held up his hand, almost instantly the surging mass was quiet, each one pausing to hear King's call to action. Many were ready for vengeance, but King said,

> "My wife and baby are all right. I want you to go home and put down your weapons. We cannot solve this problem through retaliatory violence. We must meet violence with nonviolence. Remember the words of Jesus: 'He who lives by the sword will perish by the sword.' We must love our white brothers, no matter what they do to us. We must make them know that we love them. Jesus still cries out across the centuries, 'Love your enemies.' This is what we must live by. We must meet hate with love. . . . Remember, if I am stopped, this Movement will not stop, because God is with this Movement."

Nearly eleven months later, on 13 November 1956, King sat in a courtroom as attorneys for the city of Montgomery told the judge that the city had lost fifteen thousand dollars in tax revenue from the bus boycott. It demanded remuneration from the activists. Near noon time, a stirring began among the reporters. Someone from the Associated Press handed King a slip of paper. The Supreme Court had affirmed a lower court ruling that Alabama's state and local laws requiring segregation on buses were unconstitutional. One elderly man exploded from the back of the courtroom, "God Almighty has spoken from Washington, D.C.!"

That night they had to use two churches to hold the eight thousand people who wanted to celebrate and to honor God who had accomplished the impossible. Robert Graetz, the White pastor of a Lutheran church, read aloud from Paul's first letter to the Corinthians, "Though I have all faith, so that I could remove mountains, but have not love, I am nothing. . . . When I was a child, I spake as a child, I understood as a child; but when I became a man, I put away childish things" (1 Cor. 13:2, 11). When he said that, the crowd leaped up, shouting and cheering and waving handkerchiefs. The Black child had become a man.

Twelve years later, when King was thirty-nine years old, he had been awarded the Nobel Peace Prize, met with the pope, and counted among his friends the late president of the United States, John F. Kennedy. When he was assassinated in Memphis on 4 April 1968, he was in the midst of securing rights for garbage collectors. No man was too lowly to have equality.

Thanks to the work King started, major strides have been made in the direction of equal rights. However, in too many ways the nation he sought to unify is still splintered, his vision of an integrated America still unfulfilled, and his name, in the thinking of many citizens, is vaguely linked with communism, adultery, and the welfare state. The national holiday in his honor has been condemned even from pulpits of the church.

What went wrong with the dream? Who was the real Martin Luther King, Jr.? Americans of every color need to take a hard look at the African-American experience and the source of the rumors about this man. America needs to understand the thinking that keeps the races apart and to do whatever it takes to change it.

THE TRUTH ABOUT UNCLE TOM

Before there were Pilgrims, there were slaves. From the first day a Black man arrived in America, as King said in "Nonviolence and Racial Justice," he was treated as "a thing to be used, not a person to be respected."

America, from the beginning, has been ambivalent about race. Men like Thomas Jefferson signed the words "all Men are created equal" and yet remained slaveholders. Many of our Founders felt uneasy about their slaves, but it was apparently easier to suppress their feelings than to deal with slaves as real men and women. The implications were too overwhelming.

The original Constitution of the United States was a remarkable document, but it was a compromise. There were men who hated slavery and men who used it, and both had to form a union. In the years to come, the divisiveness over that issue would never go away. The infected wound has never healed.

In 1852, Harriet Beecher Stowe, a northern housewife deeply troubled by the enforcement of the Fugitive Slave Law, said she had decided "to bring the subject of slavery, as a moral and religious question, before the minds of all those who profess to be followers of Christ in America." Her story of a kindly Christian slave who died a brutal death rather than betray his fellow slaves moved the nation to shame. Ironically, the book Abraham Lincoln said started the Civil War was a monument to the power of nonviolent love. Somehow, in the decades after the Civil War, the man with the strength to love and forgive became a symbol of the problem of American Blacks instead of the solution.

"Power at its best is love implementing the demands of justice," Martin Luther King, Jr., would say a century later. Love is not "some sentimental emotion." Jesus knew that. In "Nonviolence and Racial Justice," King wrote, "It would be nonsense to urge men to love their oppressors in an affectionate sense. 'Love' in this sense means understanding good will. . . . It is the love of God working in the lives of men. . . . We rise to the position of loving the person who does the evil deed while hating the deed he does."

AFTERMATH OF THE CIVIL WAR

King likened Lincoln's Emancipation Proclamation of 1 January 1863 to "a great beacon light of hope to millions of Negro slaves who had been seared in the flames of withering injustice." Once the Emancipator was dead, his noble aims seemed to die with him. The "Christian" nation gave the former slaves their freedom, but it did not give them restitution or love. King wrote:

> He was not given any land to make that freedom meaningful. It was something like keeping a person in prison for a number of years and suddenly discovering that that person is not guilty of the crime for which he was convicted. And you just go up to him and say, "Now you are free," but you don't give him any bus fare to get to town.

The Blacks were free, but they were illiterate, unskilled, usually separated from their families, and greatly feared. Even though many African-Americans, like Uncle Tom, were Christians, their former slaveowners expected them to cast off their faith and rise up in vengeance for all the years of oppression.

Negro rights had been imposed on the South, but, except for a few kindly souls, the Whites fully intended to control those rights. Instead of recognizing that Christian love and restitution for past wrongs would resolve their conflict with the African-Americans among them, local authorities simply bided their time until they could regain power over Blacks once again. The Whites couldn't own slaves any more, but they could control access to work, to the ballot, and to any influential place in society. The South had lost the war, but it hadn't surrendered its thinking. Southerners went to church, but they didn't listen to the Gospel. God had never given any one person dominion over another, but the Whites took it anyway. In the process, they became slaves themselves, slaves to the worst of their sinful nature.

Shortly after the Northern occupation troops left, Southern conservatives introduced Jim Crow laws. They established segregation. They forbade anyone to vote unless his grandfather had been a voter. By personal contempt and local law they stripped away the Blacks' newfound dignity. Instead of following the biblical admonition to take care of the poor and weak, they slammed the door in their faces. Instead of loving those they perceived as enemies, they allowed the Ku Klux Klan to rise like a demon spirit from the ashes of their fears.

In 1896, the U.S. Supreme Court in *Plessy v. Ferguson* refused to allow federal interference in state and local segregation laws. A Louisiana statute of 1890 had allowed separate traveling facilities for White and Black train passengers. This statute was challenged by a man who was "seven-eighths Caucasian and . . . one-eighth African." Although the Thirteenth, Fourteenth, and Fifteenth Amendments had been ratified after the Civil War to ensure the rights of Blacks, the Supreme Court ruled that Louisiana's "separate but equal" statute was still legal. Private rights should still be dealt with at the state and local level, the Court said: Equality before the law was not "intended to abolish distinctions based upon color, or to enforce social, as distinguished from political, equality, or a commingling of the races upon terms unsatisfactory to either." This "separate but equal" decision would be the basis for law for over half a century.

Beginning to See the Light

By 1954, the U.S. Supreme Court had begun to broaden its interpretation of the Fourteenth Amendment to include greater jurisdiction over the states. As a result, the National Association for the Advancement of Colored People (NAACP) finally succeeded in persuading the Court to rectify local segregation. In *Brown v. Board of Education,* the Court ruled that Black schoolchildren who were forbidden to attend White public schools in their neighborhoods had been subjected to illegal discrimination. These supposedly "separate but equal" schools were underfinanced and poorly equipped.

In ruling for the plaintiffs in *Brown,* Chief Justice Earl Warren wrote for the majority: "To separate them from others of similar age and qualifications solely because of their race generates a feeling of inferiority as to their status in the community that may affect their hearts and minds in a way unlikely ever to be undone."

The plaintiffs had been deprived of the equal protection clause of the Fourteenth Amendment, and they must be allowed to attend integrated schools. Warren wrote: "We conclude that in the field of public education the doctrine of 'separate but equal' has no place. Separate educational facilities are inherently unequal."

Instead of condemning the decision in *Plessy,* however, the Court saved face for rule by precedent by suggesting that perhaps those justices were not aware of the psychological effects of "separate but equal" accommodations. Possibly they did not know that segregation could retard Black children's educational and mental development.

As commendable as this landmark ruling was, it did not get to the heart of the matter of segregation. Neither *Plessy* nor *Brown* dealt conclusively with the fundamental questions of equality and "unalienable" rights. Black children should be allowed to attend their neighborhood schools not because such permission would help them avoid emotional strain or even because it would enhance their academic performance. They should be admitted to the school because they are just as much citizens as White children. They are just as intelligent, just as educable, and just as able to conform to the rules. They have a right to life, liberty, and the pursuit of happiness, not because they can persuade a majority of nine justices to take their side, but because these rights are granted by the Creator and affirmed in American law.

Brown also failed to deal with the faulty tradition of law by precedent, which replaced law based on absolute biblical standards with law that evolves. With no solid foundation on the laws of nature and of nature's God, rulings related to civil rights have had a checkered history.

CONSTITUTIONAL POWER STRUGGLE

When King began his activism, segregationists had used the Constitution for more than 150 years to block federal interference in their treatment of the Negro. They relied on the Tenth Amendment, which said, "The powers not delegated to the United States by the Constitution, nor prohibited by it to the States, are reserved to the States respectively or to the people." For generations, state and local governments had used this very important element of federalism as a loophole, and the Supreme Court, with the cooperation of Congress, was beginning to close it.

During King's lifetime, a federal Civil Rights Commission was established (1957), a Civil Rights Act was passed (1964), and a Voting Rights Act went into law (1965). Because of this positive experience with federal activism, however, civil rights activists became suspicious of anyone espousing strict constructionism, or an interpretation of the Constitution according to the Founders' intent. Thus, when President Ronald Reagan nominated Robert Bork to the U.S. Supreme Court in 1987, a nationwide crusade was launched to defeat him. The charge was made that he would set civil rights back twenty years. What his detractors had in mind was that Bork would restore the kind of home rule from which the federal courts had rescued the Blacks. Based on this faulty assumption, they had no other option but to defeat him.

In the process of restoring legitimate rights to African-Americans, the Supreme Court could have resorted to a strict interpretation of the Constitution and the actual charter of our nation, the Declaration of Independence. The problem all these years has not been with the documents that are the law of the land, but with their faulty interpretation. By hindsight, it is clear that the Founders could have outlawed slavery just by adhering to their own documents.

The U.S. Supreme Court in *Dred Scott v. Sandford* (1857) was just as activist as modern courts, but at that time the private preference of the justices was more inclined against Blacks than for them. The Southern majority on the Court ruled that Dred Scott was not freed, as he hoped, by virtue of moving to a free state. Their reasoning was based on their assumption that under the law Scott was not even a person, but property. Enlarging on this misbelief, the Court at the same time invalidated the Missouri Compromise of 1820. It objected to that attempt by Congress to prohibit slavery in the Louisiana Purchase because it allegedly violated the rights of property guaranteed by the Fifth Amendment.

Today, most people have no trouble agreeing with Abraham Lincoln's contention that he was not bound by the *Dred Scott* decision because it applied only to one individual case. However, when the same principle is raised in regard to *Roe v. Wade,* which unleashed the murder of millions of unborn Black children, it creates controversy. America desperately needs to return to *Lex Rex,* the law is king, not the personal opinions of the Supreme Court. We need to restore the balance of powers, and elect officials who will legislate according to God's law and the legitimate desires of the people.

Warfare over School Desegregation

The Court had called for "all deliberate speed" in the desegregation process, but this was interpreted by segregationists as a license to do as little as possible to implement it. Between 1954 and 1974, when integration languished in spite of *Brown,* the federal courts gradually expanded their influence over the nation's public schools. Since *Brown* had only applied to de jure segregation—that which was imposed by statute—local courts continued to find loopholes to perpetuate de facto segregation. However, in the 1968 case *Green v. County School Board of New Kent County, Va.,* the Supreme Court stated that school boards could no longer maintain parallel school systems for Blacks and Whites. They must "take whatever steps might be necessary to convert to a unitary system in which racial discrimination would be eliminated root and branch." In a word, the Court wanted results.

Three years later, in *Swann v. Charlotte-Mecklenburg* (1971), the Supreme Court ruled that district courts should order school boards to take any measures necessary to eliminate segregation, regardless of the cause, even measures that were "administratively awkward, inconvenient and even bizarre."

Southern school districts, tired of taking the brunt of desegregation decisions, began to complain that Northern de facto segregation was just as pervasive as Southern de jure segregation, even though not enforced by law. Because the Supreme Court and Congress were taking a stand against segregation, integrationists increasingly turned to Washington for relief. Without local involvement, however, the transformed schools were white-washed sepulchers. The schools looked integrated, but inside they were full of anger, resentment, and hate.

In Boston, for example, which had the oldest integration law in the nation, Whites, Blacks, and other minorities predominated in various schools, depending on the ethnic character of each arrogant neighborhood. In the spirit of the times, U.S. District Judge W. Arthur Garrity ruled that the Boston School Committee had conspired to segregate its schools and major changes must be made. He endorsed a plan to desegregate the schools by a massive busing effort, transporting students each day many miles across the city. The transfers were made without regard for the individuals or families involved, but solely on the basis of race. Just as in the days of Jim Crow laws, someone had to analyze the ancestry of each student to decide who was "White." Just as in the days of Reconstruction, few changed their thinking to bring it under submission to Christ.

J. Anthony Lukas, in his Pulitzer-Prize-winning account of the Boston busing crisis, *Common Ground,* said that Judge Garrity had a sincere commitment not only to the Constitution but also to divine law. Raised and educated as a Catholic, Garrity believed that Boston's segregation was immoral and intolerable. Instead of operating within the boundaries of his position as a judge, however, Garrity extended his jurisdiction over a multitude of school affairs. When the School Committee defied him, he even became involved in personnel decisions and building maintenance.

In traditional law, when plaintiffs are found to have just cause for a grievance, they must be compensated for their losses. The Boston plaintiffs, complaining of de facto segregation, represented generations of grievances. Lukas wrote, "Judges may maintain the legal fiction that they are merely trying a lawsuit between two parties, but their remedies affect the rights of parties who, strictly speaking, are not even represented before the court. A judge in such a case is no longer primarily concerned with adjudicating past wrongs; he is seeking to alter the future behavior of large sections of the population. Though he may still see himself as a neutral arbiter, he is, in fact, making social policy."

The social policy decisions of Judge Garrity, like others in the South two decades earlier, exploded into violence. On 12 September 1974, the first day of court-enforced busing to eliminate de facto segregation, most of the affected eighty schools made the transition peacefully. However, Black students who were bused to South Boston High School were greeted by angry, vocal White crowds. At the end of the day, en route to their home neighborhoods, the buses were pelted with eggs, beer bottles, soda cans, and rocks, shattering windows and injuring nine students.

Further scenes of escalating violence would be repeated throughout the decade, with attackers on both sides. Desegregation in the North was characterized by "White flight" of families to the suburbs, not solely on the basis of racism but also for fear of their children's safety, a desire to be close to school, and frustration with the constant tension and restructuring. In the South, private schools sprang up that were exclusively for Whites.

No matter what the courts did, they seemed never to persuade the American people to believe a simple fact: Every human being is created equal to every other, and we are called to love one another.

The Racist Thinking of Americans

In 1988, *Life* magazine commissioned a survey of prejudice in America. Pollsters Tarrance and Associates discovered that 36 percent of Whites and 57 percent of Blacks rated themselves as "not at all prejudiced." The remainder, however—nearly two-thirds of the Whites and almost half of the Blacks—admitted that they held on to some degree of prejudice. That is a lot of people, and many of them, every Sunday morning, religiously go to church.

Prejudice is unbiblical and un-Christian. It is time we set the record straight. God is no respecter of persons. He makes no distinction between rich or poor, Black or White, Indian or Oriental or Occidental. He loves us, and He told us to love one another. God doesn't expect us all to be alike. He is the one who divided languages and established nations, but within ethnicity and normal attitudes of community pride there is no place for hate, reproach, or bigotry. Those are sins against God.

We have allowed ourselves to accept many misbeliefs and misconceptions that have become brick and mortar in the walls between the races. These myths include the following.

The Mark of Cain. According to one theory of racial superiority, when Cain killed his brother, Abel (Gen. 4:1–16) God "marked" Cain with dark skin. Thus, all non-Whites are descendants of Cain and cursed by God. There is no biblical evidence to support this interpretation. Even though God did hold Cain accountable for his act of murder, the sign was something helpful. It was given for protection, not condemnation. God expressly said, "Whoever kills Cain, vengeance will be taken on him sevenfold" (Gen. 4:15, NASB).

The Curse of Canaan. After Ham insulted his father's dignity by telling his brothers about Noah's drunken nakedness (Gen. 9:21–27), Noah cursed his son and his grandson, Canaan. He said, "Cursed be Canaan; a servant of servants he shall be to his brothers" (Gen. 9:25, NASB). Even if it could be established that all Blacks are descendants of Canaan, however, which is impossible, a curse resulting from personal sin would not become a norm for all generations to come.

Enslavement of Aliens. Moses told the Israelites not to enslave their fellow citizens, but did allow them to take slaves from the surrounding nations (Lev. 25:39–46). Since the slaveholders of America took slaves from Africa, they argued that they were only following the Old Testament model. This myth overlooks that the American slaveholders were themselves aliens in the United States. Israel's slaves, moreover, were prisoners of war in an ancient era when foes became servants.

Silence of Jesus. Since Jesus never explicitly forbade slavery, some have assumed He condoned it. The absence of word-for-word condemnation, however, is far from a commendation. In reality, Jesus clearly stated his opposition to enslavement in these words: "He has sent me to proclaim release to the captives, And recovery of sight to the blind, To set free those who are downtrodden" (Luke 4:18, NASB).

Christ did not come the first time as a political liberator, but He did preach an inner liberation that was superior to the whim of the world's rulers. Jesus and His people were captives in their own land, yet He was able to treat His oppressors with respect without relinquishing His own dignity. This did not mean He was silent in the face of injustice nor did He expect others to be passive and abused. The scribes and Pharisees well knew His indignation.

Paul's Acceptance of Slavery. In his epistles to the churches, Paul described the ideal relationship between masters and slaves (see Eph. 6:5–9; Col. 3:22–25; 1 Tim. 6:1–3). Some have interpreted these instructions as tacit approval of the institution. Paul, however, was only demonstrating to the individuals caught up in an evil system that God could make something good come out of anything. Both slave and master are degraded by slavery, but Paul was telling them that if they respected one another and abandoned the ritualistic harshness and hate that usually characterized such relationships, they could glorify God even in the midst of evil.

Separate but Equal. Segregation is never equality. It is not a sin to live in a community where others of similar background and interests also live, nor to attend schools and churches together. When this togetherness becomes exclusiveness and haughtiness toward innocent individuals who are simply different, then the law of love is broken.

The doctrine of sacredness, which King learned from Professor L. Harold DeWolf of Boston University, states that each human life is sacred because each individual is made in the image of God. King said in a 1965 speech: "The innate worth referred to in the phrase, the *image of God,* is universally shared in equal portions by all men. There is no graded scale of essential worth. . . . The worth of an individual does not lie in the measure of his intellect, his racial origin, or his social position. Human worth lies in relatedness to God. . . . Segregation stands diametrically opposed to the principle of the sacredness of human personality. It debases personality."

Inferior Races. In first-century Athens, the intellectual center of the ancient world, the debaters at the Areopagus considered themselves superior to other, simpler men. When the Apostle Paul traveled to their city, he confronted them with the statement that God "made from one blood, every nation of mankind to live on all the face of the earth" (Acts 17:26, NASB [margin]). There were not several levels and races of people, but only one human race.

It is no wonder that many of them sneered and walked out on him. The same reaction has greeted civil rights advocates in the twentieth century. Although today's segregation is justified publicly as amoral personal preference, the root is the same: One group considers its own race superior to another and ignores the Word of God. There is one human race. One Lord. One faith.

The Idolatry of Racism. One of Martin Luther King's professors at Morehouse College, George Kelsey, said, "Racism is a faith. It is a form of idolatry." Racists examine themselves and make their own characteristics a standard of perfection. A certain type of person becomes the measure of all things. King wrote in *The Making of a Mind,* "Racism . . . is the arrogant assertion that one race is the center of value and object of devotion before which other races must kneel in submission." Anthropologist Ruth Benedict said that racism is the "dogma that the hope of civilization depends upon eliminating some races and keeping others pure." Supremacy arguments are not limited to Whites or Blacks, Americans or Europeans. Racism is a plague on all of us.

Most Americans have no difficulty condemning Hitler for the genocide of the Jews, but more than half secretly believe that one race is superior to another race. The church should take the lead in capturing those thoughts and making them obedient to Christ (2 Cor. 10:5). We must become absolutists against all forms of racism.

Apartheid. Martin Luther King expressed a kinship with all oppressed peoples, and especially those in South Africa. It was in that troubled land that Gandhi in 1907 implemented the first *Satyagraha,* or nonviolent resistance.

Gandhi spent his life searching the religious literature of the world for the common elements of nonviolent protest. Although he was a Hindu, he was successful in defining what would work because he believed that one God had established certain universal moral laws that all men should obey. He said, "I worship God as Truth only. I have not yet found Him, but I am seeking after Him."

Apartheid—suppression by the White minority of the Indians, Blacks, and Coloreds (mixed races) in South Africa—became public policy in 1948. Although some concessions have been made in recent years, there has been no obvious change in the thinking that perpetuates it. Before any final resolution, Whites will have to accept Blacks as human beings.

Black Supremacy. Just as White supremacy rules South Africa, Black supremacy rules the American Black Muslim movement, the Nation of Islam. Under leader Louis Farrakhan, many of its members have become model citizens, and even prison inmates have been rehabilitated. These positive gains, however, come at the cost of absolute submission to belief in Black superiority, rejection of Christianity, and adherence to a proviolence mutant of the Muslim faith. Muhammad himself is claimed to be Black, and any disloyalty to a Black man is not tolerated.

During the 1984 presidential campaign, the *Washington Post* reported on 13 February 1984, "In private conversations with reporters, [Jesse] Jackson has referred to Jews as 'Hymies' and to New York as 'Hymietown.'" Nine days later the *Post* attributed the information to a Black reporter named Milton Coleman. In the furor that followed, Jackson apologized for the remark. Farrakhan, however, became incensed, not at Jackson's remark but at the "traitor" Coleman who had exposed another Black man to public ridicule. King had rejected such infighting, but after his death, increasing militancy on both sides renewed the Black-against-White wedge he had carefully removed.

Black Power. Domination of one Black man over another, of White over Black or Black over White, is not caused by social conditions. It comes from a universal temptation of one person to take dominion over another. When God created Adam and Eve, He gave them dominion over the beasts, but Satan offered them equality with God as well as dominion over man (Gen. 3:5).

When King and the Southern Christian Leadership Conference began to open the door for Blacks to reenter society as equals, they incorporated Christian principles of sacrificial love for one another—coined "excessive altruism"—and love for one's enemies. With this foundation, along with disciplined training in nonviolence, they were successful in winning over their adversaries and moving the hearts and minds of the nation, much as Stowe's novel had before them.

Younger Blacks, less accustomed to restraint and less acquainted with Christ and His message, had no such scruples. They reverted to Nietzsche's will to power. The term "Black Power" was popularized in the Civil Rights movement beginning with the June 1966 Freedom March through Mississippi. The spokesman was Stokely Carmichael, chairman of the Student Nonviolent Coordinating Committee (SNCC). James Meredith, who four years earlier had been the first Black to integrate the University of Mississippi, had just been shot, and the angry young radicals were challenging King about his insistence on love and nonviolence. Carmichael found the term "Black Power" irresistible to the crowds, so he used it. King had no objections to Blacks having power, said his wife Coretta. "He merely was protesting the violent context into which the slogan was being placed, and the deliberately provocative way in which it was being shouted."

Carmichael responded to King, "Power is the only thing respected in this world, and we must get it at any cost." Four months later, Carmichael told a predominantly White audience at the University of California at Berkeley that he advocated shooting and bombing because hatred would be a catalyst for change through Black Power. He quoted the Latin American revolutionary Che Guevera concerning "hatred as an element of the struggle, relentless hatred of the enemy that impels us over and beyond the natural limitations of man, and transforms us into effective, violent, selected and cold killing machines."

This was the will to power that King had rejected. In *Where Do We Go from Here?* he said: "Black Power has proved to be a slogan without a program. . . . We can no longer afford to worship the God of hate or bow before the altar of retaliation. We still have a choice today: nonviolent coexistence or violent co-annihilation."

"Love your enemies" was not merely an exercise in self-discipline imposed by Jesus. In the context in which He spoke, in the Sermon on the Mount, He said that loving our enemies is one way that we imitate God. God does not withhold sun and rain from those who hate Him. He provides liberally for all. Likewise, those who call themselves Christians cannot justify withholding rights and opportunities from another race because it is perceived as an enemy. All are equal under the law.

Economic Equality. When the states ratified the Thirteenth, Fourteenth, and Fifteenth Amendments, all citizens were to be guaranteed equal protection under the law. This was the law of the land and the law of God. When the states violated these provisions, they were justly reversed by the Court.

None of those Amendments, nor the Declaration of Independence itself, could guarantee economic equality, only equality of opportunity. In Romans 13, Paul described the role of civil government as the rewarder of those who do good deeds and the punisher of those who do evil. It is not to provide food and clothing to multitudes but to encourage those groups who do so.

When Martin Luther King campaigned for a guaranteed annual wage, his theory was not supported by American or biblical law. This campaign did not mean King was a communist. The Federal Bureau of Investigation, even at the behest of its angry director, J. Edgar Hoover, could never find a shred of evidence to substantiate that claim. King, however, like other social activists of the twentieth century, unwittingly accepted a philosophy advocated by Marxists as well as other, more compassionate idealists and committed Christians. Their plan, in different forms, has involved the restructuring of the biblical principle of private property. There is a way to help the poor in America, Black and White, but it is not through permanent government subsidies.

In political campaigns as well as in Christian seminars, it is widely accepted that there should be some way to take the "excessive" wealth of the rich and give it to the poor. There is widespread popularity of a variable income tax, for example, that takes more money from the rich than it does from the poor.

This strategy makes some basic assumptions that are wrong.

Anyone above a certain level of income must have obtained it through fraud or the oppression of employees.

The poor are poor because they are victims of these oppressors and deserve to be remunerated.

> The ideal society in antiquity had no private property, but members shared all things in common.
>
> The goal of society should be a return to that ideal communal society.

Some of these faulty assumptions were even held by John Locke and William Blackstone, but they are not supported by a biblical model. James Kent, in his 1824 *Commentaries,* revealed a better understanding of this subject from a biblical perspective: "To suppose a state of man prior to the existence of any notions of separate property, when all things were common, and when men, throughout the world, lived without law or government, in innocence and simplicity, is quite fanciful if it be not altogether a dream of the imagination. . . . It has been truly observed, that the first man who was born into the world, killed the second; and when did the times of simplicity begin?"

Those who deny the authenticity of the Genesis account of Creation have invented the myth of the innocent society, but they have been unable to recreate it because it never existed. God never granted ownership of private property to civil governments. He gave it to families. It was a gift from God for the perpetuation of the family unit.

Each individual who heads a family, even a single person, labors to provide the necessities of life. Abraham, Isaac, and Jacob owned property, and when Jacob took his family to Egypt, they alone retained private property after the famine because the Egyptians had sold themselves to Pharaoh in exchange for grain. When the Israelites eventually entered the Promised Land, God assigned them land by families. The state did not own the land. The families did, and that was their incentive to flourish.

In the early church, Peter told Ananias that while he held his property, it was his own (Acts 5:3–4). Even the church does not have jurisdiction over its members' private property. Only cults demand full control over their adherents' wealth. Only in socialism or communism does the state control wealth. To the Founders, private property could never be taken without one's consent.

Udo Middelmann, in his 1974 work *Pro-Existence,* observed: "As Christians speaking the gospel into the world today, we must never forget this: The right to own property is presupposed in Scripture, and it is established on the ground that man is a creator. This becomes the basis for our struggle as Christians against social injustice."

One danger, said Middelmann, is that by "social legislation society will be pulled into an uncreative redistribution of wealth." God intended a man's work to be a blessing, an opportunity to fulfill his potential. When society encourages individuals not to work by subsidizing their existence, this is an injustice both to recipient and to donor.

Americans applauded recent moves to reform the welfare system and other government efforts to help the poor become self-sufficient, such as letting them buy public housing units and offering encouragement for enterprise zones in the inner city. Nevertheless, we in the church have a tremendous responsibility to improve the lot of the poor on a permanent basis by taking our rightful place among them.

When the church abdicated to the civil government the responsibility to feed the poor, it allowed the poor of all races to think that the state and the rich people paying taxes were their source of supply instead of God. One of the reasons the Scriptures repeatedly remind God's people to help the poor is that in addition to these material gifts they can also give love, and with love, share the source of love, God Himself. God could feed people with the ravens (as in the case of Elijah) if He wanted to, but it is His choice to use His people as agents of His kindness. How sad that the church has neglected the trust He has placed in it. How greatly people need to know that the righteous will not be forsaken by God (Ps. 37:25).

The Black Father. "Being a black man in America is like being a spectator at your own lynching," wrote novelist Ishmael Reed in *Life* magazine. "Everybody gets to make a speech about you but you." In what he called the "daily slander" of commentary on Blacks, there are "cartoon images presented of black men: the criminal, the athlete, the clown, the entertainer, the good nigger, the brute."

The Blacks who fit none of these descriptions are rarely recognized, people like the parents of Martin and Coretta King, who gave them the spiritual and academic depth needed to overcome the Black stigma. The Black family is in trouble, and God has the answers. Who will go and tell them?

Suffering. Suffering can bring out the worst in us, or it can polish and harden and strengthen the precious stones God has built into our foundation. When little girls were killed by a bombing of the Sixteenth Street Baptist Church in Birmingham, Alabama, King spoke at the funeral. He told the people, "They did not die in vain. God still has a way of wringing good out of evil. History has proven over and over again that unmerited suffering is redemptive. The innocent blood of these little girls may well serve as the redemptive force that will bring new light to this dark city."

King's own family suffered, especially under the blows of his untimely death. But they had to go on because they believed in a God of justice who would ultimately triumph. This faith took them through one of the darkest periods of their lives, one that in the thinking of many has not yet been brought to light.

COMMUNISM AND ADULTERY

From the earliest days of King's crusade, he and his wife suffered from relentless campaigns to smear their character and question their motives, but the most thorough personal attack was financed by the citizens of the United States. According to an exhaustive investigation performed by a Select Committee of the Ninety-fourth Congress in 1976, the director of the Federal Bureau of Investigation, J. Edgar Hoover, was convinced that King was either a communist or heavily influenced by communist infiltration. He also found it unconscionable that King opposed the Vietnam War. On that basis, Hoover justified a sweeping investigation of King's personal and professional life that lasted for years. His phones were tapped, his motel rooms bugged, and tape recordings allegedly documenting his activities offered to reporters as proof of immorality.

The FBI anonymously sent a composite tape to King, which his assistant Andrew Young, the current mayor of Atlanta, described as "garbled" and a "personal conversation among friends." Young and King's other colleagues were particularly incensed by the anonymous letter accompanying the tape, from which they surmised that someone was strongly implying that King should take his own life.

Director Hoover prepared a scathing monograph on King that was described by a Justice Department official as "a personal diatribe . . . a personal attack without evidentiary support." Attorney General Robert F. Kennedy ordered the first version recalled, but later versions were circulated widely, from members of Congress to world leaders.

King had been befriended by John and Robert Kennedy as early as the former's presidential campaign, but Hoover was so convincing that Robert Kennedy, then attorney general, allowed wiretaps on King. The Senate committee concluded that he probably never knew how extensive the surveillance became.

Hoover's international campaign to discredit King and destroy the credibility of the Southern Christian Leadership Conference included dispatches sent to the pope and efforts to head off the awarding of the Nobel Peace Prize to King. Even after King's death, the FBI considered a further investigation of his widow and undertook a major effort to prevent the establishment of an annual commemoration of the slain leader.

High school students are accused of being ignorant of many subjects, but in a 1988 survey of 411 high school seniors, all but 2 correctly identified Martin Luther King as the man who gave the "I Have a Dream" speech. This was what the Senate Committee wrote about the FBI's evaluation of that moment in history:

> At the August 1963 March on Washington, Dr. King told the country of his dream that "all of God's children, black men and white men, Jews and Gentiles, Protestants and Catholics, will be able to join hands and sing in the words of the old Negro spiritual, 'Free at last, free at last. Thank God almighty, I'm free at last.'" The FBI's Domestic Intelligence described this "demagogic speech" as yet more evidence that Dr. King was "the most dangerous and effective Negro leader in the country." Shortly afterward, *Time* magazine chose Dr. King as the "Man of the Year," an honor which elicited Director Hoover's comment that "they had to dig deep in the garbage to come up with this one."

After all the years of FBI harassment, invasion of privacy, and disregard for personal rights, the committee established that King had been exonerated from Hoover's charge of communist influence. According to the official report:

> The FBI has stated that at no time did it have any evidence that Dr. King himself was a communist or connected with the Communist Party. Dr. King repeatedly criticized Marxist philosophies in his writing and speeches. The present Deputy Associate Director of the FBI's Domestic Intelligence Division, when asked by the Committee if the FBI ever concluded that King was a Communist, testified, "No, sir, we did not."

When members of the Senate Committee asked Hoover's former assistant, William Sullivan, whether he or any of the others had ever raised objections to the character assassination of King, he responded:

> Never once did I hear anybody, including myself, raise the question, is this course of action which we have agreed upon lawful, is it legal, is it ethical or moral? We never gave any thought to this realm of reasoning, because we were just naturally pragmatists. The one thing we were concerned about [was] will this course of action work, will it get us what we want, will we reach the objective that we desire to reach? . . . I think this suggests really in government we are amoral.

According to this self-description of the FBI's pragmatism, in this regard they are no better than the communism they assiduously broke the First Amendment to uncover. Ironically, it was just such a philosophy—that "the end justifies the means"—that in addition to atheism, made communism intolerable to King. John Ansbro wrote in *Martin Luther King, Jr., The Making of a Mind:*

> King felt compelled to reject communism also because of its denial of the existence of eternal and unchangeable moral principles. Instead of affirming the existence of absolute right and wrong, Communists endorse any method that can promote the goal of a classless society, even if that method involves lying, violence, torture, and murder. King appealed to the words of Lenin to reinforce this charge. "We must be ready to employ trickery, deceit, lawbreaking, withholding and concealing truth."

It is difficult to admit it, but many Americans have secretly doubted that King was a leader worth commemorating. They have wondered if his crusades were darkened by immorality and subversion. Even those who have not begrudged African-Americans their rights have still wondered if they were duped by King when they joined in marches, sit-ins, and freedom rides. Few realize the depth and breadth of the philosophy that enabled King to survive as long as he did and never give up, never turn aside from sacrificing his time and surrendering his dignity to the cause of freedom.

Americans have looked too long for a perfect man to lead them. They have rejected too many who were imperfect. King knew he was a sinner. He knew all men are sinners. John Ansbro wrote: "King described as 'perilous' the tendency of some liberal theologians to regard sin as a mere 'lag of nature' that can be progressively eliminated as man climbs the evolutionary ladder. He defined man as 'a being in need of continuous repentance.'"

At the 1976 Senate hearings, the FBI admitted that its efforts to discredit King were unjustified. It was a time of repentance and rebuilding.

For those we have wronged, we, as a nation, need to repent before God. God does not hate those whom He created. He loves the world. He sent His Son because He loves them. We hate too much. We judge and condemn too much. Only God can change our thinking. Only He can redeem what has been suffered and make us whole.

A Personal Reflection

I grew up in Guthrie, Oklahoma, a town where the attitude toward Blacks, as I recall, was pretty much like that in the Deep South, only with less pride in its prejudice. I grew up thinking that all people used the term "nigger." I believe—although it might be wishful thinking—that I didn't like such terms, but I certainly did nothing about it. I remember a sign on the outskirts of town on which someone had written: "Guthrie, One White, Two Niggers." I suppose I laughed at it along with everyone else.

When I was ten, my family moved to a prominent town—Presque Isle—in the heart of Maine's potato country. At home, my parents spoke matter-of-factly of Negroes and niggers. I believe I remained silent. By the time I was thirteen, I was playing trumpet in various dance bands. It was in this environment, in pickup groups and jam sessions, that I began to have my first relationships with Black musicians. The common reference to Blacks among musicians in those days of the forties, I'm ashamed to note, involved the word "jigs." I remember playing music and talking with black people, even trying to emulate them musically, but I didn't carry it any further than that. We were just different. When the dance or jam session ended, we parted.

By the time the newspaper business carried me to New York City in 1955, I was encountering Black people on a day-to-day basis professionally, but their numbers were small. As I try to look back with honesty and accuracy, I'm afraid I find a Bob Slosser who was a "nice guy," a bit of a drinker at times, a bit foul-mouthed, a bit arrogant, but a "nice guy." Deep down inside, I took no unpopular stands on any important matters like relationships of Blacks and Whites. I went along with the crowd, pretty much as I had done as a kid in Oklahoma and Maine.

I simply lacked conviction. Claiming to be idealistic, I was not idealistic. Claiming to be principled, I was not principled. I was a fallen man who was his own god, the center of his universe. I take no comfort in the fact that many, many people were the same way.

That changed, beginning in 1965. As I've explained earlier, I finally realized my need for God and His willingness, indeed His eagerness, to change my life. Sometime after that, I discovered, at a deep level, the words spoken by the Apostle Paul to the Greek intellectuals. It was startling, even though I had read them many times. I made reference to them earlier, but here is the full text:

> The God who made the world and everything in it is the Lord of heaven and earth and does not live in temples built by hands. And he is not served by human hands, as if he needed anything, because he himself gives all men life and breath and everything else. *From one man he made every nation of men,* that they should inhabit the whole earth (Acts 17:24–26 [emphasis added]).

The point is not all that obscure. From one person God made all people, in every place, in every time. How terribly liberating it was to have this sink down into my bones. We are all descended from one man—one "blood," as the older translations record it.

I began to see the significance, the sense, of something Jesus said when someone told Him that His mother and brothers were outside wanting to speak to Him. "He replied to him, 'Who is my mother, and who are my brothers?' Pointing to his disciples, he said, 'Here are my mother and my brothers. For whoever does the will of my Father in heaven is my brother and sister and mother'" (Matt. 12:48–50).

With that exchange Jesus turned the world's system of race relationships upside down. Yes, family relationships are paramount, but so are relationships between Christians. In Christ, every woman and man—regardless of attractiveness, unattractiveness, color, nationality, prosperity—are part of my family. They are my mother, my brother, and my sister, no matter what the world says.

The discovery of those words crystallized the love God was freely pouring into my inner man. It was part of my renewed mind. The only thing left that could restrict my affection toward my Black brother and sister was my own stubborn will. Paul explained it this way: "We have spoken freely to you, Corinthians, and opened wide our hearts to you. We are not withholding our affection from you, but you are withholding yours from us. As a fair exchange—I speak as to my children—open wide your hearts also" (2 Cor. 6:11–13).

I had been a hypocrite, but that sin was nailed to the cross of Calvary and the Holy Spirit was sent to teach me from the inside out, to make God's Word real to me. Now I have "the mind of Christ" (1 Cor. 2:16, KJV), according to Scripture. I can actively and aggressively say to the Black, the White, the Hispanic, the Asian, the native American, "I love you, good brother." I expect to be taken to task should this truth waver within me.

I hold another personal view, shared by a number of friends: Revival is coming to America, and the African-American church may lead the way, simply because so many Black Christians have experienced the suffering of Christ and have been forced to trust Him when all else seemed to fail.

Neither Slave Nor Master

Abraham Lincoln said, "As I would not be a *slave,* so I would not be a *master.*" The time has come in America when both Black and White must resolve to be neither slave nor master toward each other but to walk in equality before the Lord their Maker.

Wellington Boone, a Black pastor in Richmond, Virginia, and president of New Generation Campus Ministry, said in an interview that America's first "national sin"—its tolerance for slavery—has never fully been resolved. As a result, this unsettled issue is hindering a move of God in the land. The change must come, he said, "not by laws but by moves in the hearts of men."

Members of the White community need to become involved in Christian outreaches to the Blacks, he said, and suggested the following steps.

Acknowledge and promote Christian leaders in the Black community.

Assist Blacks to communicate their message through television, radio, magazines, and newspapers. This includes the provision of air time and print space as well as editorial and technical assistance. This is not in the spirit of superiority, of course, but brother to brother as has been the pattern in the church from the beginning.

Treat Blacks as equals with equal ability and desire to succeed. E. V. Hill, pastor of Mt. Zion Missionary Baptist Church in downtown Los Angeles, told *Charisma and Christian Life,* "Those of us who have come up out of slavery and discrimination have always had the ambition to overcome and to be somebody. We were taught this when we weren't in positions of leadership, so ambition has always been there. The belief that we don't want to better ourselves is a common misconception."

Shine the light on the positive things that are happening among Blacks in America. Don't just emphasize the minority who are engaged in crime and drugs.

Encourage self-help efforts among Blacks by providing resources, materials, and expertise. Habitat for Humanity, for example, an international organization based in Americus, Georgia, has enlisted the aid of people like former president Jimmy Carter. Their goal is to work with the needy to build and restore homes with the participation of the future owner. The homes are sold without interest or profit.

Regain a concern for the lost. Boone said he was targeting the Black community, and urging others to do so, because of the people's great need for the Gospel. Hill said, "I have a great fear that Christians are losing their love for the lost and that Christianity is now becoming almost a country club. . . . If reaching the inner city becomes an objective of evangelicalism, together we could make them spiritual strongholds."

The heart of America is the Boone group's motto—One Nation Under God. In this current age is it possible to recapture the true meaning of that motto for Blacks and Whites and people of every ethnic group? I believe it is, and I believe that as a nation we have a covenant with God to do so.

For Further Reading

John J. Ansbro. *Martin Luther King, Jr.: The Making of a Mind.* Maryknoll, N.Y.: Orbis Books, 1982.

Derrick A. Bell, Jr. *Race, Racism, and American Law.* Boston: Little, Brown and Co., 1973.

J. Kent. *Commentaries on American Law.* 1827–30; New York: Da Capo Press, 1971.

Coretta Scott King. *My Life with Martin Luther King, Jr.* New York: Holt, Rinehart and Winston, 1969.

Martin Luther King, Jr. *A Testament of Hope: The Essential Writings of Martin Luther King, Jr.* Edited by James Melvin Washington. San Francisco: Harper & Row, 1986.

J. Anthony Lukas. *Common Ground: A Turbulent Decade in the Lives of Three American Families.* New York: Vintage Books, 1986.

Harriet Beecher Stowe. *Three Novels.* New York: Literary Classics of the United States, 1982.

United States Senate, 94th Congress, 2d Session, Select Committee to Study Governmental Operations with respect to Intelligence Activities. Supplementary Detailed Staff Reports on Intelligence Activities and the Rights of Americans. Report No. 94-755, 23 April 1976, vol. 3.

11

One Nation under God

It was shortly after noon on the clear day of 22 November 1963 in Ridgewood, New Jersey, a prosperous "village" in northern Bergen County. My old, battered "second car," a green Chevrolet, was on the lift for oil change and service at my favorite gas station. I was getting a lot of chores done on my day off.

The radio inside the station's small cluttered office was blaring loudly enough to be heard out at the lift by Angie, the station owner. I was hanging around.

Suddenly, the music changed to words: "We interrupt this program to bring you a news flash from Dallas. . . . President John F. Kennedy was shot at 1:30 P.M. Eastern Standard Time during a motorcade through the streets of Dallas."

I yelled at Angie, "Get my car down! I've got to get going!"

I arrived at the *Times* on West 43d Street about 3 P.M. By then, Kennedy was dead and details of his assassination were pouring in. The *Times'* huge newsroom had begun to fill with hundreds of people—reporters, rewritemen, copy editors, picture editors, make-up editors. The place was packed, but it was so very quiet, hushed, intense. Everything seemed to be in slow motion. There was only one story that night, and it was the biggest one any of us had covered.

Tom Wicker, a North Carolinian fairly new to the *Times,* had been traveling with the president that day. The affable, warmhearted correspondent made his reputation on that story. Tom had somehow lost or misplaced his reporter's notebook. Suddenly, madness broke out and he had to get on top of the story. He wrote on anything he could find—his shirtcuffs, scraps of paper, match covers, anything. It was a tour de force. He filed and filed and filed. He was magnificent, and so were my colleagues in the *Times* newsroom.

After the first edition had rolled and was cleaned up for the second, I walked out into the dark streets. The hush was there, too. Midtown was quiet, respectful, a real town, the way it always got in a giant snowstorm. People were aware of one another. They cared. But the smiles weren't there that night. Everyone—and there weren't many on the streets that midnight—seemed to stare down at the sidewalk. The city, like the country, was in shock.

The Unity of Grief

The Kennedy assassination and its aftermath were the greatest simultaneous experience any nation ever shared. Through radio, television, newspapers, and a constant flow of information from neighbor to neighbor, America seemed united as never before. It was the unity of grief, the unity of leadership, and another kind of unity, one symbolized by an elderly parish priest.

Oscar Huber, a short, stocky man, arrived on foot at Parkland Hospital in Dallas, breathless after leaving his fellow priest stuck in traffic a few blocks away. Past agitated newsmen and bewildered crowds, he was escorted through a line of policemen to the place where Kennedy's body lay. His arrival deepened the sense of lost hope. Eyes filled with recognition of the last act he had been summoned to do. But the arrival of the priest had another significance. It symbolized the great outpouring of prayer that united the nation for the next several days and made it one nation under God.

Word passed quickly to the waiting nation. By the time of the official funeral service at St. Matthew's Cathedral the following Monday, a line had formed at the Capitol that was three miles long. The presence of the American people extended beyond the streets of the city. It stretched from sea to sea. While Richard Cardinal Cushing conducted the funeral rites, everyone who could do so was praying in his hometown house of worship. Even in cosmopolitan New York a *Times* headline read, "New York Like a Vast Church."

There was no good reason for the nation to mourn Kennedy as it did. He had won barely half of the popular vote and was by no means assured of reelection. Yet there was every good reason for it to mourn. He was young. He had a dream that he and his energetic friends could make a difference in Washington. In spite of some ill-conceived policy decisions, the team from "Camelot" had begun to break down the walls of segregation, had confronted the Soviet Union over missiles in Cuba, and proposed sending a man to the moon. Kennedy had secularized foreign missions in the Peace Corps and sent out idealistic public servants.

America also mourned John Kennedy because they saw his wife and children. Jacqueline Kennedy's regal bearing, her prayers, and her participation in the rites of the church directed even those with a different religion to think more deeply about God. John Kennedy had frequently quoted Scripture in his speeches. The night before he died he told the audience at the Houston Coliseum, "Where there is no vision, the people perish" (Prov. 29:18, KJV). When he was killed, the nation did not perish, because the people believed in God and they believed in the Constitution.

BIBLICAL ROOTS OF THE CONSTITUTION

Lyndon Baines Johnson took the constitutional oath of office in Dallas, one large hand resting on the Bible of his predecessor. In the cramped and sweltering cabin of Air Force One, someone asked Judge Sarah Hughes if she wanted a Bible as she prepared to read the oath of office from an index card on which she had hastily scribbled it. Sergeant Joe Ayres, the chief steward of Air Force One, knew that President Kennedy had always carried a Bible. In *The Death of a President,* William Manchester described it: "It was an unusual copy, and very personal; even Larry O'Brien, to whom Ayres handed it, had never seen it before. The cover was of tooled leather, the edges were hand sewn; on the front there was a gold cross and, on the inside cover, the tiny sewn black-on-black initials, 'JFK.' On flights alone the President had read it evenings before snapping off the night light."

It was the beginning of a new term, but the perpetuation of an old tradition: the Bible and the Constitution as guardians of freedom.

President Ronald Reagan described this relationship of God and state in his 1987 State of the Union message: "The United States Constitution is the impassioned and inspired vehicle by which we travel through history. It grew out of the most fundamental inspiration of our existence: that we are here to serve Him by living free."

This concept of the Constitution as a guarantee that we will live free for God is not often taught in schools, nor even in the church. The idea of the Constitution as a part of our spiritual heritage seems as revolutionary as the men who wrote it appeared to their fellow colonists.

The men designated to draw up the Constitution were predominantly graduates of the church college at Princeton, established about forty years earlier during America's Great Awakening. The Constitution was not a sectarian document, but it did embody principles of biblical law, and everybody knew it. During the time between the convention and the actual ratification by the states, John Jay, James Madison, and Andrew Hamilton anonymously penned *The Federalist Papers* to explain the concepts to the public. In so doing, they often resorted to Scripture without citing chapter and verse. They knew that the citizens of the new nation differed on specifics of their religion, but all were aware of the same Creator and cognizant of the principles of government laid out in the Bible. John Jay wrote in *Federalist Paper No. 2:*

> Providence has been pleased to give this one connected country to one united people—a people descended from the same ancestors, speaking the same language, professing the same religion, attached to the same principles of government. . . .
>
> This country and this people seem to have been made for each other, and it appears as if it was the design of Providence that an inheritance so proper and convenient for a band of brethren, united to each other by the strongest ties, should never be split into a number of unsocial, jealous, and alien sovereignties.

Jay and others of the Founders knew that a workable and lasting federal government could be built on a foundation of universal truths shared by its citizens. Common interests were helpful, but without absolute truths, they were incapable of creating fixed, uniform, and universal laws that would work as well in the future as they did in the present. Human experience differed from year to year and place to place, but God is eternal.

Because all mankind is united under one Creator, the citizens of any nation can find in the Bible ideal boundaries for their civil law. The Bible is not prescriptive about every detail of civil law, and some details of Old Testament law clearly applied only to those times, but, nevertheless, there is a vast reservoir of principles that should be incorporated into any legal system. As Moses said, "What other nation is so great as to have such righteous decrees and laws as this body of laws I am setting before you today?" (Deut. 4:8).

Had Kennedy spoken at the Dallas Trade Mart as scheduled, he would have said that the strength of a nation was meaningless without the biblical standard of righteousness. His prepared speech included a citation from the Psalms, "For as was written long ago: 'Except the Lord keep the city, the watchman waketh but in vain'" (Ps. 127:1, KJV). "One nation under God" means Americans have not only a common Creator, but also a common standard of righteousness, and its source is the Lord.

In spite of America's biblical heritage, its public officials search vainly for ethics without considering the biblical standard. Some members of Congress have investigated the psychic realm, searching for answers in the world of satanic spirits.

Those in government have ceased to look to the Bible for personal and civic standards of morality because so few of the nation's churches teach the concept of the Creator's law. Some attribute this decline of church teaching on morality to a neglect of biblical law in the schooling of ministers.

Biblical law sets the standards of proper behavior for everyone, believer and unbeliever, because all are made in the image of God. The Apostle Paul said that although the law is powerless to force people to be righteous, it shows them when they miss the mark.

When individuals are born again, they receive forgiveness for breaking God's law on the basis of Christ's death for their sins. This removes their guilt, which the temple offerings could never do, but it does not remove their obligation to continue to obey the law. Christ said He came to fulfill the law, not abolish it (Matt. 5:17).

Salvation is not a license to ignore the law and live by personal spiritualism, unchecked by eternal standards. When that path has been taken by religious leaders through the ages, they have led multitudes to destruction. God gave the law for our benefit as well as to show us our sinfulness. Once individuals are born again, the Holy Spirit enables them to obey the law and reminds them to seek forgiveness when they break it. Jesus said, "Blessed are they which do hunger and thirst after righteousness, for they shall be filled" (Matt. 5:6, KJV).

The Founders understood that law was meant to protect liberties, not to destroy them. Rights were God-given, so governments were instituted to ensure those rights. The lawmakers were to write fixed laws that could not be changed at the whim of tyrannical leaders.

Oliver Wendell Holmes, Jr., a chief justice of the Supreme Court, rejected this notion of God's universal law and said that the law should be based on human experience. In each generation, the law should be determined by the will of the majority. He said, "I am so skeptical as to our knowledge about the goodness or badness of laws that I have no practical criticism except what the crowd wants."

Holmes interpreted the common law not as centuries of judicial decisions based on the Bible but as an evolving, experiential system of law. In accordance with the theory of evolution, he promoted a marketplace of ideas where all "truths" could compete until the strongest prevailed. He advocated "free trade in ideas—that the best truth is the owner of the thought to get itself accepted in the competition of the market."

The biblical model of law rejected such thinking. The law is not legalistic in the sense many have interpreted it, defining length of hair and amount of entertainment, but it does provide powerful remedies for the human tendency to lawlessness. Biblical law falls into three main categories: moral, ceremonial, and civil. These laws were implemented respectively by prophet, priest, and king.

- Moral law remains as a perpetual standard which reflects the unchanging moral nature of God, such as the Ten Commandments.
- Ceremonial law essentially ended with the sacrifice of the last Lamb of God, Jesus Christ.
- Civil law remains only as the basis for criminal codes of justice and restitution.

Church and State Separate But under God

The Old Testament law was written as a covenant between the people of a certain nation and God, but it was not written only for that time and place. God used it as an example to the rest of the world. Even without faith, those who follow the universal aspects of the law will be blessed, and their nation will prosper; "Righteousness exalts a nation, but sin is a disgrace to any people" (Prov. 14:34).

The Founders did not want a theocracy in the sense of uniting the civil and ecclesiastical leadership in one leader. They wanted neither the church to rule over the civil government nor the civil government to rule the church. The First Amendment both forbids an establishment of religion and protects its free exercise.

Even in Israel when the people demanded a king "like all the other nations," God did not make the priest Samuel their civil ruler. He chose Saul, who was not a Levite. God also did not impose His will on the people. He suggested His choice and allowed the people to confirm Saul by acclamation.

Even though church and state are separate, both are still under God. Belief in God is not a religion. It is a reality. God's sovereignty is not affected by sectarian religion. He reigns over the nation because He is the only one who can protect the complete freedom of His creation. He gave human beings rights, and He stands alone to guarantee them.

One of the rights that God guarantees is the freedom to accept or reject His Son as Savior. Thus, a nation under God does not preach Christ, but allows the free exercise of religion so that Christ can be preached. The day will come when Christ will personally rule the earth, but until that time the civil ruler is obligated to protect freedom for all religions.

The American Constitution represented many centuries of experimentation in implementing the law of God in the law of the land. It drew principles of civil liberty from the English common law and the French Huguenots, from the Protestant Reformation and the canon law that preceded it, and from the ancient nation of Israel.

When a committee met to revise the Articles of Confederation, although there was considerable agreement on principles, none of the colonies could present a model constitution that all the others would agree on. The possibility of unanimity became increasingly remote.

Then Benjamin Franklin, a man whose faith was perhaps scorned by his more evangelical colleagues from Princeton, proposed the final step that was needed for success. He told the troubled group of delegates that they needed to pray. He said: "We have been assured, Sir, in the sacred writings, that 'except the Lord build the house, they labor in vain that build it.' I firmly believe this; and I also believe that without His concurring aid we shall succeed in this Political building no better than the builders of Babel. We shall be divided by our partial local interests; our projects will be confounded, and we ourselves shall become a reproach and a byword down to future ages."

When they prayed together, some kneeling in place in the hot, close room, some raising their hands to heaven, it marked a turning point in their deliberations. They were able to find unity in spite of diversity, a principle of religious liberty that has bound the United States together ever since.

The Lord did not build the house solely on prayer, but also on His eternal principles. The Declaration of Independence and the Constitution are not equated with Scripture, but they incorporated enough sound biblical principles to stand the test of time. Some of these include the following.

People are dependent on their Creator. God grants to each individual certain unalienable rights that the state cannot take away. Only a nation under God provides proper protection of these rights.

The role of the state is to guarantee human rights. The anarchist believes that any central government stifles individual rights, but the opposite is true. Without laws to rule them, people revert to lawlessness and the law of the jungle where the strongest survives. A vacuum without law will not be filled with voluntary associations of cooperating groups, but with terrorism and destruction of individual rights.

Human nature is sinful. Because people tend to usurp power from each other, a strong Constitution must incorporate checks and balances to prevent tyranny.

Repression violates the laws of nature. Citizens have the right under God and the law to take action against tyrants by lawful means. Tyranny need not be permanently endured. Nihilists believe that a corrupt institution of society must be destroyed to bring on a new order, but that was not the biblically based method of the Founders.

Consent of the governed is essential to ensure human rights. God has not given any one man or woman dominion over another. After the Constitutional Convention, the document was not law until it was ratified by the people.

Under federalism, unity and diversity benefit a nation. Contrary to the Greek model, which many assume was the Founders' example, the United States is united by one God and a number of specified common purposes more than it is divided by regional interests. Unlike utopians who propose the cutting of all ties to family, tribe, or state in order to promote unity among the human race, the biblical model allowed for the tribes of Israel to remain separate even while they were united as one nation. Likewise, under federalism, the American states each retained sovereignty over their own affairs, granting but limited jurisdiction to the national government. In recent years, this principle has been greatly eroded.

Pluralism can be a blessing or a curse. According to the biblical model, all ideas have a right to be heard because people are made in the image of God and granted an equal part in the dominion mandate. Their opinions can be weighed by individuals against the standard of God's Word to determine which are valid. Modern pluralism accepts no standard and insists on a marketplace of ideas to find truth, which the majority then enforce as law. This is a form of tyranny.

Separation of church and state is not separation of God and state. The Founders forbade a church-state (like Iran) or state-church (like Germany). Civil rulers, however, are not forbidden to speak of God or their personal faith or to touch the conscience of the nation. Like any other citizen, rulers have freedom of religion, although as civil rulers they could not be evangelists nor hold an ecclesiastical office while in public service.

The suppression of religion in the guise of freedom was the technique of Benito Mussolini's fascism. Mussolini's vocal opponent, Alcide de Gasperi, survived the war only because he was sheltered by the Vatican. He emerged to restore the devastated Italy on the principle of absolute laws. De Gasperi said on 28 June 1925, "The theoretical and practical principles of fascism are the antithesis of the Christian concept of the State, which lays down that the natural rights of personality, family and society exist before the State." Historian Paul Johnson wrote in *Modern Times,* "Hence when fascism collapsed, de Gasperi was the only unsullied major figure to offer the Italian people an alternative to it which was not another form of statism."

PRINCIPLES OF SELF-GOVERNMENT

When Jesus preached to the people about the kingdom of God, He used the example of a flock of a hundred sheep. Only one was missing, but the shepherd left the ninety-nine to search for the one. In one nation under God, each individual citizen is just as important as another.

Part of the application of this principle concerns the various spheres in which an individual operates. Each sphere has a certain jurisdiction separate from every other and is relatively sovereign. An individual usually functions in several spheres concurrently. These independent governments include the areas of self, family, church, voluntary associations, and civil government. This is not a hierarchy, with one level dominating another, but they are separate entities. The principle is sometimes called "sphere sovereignty."

Self-Government. "God so loved the world," said Jesus "that he gave his only begotten Son, that *whosoever* believeth in him should not perish, but have everlasting life" (John 3:16, KJV). Self-government assumes belief in a Creator in whose image people are made and to whom they are accountable. God created individuals to be self-governing so that they could personally determine what they would do about Jesus. He gave them dignity and worth. Church, state, and associations to which they consent to belong must allow them space to govern themselves.

Family Government. According to the biblical model, a family begins when a man leaves his father and mother and takes a wife. Marriage was ordained at creation, preceding all other spheres of association. It is assumed that a family is established for the life of the partners. Family government includes the husband as the head, but he is to treat his wife as he would like to be treated himself. The father is to love and bless his children, training them but not provoking them to wrath. The family is guided by the law of love, and the rod of correction for children. Each family member retains areas of self-government as an individual.

Church Government. In a church, members are freely associated under a voluntary covenant that can be terminated at will. The covenant with God is permanent. Members submit to church discipline on certain matters, but, since only God can perfectly judge the heart, individuals still retain areas of sovereignty independent of the church. The church wields the sword of the Spirit, the Word of God.

Civil Government. The Bible does not prescribe a certain form of civil government. The Founders decided that a federal republic would diffuse authority enough to ensure liberty yet also provide national unity. It was a combination of local and national rule by elected officials. The biblical principles defining how an ideal civil government should function are found in Rom. 13:1–7. These principles include:

- submission to the governing authorities because they are designated by God
- expectation of punishment for disobedience: the state as an agent of wrath
- commendation for those who do well
- taxes to support those who govern

Civil rulers cannot interfere in family government, tell parents how to raise or educate their children, or interfere in a husband-wife relationship, but can only intervene in cases of criminal offense. This principle of liberty is frequently abused.

The civil government is authorized to stop wrongdoers and wield the sword of justice, but it must operate according to the principle that law is king. Where civil rulers usurp the right to interfere with sphere sovereignty, whether individual, family, church, or association, the people suffer accordingly.

In November 1988, Douglas Stanglin and Jeff Trimble of *U.S. News & World Report* made an interesting observation about current developments in the Soviet Union: "The Russians have a saying: Good czar, good times; bad czar, bad times. But today's Soviet human-rights activists, emboldened by *glasnost,* reject folk logic that subjugates individuals to the whim of a powerful ruler. Increasingly, they demand rights guaranteed by law, regardless of who sits in the Kremlin. . . . By calling for legal and constitutional safeguards, they have upped the ante, demanding limits, in effect, on party and government."

As free Americans, we must maintain legal safeguards against a "bad czar."

REPRESENTATIVE GOVERNMENT

The greatest safeguard and one of the least appreciated is the opportunity for any citizen to participate in government. Although it is often the lesser officials who take actions outside the law, they are answerable to elected officials, whom voters can inform, elect, or replace.

In the early days of our nation, representation of the citizens in decisions made about their civil government was considered a basic right of Englishmen. When Samuel Adams organized the Committees of Correspondence, he urged that representatives of the people be chosen at legal meetings in each locality. Although the right to vote had been limited to male property owners at first, men like Thomas Hooker, a Puritan preacher, led the way to the inclusion of all citizens.

Hooker was a close friend and colleague of John Winthrop, colonial governor of the Massachusetts Bay Colony, but he disagreed with Winthrop's system of civil government. Winthrop still subscribed somewhat to the British prejudice against the commoner, believing that only those properly trained and educated should vote and hold office. Hooker was more in tune with the policies of the Plymouth Separatists who had framed the Mayflower Compact. He wrote, "There must of necessity be a mutual engagement, each of the other, by their free consent, before by any rule of God they have any right or power, or can exercise either, each towards the other." When magistrates are elected for life, as they were in Massachusetts, he said, it "leads directly to tyranny."

Although Hooker retained his ties to his Massachusetts brethren, he moved to Connecticut where the people drew up the Fundamental Orders of Connecticut. This document is considered the first constitution, although it reflected other compacts and regulations throughout the colonies. It made the unusual provision of allocating certain voting rights for servants and forbade a religious test for office. This separation of church and state was, as always, not a separation of God and state. As the American Bar Foundation described it, "The governor and magistrates were given power, as in Massachusetts, to administer justice according to the laws of the colony and in the absence of applicable laws according to the word of God."

FEDERAL REPUBLIC

Federalism is an extension of the principle of sphere sovereignty to the national level. When individuals cross a state border, they enter a new political system with its own officials, taxes, and laws. Yet these independent states have also agreed to cede certain rights to the national government for the mutual protection and support of all. It is significant that the authority of federal officials was granted by the states, not the opposite. The federal government was to be the servant of the people, not their master. The term "free and independent states" was adopted in a resolution by the Continental Congress of 1776.

That arrangement, however, began to deteriorate when the federal government started to return funds it had collected in taxes for use by the states. It seemed like a windfall to the states, since they did not have to collect the money themselves, but it became a weapon for control. In addition, the insistence of certain states on abrogating the rights of their Black citizens invited federal intervention that has never been completely withdrawn.

According to the findings of the Working Group on Federalism created under the Reagan administration, "The states, once the hub of political activity and the very source of our political tradition, have been reduced in significant part to administrative units of the national government."

Although some fear that a return to states' rights would bring about a loss of individual rights, when the citizenry actively participates in the processes of government, the opposite is true. The state, in closer proximity to individuals and their associations, can be made more responsive to local pressure for legal reform. When state and local governments are not held hostage to decrees from Washington that affect the sovereignty of individuals and groups, rights are increased, not decreased.

Balance of Powers

The Constitution established a working relationship not only between the state and national governments, but also between the three main branches at the federal level: executive, legislative, and judicial. George Washington, in his farewell address of 17 September 1796, warned his colleagues that the nation would suffer if any of the branches refused to curb their appetite for power and "confine themselves within their respective constitutional spheres." He added: "The spirit of encroachment tends to consolidate the powers of all the departments in one, and thus to create, whatever the form of government, a real despotism. A just estimate of that love of power, and proneness to abuse it, which predominates in the human heart, is sufficient to satisfy us of the truth of this position."

Washington and the other framers understood that human beings are sinners and need the restraint of the law and a sense of responsibility for others as an encouragement for them to be righteous. A Christian is not exempt from this requirement. The principle of balance, as it is incorporated into the Constitution, is continually tested, and each branch that bends the Constitution justifies its means by a worthy end. If, as Washington said, changes are needed in the operation of the civil government, sufficient legal means are available instead of illegal ones. He said: "Let there be no change by usurpation; for though this, in one instance, may be the instrument of good, it is the customary weapon by which free governments are destroyed." In the end, he said, the overbalance of power yields a "permanent evil," instead of "any partial or transient benefit which the use can at any time yield."

The Constitution is a covenant. It is an agreement between those who hold office and those who put them there. God makes covenants, sometimes unilateral ones. He gave Noah a rainbow as "the sign of the covenant I am making between me and you and every living creature with you, a covenant for all generations to come" (Gen. 9:12). A covenant always contains a bond. It involves more than one party, has an element of reciprocity, and invokes a common purpose. It binds each party, signifies a commitment, and unites partners. Unless specified otherwise, it remains in force in perpetuity.

God made the first covenant, and because people are made in God's image, they, too, may make covenants with each other. God is always a witness to a covenant, a fact that was once written into the terms of an agreement. Whoever breaks a covenant not only has harmed another person but also has acted against God.

The colonists had an agreement with the king of England, but the king broke its terms. When the colonists wrote a new covenant with one another, they concluded the Declaration of Independence with this covenant language: "And for the support of this Declaration, with a firm reliance on the Protection of Divine Providence, we mutually pledge to each other our Lives, our Fortunes, and our sacred Honor."

DEBT AND TAXES

The covenant of the Constitution limited the powers of government. In the area of taxes, however, the civil government now wields such great power that many analysts say that it has far exceeded its legal authority.

When the Constitution was ratified, the right of taxation was included to pay for salaries and services necessary for certain specified purposes. Before long, these legitimate uses of tax money were expanded into the vast area of the "general welfare."

According to every analyst of the 1988 presidential campaign, the national deficit had become a problem that everyone wanted solved. The solution offered by analysts (but rejected by the winning candidate,

George Bush) was raising taxes. Additional taxes are not needed. What is needed is drastic reform.

Until recent years, even though the federal government had begun to enter the spheres of influence previously reserved to the family, church, and private associations, enough taxes were raised to cover its services. The national debt rose only in time of war and was usually retired during peacetime. Beginning with the Kennedy administration, however, deficit spending became a way of national life. Lyndon Johnson continued this trend with the War on Poverty and other social programs, increasing the amount of money in circulation as well as tax revenues. "The danger of the kind of welfare state Johnson was creating," wrote Paul Johnson in *Modern Times,* was that it pushed people out of the productive economy permanently and made them dependents of the state." Legislation regulating welfare grants inadvertently encouraged single-parent homes, causing a massive breakup in families, especially among poverty-stricken Black Americans. Another federal agency, the Legal Services Corporation, paid for the divorces.

When the principle of sphere sovereignty broke down, families and individuals suffered, and the church, which had abandoned its role to the federal government, was not there to help them. Outside its God-given authority, the civil government's financial structure began to crumble. Disobedient to God, the churches began to fall on hard times.

Charity toward the poor is supposed to be voluntary, guided by the law of love. When the civil government takes on the role of financial supporter, charity becomes compulsive. People are forced to give because they are forced to pay taxes. This is not only an excessive, illegal burden on the taxpayer, it also destroys the recipient it is supposed to help.

God told His people to minister to those in need so that they could demonstrate His love, not just so hungry people could get fed. He also knew that acts of charity enrich the ones who give and draw them close to God as well. He said "to divide your bread with the hungry, and bring the homeless poor into the house; when you see the naked, to cover him; and not to hide yourself from your own flesh." If you do those things, He said, "Then your light will break out like the dawn, and your recovery will speedily spring forth; and your righteousness will go before you; the glory of the Lord will be your rear guard. Then you will call, and the Lord will answer" (Isa. 58:7–9, NASB).

Jesus also urged ministry to the poor and said that in so doing they were ministering to Him. He said, "Truly I say to you, to the extent that you did it to one of these brothers of Mine, even the least of them, you did it to Me," but "to the extent that you did not do it to one of the least of these, you did not do it to Me" (Matt. 25:40, 45, NASB).

If the American people truly want to end budget deficits, the church will have to take the lead in resurrecting its long-neglected ministry to the poor. Individuals and families will have to learn how to keep themselves out of debt. The citizenry will also have to pressure their elected officials to stop bankrolling projects that have nothing to do with their constitutional mandate.

When the poor suffer, the nation suffers. No plan to rob the rich to help the poor will have the blessing of God. A change of emphasis from church growth to church outreach would have a dramatic effect on those in need and restore much needed stability to the national budget. No civil servant can provide what the church can offer: love, availability, advice, training, literacy, babysitting, and salvation in Jesus Christ.

A good friend and teacher, Terry Fullam, rector of St. Paul's Episcopal Church in Darien, Connecticut, reminded me one day that the church, in many ways, exists for the benefit of those not yet a part of it.

AMERICA'S CONTRIBUTION TO THE WORLD

Unlike personal and family financial aid, national defense is an item listed in the Constitution. Historically, controversies that have arisen in that area concern the priorities for the use of our armed forces. When John Kennedy took the oath of office he said: "Let every nation know that we shall pay any price, bear any burden, meet any hardship, support any friend, oppose any foe to assure the survival and the success of liberty." Although the country applauded his bold statement, it soon found itself unwilling to pay the price for such sweeping rhetoric. The war in Vietnam, which Kennedy pursued, would eventually refute his inaugural words. It finally became obvious that America was not willing to pay the price of war for every nation's liberty.

When John Winthrop arrived in New England on 8 June 1630, the beauty of the land inspired him to believe that this was the one place on earth where a covenant people of God could launch a noble experiment in government that would bring honor to the Lord. He wrote:

> We must delight in each other, make one another's condition our own, rejoice together, mourn together, labor and suffer together, always having before our eyes our Commission and Community in this work, as members of the same body. So shall we keep the unity of the Spirit in the bond of peace. . . .

> He shall make us a praise and glory, that men of succeeding plantations shall say, "The Lord make it like that of New England." For we must consider that we shall be as a City upon a Hill.

The idea of the United States as a city upon a hill is still invoked today as the wistful hope of Americans. Those words, which were said first by Jesus in the Sermon on the Mount, have been used to export missionaries, and they have also been used to export war. America's "manifest destiny" has included noble efforts to make the world safe for democracy. In the meantime, however, our own democratic principles have languished, and fewer and fewer citizens are willing to get involved in the system. In the 1988 election, almost 100 percent of the incumbent members of Congress were reelected. It is unlikely that all of them were the best persons for the job.

When John F. Kennedy died, a dream died with him. It was the dream of his young team of idealists that if only someone would give them the chance, they would change America. In the speech he gave at the Houston Coliseum the night before his assassination he included the biblical message, "Your old men shall dream dreams, your young men shall see visions" (Joel 2:28; Acts 2:17).

John Kennedy enthusiastically approached his presidency with an aim to reform and stimulate America to a new plateau of greatness. Breaking into the political system, however, is an extremely difficult task. Like Kennedy, Christian activists have only begun to share their visions of a revitalized America in the corridors of power in the nation's capitol. Some church groups think they shouldn't even try. Others say that even if it is right for Christians to enter politics, they should not define their positions in terms of biblical principles. In 1981, representatives of fifteen church bodies signed this statement: "On theological and ethical grounds, we reject the assumption that human beings can know with absolute certainty the will of God on particular public policy issues. Many in the religious right seem to have forgotten the clear biblical witness and central Christian acknowledgment that all of us are finite, fallible, and sinful. They make claims to knowledge of God's will for our nation that no Christian is entitled to make."

Charles Colson, former assistant to President Richard Nixon, said in his book *Kingdoms in Conflict,* "Who's to say religion and politics shouldn't mix. Whose Bible are they reading anyway?" Christians should be involved in the civil government and use God's law to judge the laws of the land because that is part of Christ's commission to believers. Jesus said, "Go and teach." Paul said even of unbelievers that "what may be known about God is plain to them" (Rom. 1:19). John Winthrop said that we are to be a city on a hill.

The only way America can have any light to offer the world is if its people are righteous and just. The Holy Spirit leads into all truth. Without Him, it is possible to find some truth because God graciously provides it to all His creation. It is, however, only with the extra measure of His Spirit that one is able to transcend the desire for personal power and private agendas to work for the good of the nation and for its God.

There has been considerable fear expressed that Christians want to get involved in politics to establish a fascist state and impose Christianity on the population. Christian Reconstructionists are especially attacked on this front.

However, wrote Joseph N. Kickasola of CBN University, "Reconstructionists [seek] to infiltrate the institutions which exist throughout a culture and rebuild them along biblical lines. . . . What is important is a bottom-up-ism, grassroots—transforming, moral and spiritual change. This will require the salvation of souls and world mission, as well as legislative reform, for we cannot allow our social base and religious liberty to deteriorate in the meantime. . . . The Civil War taught us that the sword cannot resolve what is possible only through the pulpit."

The Reconstructionists, like many of the framers, are deeply influenced by Calvinism. Instead of establishing a theocracy in America, many want only to recapture their rightful place among the people, the true sovereigns in the land.

Former President Reagan said: "In those other constitutions, the government tells the people what they are allowed to do. In our Constitution, we the people tell the government what it can do and that it can do only those things listed in that document and no others. Virtually every other revolution in history just exchanged one set of rulers for another. Our revolution is the first to say the people are the masters, and government is their servant."

As Americans we have sometimes exported weapons of war when we should have exported weapons of peace. A city on a hill should demonstrate that "we the people" can function as a nation under God, following His law and our own constitution as evidence that His plan works.

In the concluding chapter of the Bible, John saw a tree in the new Jerusalem that was watered by the river of the water of life: "And the leaves of the tree are for the healing of the nations" (Rev. 22:2). That prophecy will not be completely fulfilled until Christ returns, but there is no reason we cannot, in a small way, begin the process now.

For Further Reading

Alexander Hamilton, James Madison, and John Jay. *The Federalist Papers.* New York: New American Library, 1961.

Benjamin Hart. *Faith and Freedom. The Christian Roots of American Liberty.* Dallas: Lewis and Stanley, 1988.

Paul Johnson. *Modern Times.* New York: Harper & Row, 1983.

Joseph N. Kickasola. "The Bible, Ethics, and Public Policy." *Journal of Christian Reconstruction,* 11 (1985).

"Christian Theological Observations on the Religious Right: A Statement by 15 American Church Bodies." *Face to Face: An Interreligious Bulletin,* 8 (Winter 1981).

William Manchester. *The Death of a President.* New York: Harper & Row, 1963.

Peter Marshall and David Manuel. *The Light and the Glory.* Old Tappan, N.J.: Fleming H. Revell, 1977.

Richard L. Perry, ed. *Sources of Our Liberties.* Chicago: American Bar Foundation, 1978.

Part 4

The Church

The Church's one foundation
Is Jesus Christ her Lord . . .
With his own blood he bought her,
And for her life he died.
Samuel J. Stone

12

That We May Be One

On a hot July day in 1983, 5,000 people streamed into Amsterdam. Inside a huge, stuffy auditorium, blue-jacketed stewards and stewardesses orchestrated the seating of the awestruck men and women who had gathered from 130 countries.

On the platform was a distinguished looking man of powerful gentleness known worldwide for his ability to command the attention of a crowd. In a matter of moments this man could convince anyone from sophisticated businessman to awkward adolescent that he or she should take an embarrassing, bold step. At his word, thousands would humble themselves and stream forward to accept Jesus Christ as Lord and Savior.

That man, of course, was Billy Graham. The event was the International Conference for Itinerant Evangelists.

Graham had envisioned such a conference for years. Ever since he was a young evangelist he had searched for ways to help others who had the same calling as he. Finally, a massive conference had come together, and he gave the credit to God. As he would say later, "As we look back, we can sense His guidance in every step."

As Graham watched the thousands flow into the hall, he said, "Their faces, with eager smiles and shining eyes, showed the enthusiasm with which they had come." Each one, at great financial sacrifice and often with the help of hundreds of donors, had come from squalid city slums and from tangled jungles, on foot and on horseback, by car and by train. They had come to learn better ways to tell their world the good news about Christ.

Each individual had his own story. Each had struggled with his own sinful nature. Each had come to understand the Gospel for himself. Each had accepted the teachings of Jesus Christ, some of which, like this statement affirmed at the conference, were very hard indeed: God loves every human being, who, apart from faith in Christ, is under God's judgment and destined for hell.

MIXED MESSAGES

Through the centuries, that "good news" has bitterly divided the members of the church. They have questioned how a loving God could send anyone to hell, and in the process they have doubted the accuracy of the Scriptures that tell about it. As a result, the church since the beginning has given the world mixed messages. It is time, once again, to call a halt to this division. We must affirm as one church: Jesus is who He said He is. The Bible is true.

Jesus confronts us once again: "There are some of you who do not believe" (John 6:64, NASB). When His hard sayings had proven too much for some of His listeners, they left Him. Turning to His disciples, He asked, "You do not want to go away also, do you?" Simon Peter answered, "Lord, to whom shall we go? You have words of eternal life" (John 6:67–68, NASB).

I think it is time to make it very plain that only Jesus Christ has the words of eternal life. Each person on earth has only two choices: believe and find eternal life or refuse to believe and fall under God's judgment.

This is not a good time for such absolutist thinking. America is in the midst of the greatest watering down of absolutes in its history. As a result, our society is applying truckloads of Band-Aids and accomplishing nothing. America needs a miracle of God, but it will only come on His terms. Our forefathers made covenants with God for this land, and I believe He will honor those as He did with Israel (Lev. 26:45) if we will repent for our sins and treachery against Him. The church itself must restore its faith that Jesus Christ is who He says He is and that the Bible is true. Before that can happen we will have to straighten out some thinking in the church.

THE BIBLE AS MYTH

In 1962, the prestigious Newbery Award for children's literature went to a work the author unashamedly called "a theological book." An immediate bestseller in the secular market, it remains an all-time favorite among believers and unbelievers alike.

The book is *A Wrinkle in Time.* It marked the end of a ten-year struggle by author Madeleine L'Engle to find someone who would publish her work. She said in an interview, "You can't name a major publisher who didn't reject it." Eventually Farrar, Straus and Giroux in New York picked it up, and in the decades since then it has undergone forty-seven hardcover printings, a remarkable accomplishment.

A Wrinkle in Time is an adventure of three children into the world of evil. They succeed in their quest because they have the assistance of a helpful witch (complete with broomstick and black hat), a medium (with crystal ball), a former star (from outer space), and an ethereal creature who quotes philosophers (by name) and the Bible (anonymously). L'Engle said she has come under fire for using such characters as helpers, but considered them a "joke," no less harmful than Halloween. She is totally opposed to Satan worshipers, she said, but considers these in a different category. Those who can't understand her reasoning have no appreciation for the imagination, she said.

L'Engle has been so successful with her writing that she is now a regular speaker on Christian college campuses, and especially at Wheaton College where the Billy Graham Center is located. In the process of teaching her eager listeners how to write imaginatively, she explains that the Bible portrays "truth" (as opposed to "facts") through the medium of myths. She explained that she refers to German theologian Karl Barth who said, "'I take the Bible far too seriously to take it literally.'"

How do her audiences respond to her view on the Bible as not literally true? "People are interested," she said. "They want to question." If "you take it literally, you lose all the depth."

Taking the Bible Literally

L'Engle represents a growing number of academicians and preachers who believe it is necessary to wean the church away from its insistence on biblical absolutism. For example, she said it is wrong to tell people what the Evangelists conference affirmed, that apart from faith in Christ every human being is under God's judgment and destined for hell.

Jesus talked about hell in the same way he told parables, L'Engle said. "When Jesus wanted to put in a thumbtack he used a sledgehammer," she said. "He exaggerated. Are we supposed to believe that that man had a beam in his eye? Jesus spoke in parables. Many of them are wildly exaggerated because he's making a point for people who *will not hear what he says.*"

It is impossible to believe in God's infinite love and also believe in hell, she said. "I don't think God's love is so weak that it'll quit." Quoting a Russian philosopher and theologian, she said that "belief in hell is lack of faith in God, for it is to attribute more power to Satan than to God."

What do L'Engle's comments have to do with the public-policy issues raised in this book? They are significant because they represent an influential portion of the modern church that is not helping to affirm God's love, regardless of its intentions. Instead, it is negating His sovereignty.

Such a position displays human beings as able to save themselves instead of desperately needing to be saved by God. That kind of thinking suggests to the American church that it is possible to legislate God out of public life and still solve its national problems. Expanding the imagination is a worthy goal, but children's books about witches are not harmless even when introduced in jest. There is a real battle going on between good and evil, and witchcraft is a part of it. It is not our place to judge anyone's heart or anyone's faith, but it is necessary to sound the alarm about what such thinking is doing to America and how it is destroying the church.

THE POWER TO TAKE DOMINION

The Bible records that God's first instruction to Adam and Eve was this: "Be fruitful and increase in number: fill the earth and subdue it" (Gen. 1:28). That instruction has not been fulfilled because people, although made in the image of God, have lost their regard for the truth that God is the center of all things. The church, which the Bible calls the body of Christ, is too weak to take dominion over the earth because its members are warring against one another. In this age of openmindedness, many would argue that the church could be unified if all the individual groups would be more neutral. I disagree. I am arguing for unity on the basis of absolute partisanship: the Bible is true and Jesus Christ is who He said He is.

CHRIST'S GOSPEL: BAD NEWS OR GOOD?

As uncomfortable as the doctrine of judgment and Christ's atonement is today, it is something that will never stop being true. It began with the conscious decision to disobey God in the Garden of Eden. It was resolved on the cross. Denial of God's judgment and atoning love brings hell on earth and unfortunately ends with a final, personal hell.

Graham said: "Hell is not the most popular of preaching topics. I don't like to preach on it. But I must if I am to proclaim the whole counsel of God. We must not avoid warning of it. The most outspoken messages on hell, and the most graphic references to it, came from Jesus Himself. He spoke of hell as 'outer darkness,' where there will be 'weeping and gnashing of teeth.' He contrasts 'everlasting punishment' with 'life eternal' [Matt. 25:46]. He describes hell as a place of torment and agony and fire [Luke 16:23–24]."

An understanding of Christ's atonement for sinful people is not bad news but good. Instead of love and judgment being contradictory, it is precisely an understanding of God's judgment that shows how great His love is.

Madeleine L'Engle is clearly a strong woman of extraordinary talent, which makes her work, like that of so many gifted people, capable of causing confusion and muddiness among people in these days of relativism and uncertainty. Too often such artists, unwittingly or not, tend to make God in their own image. As a young writer and editor, I was dangerously vulnerable to them.

Knowledge of God's Power

It is important for each of us to be saved by understanding that we escape hell by believing in the Lord Jesus Christ. It is also important for us to take that knowledge of God's incredible power to save us and begin to do His work. The church has been chosen to accomplish God's purposes on earth. Once one understands who Jesus is and the absolute reliability of His Word, he gains the confidence and power necessary to go out and change the world. This is not done according to some personal agenda but, like those evangelists in Amsterdam, according to a plan revealed by God Himself. That is why I have stressed throughout this book what the Bible says about families, education, law, and government, not someone's opinion of what will work. All of us must look to the biblical model, not some personal crusade, especially not an effort to undermine the Bible and the work of Christ. Armed with the spiritual weapons of the Lord, we can be like the saints who preceded us, including Paul the apostle. We can be "God's fellow-workers" (2 Cor. 6:1).

Yes, God has chosen to use His people—the church—to accomplish His purpose on earth. That means we are expected one day, in the eternal kingdom of God, to rule and reign with Christ, but first, we have a lot to learn. In what we call the Great Commission, Jesus said to His followers, who became the church: "All authority in heaven and on earth has been given to me. Therefore go and make disciples of all nations, baptizing them in the name of the Father and of the Son and of the Holy Spirit, and teaching them to obey everything I have commanded you. And surely I am with you always, to the very end of the age" (Matt. 28:18–20).

I want to emphasize the importance of converting people, but I want to emphasize equally the importance of "teaching" the people the complete Word of God. Jesus is the Living Word. The Bible is the Written Word, and it has to do with "everything I have commanded you." It is a book for all of life, not only for devotional life.

The "everything" in that Great Commission has everything to do with everything. Jesus was talking about the way the world works, a world that was set up by Him and held together by Him (Col. 1:16–17).

PARADOXICAL PRINCIPLES OF LEADERSHIP

The church is supposed to show the world the value of God's Word in addressing the issues of the day. Jesus said He is the way, the truth, and the life (John 14:6). The church must demonstrate that truth. Notably, however, the church's leadership is to be based on principles paradoxical to modern understanding.

In the beginning of the Sermon on the Mount, Jesus spoke what we have come to call the Beatitudes. Most of us know something of them: "Blessed are the poor in spirit, for theirs is the kingdom of heaven. . . . Blessed are those who mourn. . . . Blessed are the meek . . . those who hunger and thirst for righteousness . . . the merciful . . . the pure in heart . . . the peacemakers" and so on (Matt. 5:3–10).

Many years ago my reaction to that list of virtues was not good. I perceived only weakness and the necessity to have the personality of a milquetoast. I didn't recognize the strength of the passage until my mind, my thinking, began to be renewed. Then I saw strength, especially when I juxtaposed two key sentences that follow quickly after the Beatitudes. For Jesus said plainly that those possessing such virtues were to be "the salt of the earth" and "the light of the world" (Matt. 5:13–14). Those were not the qualities of a human doormat, an overbearing, deferential weakling, or a retiring wallflower.

Think about it. All of those virtues, from poverty of spirit to perseverance under persecution, were to be manifested, not in ivory-tower seclusion but in strong, healthy, day-to-day interaction with people from all walks of life. Those who manifested the virtues with God-given strength and wisdom were to be salt and light; they were, in the supernatural course of events, to become leaders. Why? Because they knew the way things worked. They knew where they were going.

Can a kind, gentle, compassionate individual actually be a strong leader? You can hear the challenges now. Leadership calls for rough-riding domination, skeptics say. The will to use power. Martin Luther King, Jr., struggled with that very issue. How can such a person change the world around him?

The biblically thinking leader can change the world quite simply, at least from God's point of view. This is how Jesus described the men and women He wanted to follow Him, becoming leaders in fulfilling His purpose on earth: "The kings of the Gentiles lord it over them; and those who exercise authority over them call themselves Benefactors. But you are not to be like that. Instead, the greatest among you should be like the youngest, and the one who rules like the one who serves. For who is greater, the one who is at the table or the one who serves? Is it not the one who is at the table? But I am among you as one who serves" (Luke 22:25–27).

The leader is to be like one who serves. Add the following statement, and the picture becomes clearer: "Whoever humbles himself like this child is the greatest in the kingdom of heaven" (Matt. 18:4).

On top of servanthood, the leader is to be like a little child—humble, eager to learn, enthusiastic, trusting, persevering. Put all those elements together, fully immersed in faith, hope, and love, and you have a picture of the people who will rise to leadership of the world in its dark hour.

Madeleine L'Engle said she knew Christians who seemed to relish the fact that they were saved and others were lost. She called it "elder brotherism," and it rightly offended her. She said, "We all tend to be elder brothers. We do not want God to give a party for the prodigal son" when he comes and says, "'Daddy, I'm sorry.' We don't want him to have a party. He was bad."

Those who bear Christ's message must be humble, realizing that "there but for the grace of God go I." They must not lose the Madeleine L'Engles of the world through their arrogance and lack of compassion.

Believers alive today cannot expect to usher in the fullness of the kingdom of God. That is the job of the Lord and His angels. But God still foresaw human beings, His greatest creation, as "subduing" the world until He comes. He made things that way. The church—all believers—must recognize in total love and humility that they are being called upon for leadership, and they must prepare for that.

Suppose the church was given authority today to rule the nations with the Lord. We wouldn't have any idea how to proceed because we have walked away from the world in too many instances, despite the fact that the church is told to be *in* the world but not a part *of* it.

Jesus said it first and it applies to us: "My kingdom is not of this world" (John 18:36). He also said we were to be His witnesses, His evidence, throughout the world (Acts 1:8). We are to occupy it till He comes, making it possible for the gospel to be preached in all the earth (Matt. 24:14).

We *must* hear the Lord's call for us to proclaim His lordship over everything. We have too often been satisfied with our personal piety and occasional bursts of evangelism while neglecting God's admonition to learn how the world works. We have not taken our proper authority over marriage and family, education and values, law and government, or mastered the media that so persuasively transmits an unbiblical world-view. The church *can* master these arenas of warfare because it has been redeemed and empowered by the Master. Neglect of these arenas means neglect of God's calling.

Yes, we have had some wonderful surges of spiritual renewal in the twentieth century, but they have too often fallen short of changing the society and the culture of America. Truly meaningful renewal must change society. Secularized good will and ingenuity, no matter how well intended, will not and cannot overcome man's problems.

Why? Because our available good will and ingenuity fall far short of the scale needed. Our problem is serious, dating all the way back to the Fall, as reported in the Bible's book of Genesis, and the vast amount of elapsed time has severely increased the complexity of that problem. The entire creation has been infected.

THE CHURCH STUMBLED

In the seventies, Christians took steps that appeared to lead toward fortifying the church by building the strength of local congregations. Teaching began to go beyond mere evangelism and also emphasized discipleship. Individuals were not only receiving Christ as Savior, but also learning from mature Christians what it meant to make Him Lord. Obviously, Satan was displeased with this development, and he exploited flaws in the renewing church to wreck the movement.

The teachers were onto something good with their discipleship efforts, but some of them fell into what might be called dictatorial error. Some poorly prepared "shepherds" developed haughty, domineering attitudes that tore the renewal apart and derailed a movement that had been expected to make the local church what it should be. The steaming controversy set back many churches in their plan to become what the New Testament describes.

Then came the infamous "Jonestown" horror, as a pastor, Jim Jones, spun out of reality and led a congregation to Guyana and ultimately to death by mass suicide. Even though Jones trashed the Bible and blatantly told his followers that he was God, because he was a minister the whole church suffered by association. This terrible story provided the finishing touch to the shepherding movement and gravely weakened the influence of churches on their local communities.

After that came several prosperous years among numerous so-called mega-churches with flourishing television ministries, where thousands and thousands of souls were saved. Questions were raised in some places about superficiality, cheap grace, materialism, and worldliness. One began to hear statements like, "Lives have been changed, but lifestyles have not." Church memberships began to drop, and financial difficulties arose. Many lost true discipleship training.

It is important to recall that the discipleship movement was spawned from passages of Scripture that reveal the church as "the Body of Christ," with a strong emphasis on lay ministry and the truth that every Christian is a minister with a call to service. That service is not always in the ordained ministry but frequently in the marketplace. The unconscious retreat from those truths again caused a turning inward, into personal piety without marketplace involvement. This relegated Christianity to the pew and Sunday school, which delighted the secularists who were pushing hard to remove every trace of religion from society.

One of the key passages that were stressed in discipleship activities comes in 1 Corinthians 12–14. It teaches unity within the diversity of the church—the Body of Christ—and elaborates on the various gifts and ministries that are expected to operate. A church should see itself as a living organism rather than an institution. Every member is to participate in the life of the church so that all will be strengthened, nurtured, and healed, able to live effectively in the world.

Additional powerful teaching came from Ephesians 4, which also stresses unity and shows specifically that each of God's people is to be involved in ministry and service, to build up the body of Christ and bring it to maturity (Eph. 4:1–16). Understanding and implementing these truths is critical to making the church what the New Testament intends. Without them, a church service becomes a performance by a handful of people—mostly ordained clergy—and the church deteriorates, undernourished, and unable to bear a witness to society.

It is terribly important for all the church to know and to live as though it believes that in Jesus Christ, the Head of the Church, resides all wisdom and knowledge (Col. 2:3). The world desperately needs Him. The church must see that Almighty God, the totally sovereign Lord of the universe, chose to reveal that wisdom and knowledge through them: "[God's] intent was that now, through the church, the manifold wisdom of God should be made known to the rulers and authorities in the heavenly realms, according to the eternal purpose which He accomplished in Christ Jesus our Lord" (Eph. 3:10–11).

The world can fight it, but the truth remains that God, the Creator of everything there is, has chosen to fulfill His purpose for the world through His people. He could have done it any way He desired, but He chose this way—revealed and explained in Holy Scripture—working through vessels of clay that contain the all-surpassing power of God (2 Cor. 4:7).

THE DISCOURAGEMENT OF DISUNITY

As we wring our hands over the state of the nation we would do well to remember that the state of the nation is no better or worse than the state of the church. Why? Because they are inextricably linked, as is illustrated in the founding documents of America. In a report for the Brookings Institution in Washington, James Reichley, whom I interviewed as he was bringing the document to completion, wrote that the Founders never intended for the Constitution's First Amendment to prevent "acknowledging dependence of civil society, as all of life, on transcendent direction."

"The First Amendment," he said, "is no more neutral on the general value of religion that it is on the general value of free exchange of ideas or an independent press." He wrote that the Founders' view coincided with the Judeo-Christian belief that "man is inherently inclined to sin" and is thus inclined to pursue his own ends, sometimes to the detriment of others.

Something can be done about our sinful nature and the general unawareness of God's purposes. The Bible explains it. We in the church must take our salvation, plus the biblical world-view that has been given to us, and then be what we are—the Body of Christ, directed to serve all people as God directs us.

Here is a crucial point: We have already been given enough unity to do the job, if we will but accept it and purpose ourselves to live in it, without dilution or compromise of the full Gospel. God gave the church weapons of warfare that are different from those of the world. They are not only different, they are more powerful. Paul told the Corinthians that they ignored that fact to their peril. He said: "I think I shall have to do some plain speaking to those of you who will persist in reckoning that our activities are on the purely human level. The truth is that, although we lead normal human lives, the battle we are fighting is on the spiritual level. The very weapons we use are not human but powerful in God's warfare for the destruction of the enemy's strongholds" (2 Cor. 10:2–4, PHILLIPS).

In 1988, a book on this spiritual warfare became a runaway best-seller in Christian bookstores. It is Frank Peretti's *This Present Darkness.* In 1978, when Peretti was assistant pastor of the Dockton Community Church in Vashon Island, Washington, he watched with growing alarm the increasing compromises with witchcraft and reincarnation masquerading as the New Age movement. He said in an interview, "I really resent the way that demonic powers are dressing themselves up as such benevolent, wise persons." He decided to "tear the mask off the critters and show them for what they are."

Peretti's book is the fictional account of what can happen when a town compromises with "the world rulers of this present darkness" (Eph. 6:12, RSV). Employing graphic descriptions of sinister demons and powerful, warring angels, Peretti presents a duel to the death, but his true heroes are simple church people who pray.

Ephesians 6 (from which Peretti took his title) describes these major elements of spiritual warfare:

- be strong in the Lord (not yourself)
- put on God's armor against Satan's tricks
- recognize that your true enemies are not human beings but powerful evil forces in the unseen world
- clothe yourself with truth, righteousness, and the gospel of peace
- carry the shield of faith and the sword of the Spirit (the Word of God)
- pray in the Spirit at all times

In the marvelous fourth chapter of Ephesians, Paul told the church to keep the unity it has, to preserve it, nurture it, and use it. Maintain and attain. It's the law of use: fully and creatively use what God has given you, and you will receive more (Matt. 25:29).

The time is now, beloved. We have everything we need to change the way America thinks. We must learn *how* to use it and then we must *use* it. To do this, we need a strong, unified church.

The most unloving act we could commit would be to continue buying the lie that "Christians have no place in secular life" and thus do nothing. Just think about the children who, despite their families' efforts, grow up receiving a constant and consistent barrage in school, on television, in the country's law and government—everywhere—that there is no personal God, that there is no absolute truth, that people are on their own as they try to survive in this world. What will these children do? They will grow into hurting, lost adults who will ultimately go to hell.

THE PARABLE OF THE TRAIN

I want to close this book about the importance of the thought life and work life of America with a parable, asking you to pray about what you are going to do.

American society is like a train. Traditionally, the main influences on this train have been the family, church, law and government (including the public schools), and the media.

Now every train has a destination, which is determined by those who run it. The execution of the trip to the destination depends on the way the tracks are laid and on the engineers.

Originally, the train was run by people who believed that God, through them, should determine the destination of the train. They used the Bible as a guide and expected the engineers (and the others working on the train) to operate this train of American society according to their wishes.

The passengers—those who determined the destination—were free to come and go on the train, regardless of their religious beliefs.

The rest of society—its citizens—when they weren't riding the train, spent most of their time living in houses along the train tracks. They didn't have much direct control over the train workers, except in periodic elections and, of course, in choosing the newspaper they wanted to receive.

All in all, they pretty much agreed on the same master plan for the train.

Now, you must understand that the train tracks—which are central to the performance of the master plan—are actually education: the schools. In the early decades of American history, the people laid tracks according to certain basic principles from the Bible. When the principles were followed, even if all the passengers didn't agree on them, the train moved steadily toward its destination, avoiding derailments and collisions.

Part way through the journey, the railroad workers began to be influenced by certain noisy passengers who insisted that biblical principles were no way to run a railroad. Before too long, the workers started to believe the malcontents and decided it was time to take some liberties with the master plan.

Eventually they changed the destination. Soon the track layers—educators—decided that biblical principles were altogether too confining.

After all, only ignorant people would blindly follow a rule book. Smart people thought up new ideas based on experience and intuition. Anyone could see it was too restricting to chip and bore a tunnel through a mountain instead of going around it, or to follow a straight path when it was possible to add a few breathtaking curves to heighten the excitement.

When the education track layers announced the new progressive plan, designed to direct the train away from the confining standards of the past, some workers complained and left. Most of those who stayed agreed to give the new plan a chance, and the educators began to lay track according to the new submaster plan.

Now there were a few remaining rail layers who believed in the old master plan, but they were so outnumbered that they were ridiculed and labeled as reactionaries and fundamentalists. Effectively silenced, they either left the railroad business or formed small societies to try to develop strategies for change. Most of the time, however, the pitiful hand tools of these little groups were no match for the powerful, government-financed machines now laying the track.

Instead of being filled with people from all religions and belief systems, the train of American society became more and more restrictive. In the beehive of activity among elected representatives, bureaucrats, and lobbyists onboard, few really understood the new destination and complained little about the new direction of the track. Most of them had undergone the same educational indoctrination as the rail layers, and furthermore this new direction offered a lot of thrills.

The bulk of the American people still lived in the towns and cities near the tracks, but they were not as close to the railroad workers and passengers as before. Their choice of news from the train was restricted by an elite group of journalists who had moved onboard the train and established their own headquarters. These journalists, in addition to the government education they shared with everyone else, also had decided that they alone could be trusted to dispense "truth" to the people.

The trainworkers and the passengers disagreed on many things, but most of them accepted with little discussion the new personnel and the change in destination. Regardless of their religious practices on their own time, they thought it was best for the railroad if they kept that area of their lives strictly segregated from their work on the train.

In the towns and cities along the way, people began to wonder if the things they were reading in the newspapers told the whole story about the people on the train. They also wondered why there were so few stories about themselves and their churches.

These people attended the same government schools and were also taught that they must avoid a biblical "bias," but at least once a week they heard a slightly different story. They learned about the old days when there was a different destination and fewer train derailments and collisions.

Some tried to run after the train and shout instructions to the people on board, but the train was too fast and too powerful.

A few caught the train when it stopped at stations to unload government gifts and newspapers, but by then they were so out of breath from running that they couldn't say anything very convincing. When they looked around for fellow townspeople to agree with them, the folks were too busy snatching up benefits and reading newspapers to get involved.

The best opportunity the believers had to talk to people on the train was when it frequently ran off the tracks, usually in an area where the tracks had been laid with a strange curve in order to take advantage of a new scenic route.

At these times the passengers and the workers would be so hard-up that a few church people would be allowed to trickle in and take care of the victims. However, they were kept under the supervision of wise experts who monitored their conversations for any biblical content. As soon as the passengers were well enough to travel, the train would roar off, bent on the progressive destination.

Finally, a few believers began to meet together secretly in towns and villages to see if they could change the train's direction and *prevent* some derailments and collisions instead of always mopping up after them.

Unfortunately, some of the leaders of these secret societies built such large groups that they forgot Who was supposed to be running the train. They began laying a series of tracks parallel to the main track and establishing themselves as engineers. Their new trains were so competitive with one another that they never became any threat to the main line.

Then another plan arose. By that time many of the upstart engineers had fallen in disgrace and sold their trains to the highest bidder. But some of the people who had worked for them suddenly realized that God owned the main line and all the people who were running it were nothing but usurpers. The train belonged to God and His people.

Believers hadn't always done the best job running the train even in the old days, but at least it was going to the right destination. At least in those days people had been free to come and go on the train regardless of their religious beliefs.

They decided to work together with all the other alternative train builders to learn the skills they needed to run the main train, and to do it better than it had ever been run before. They would make a pact with God and one another to live according to biblical principles and not allow anyone to forbid them to speak out. They would study and sacrifice until they were ready to work *on* the train instead of running or building alongside.

They called their program One Nation Under God.

BOB SLOSSER, journalist and author, is the president of CBN University, a graduate institution in Virginia Beach, Virginia. He was formerly an assistant national editor for the *New York Times;* night news editor for the *New York World-Telegram* and the *Sun;* editor of *The National Courier;* and executive vice-president for creative development at the Christian Broadcasting Network. He is the author or coauthor of twelve previous books, including *Reagan Inside Out, The Secret Kingdom* (with Pat Robertson), *Miracle in Darien, Child of Satan/Child of God* (with Susan Atkins), and *The Miracle of Jimmy Carter* (with Howard Norton). He and his wife, Gloria, live in Virginia Beach.

CYNTHIA ELLENWOOD is a freelance writer, the author of numerous articles and curriculum materials, including children's neighborhood evangelism. As a registered nurse she specialized in remotivation and medical care for the elderly. She holds a master's degree in journalism from CBN University and was a founder and editor of *The Standard,* a public-affairs journal with a biblical perspective. She lives with her son and daughter, Paul and Lorien, in Virginia Beach.